Kinds Come First

Kinds Come First

Age, Gender, Class, and Ethnicity Give Meaning to Measures

Jerome Kagan

The MIT Press
Cambridge, Massachusetts
London, England

This book was set in Stone Serif and Stone Sans by Jen Jackowitz. Printed and bound in the United States of America.

Library of Congress Cataloging-in-Publication Data is available.

Names: Kagan, Jerome, author.
Title: Kinds come first : age, gender, class, and ethnicity give meaning to measures / Jerome Kagan.
Description: Cambridge, MA : MIT Press, [2019] | Includes bibliographical references and index.
Identifiers: LCCN 2018059566 | ISBN 9780262042932 (hardcover : alk. paper)
Subjects: LCSH: Life change events--Psychological aspects. | Life cycle, Human--Psychological aspects. | Social classes--Psychological aspects. | Ethnicity--Psychological aspects. | Gender--Psychological aspects. | Social psychology.
Classification: LCC BF637.L53 K34 2019 | DDC 158.1--dc23 LC record available at https://lccn.loc.gov/2018059566

10 9 8 7 6 5 4 3 2 1

Contents

Preface

The primary theme of this slim book is easy to state: It is a critique of the popular premise that a particular value on a reliable measure probably possesses the same theoretical meaning for human participants who vary in developmental stage, gender, social class, or ethnic group. The health consequences of a behavior, say excessive drinking of wine, beer, or whiskey, are ambiguous because the level of risk usually depends on the life stage, gender, class, and ethnicity of the person. Nonetheless, one research team ignored these categories when they reported that anyone who drank more than 100 grams of alcohol per week (more than seven glasses of wine) were at a higher risk for a serious illness (Wood et al., 2018).

Statements about popular psychological constructs, such as attention, anxiety, learning, memory, or regulation, are often silent on the subjects who provided the observations. The assumption that most psychological measures have meanings that transcend the kinds of agents providing the values reflects a premature hope of discovering broadly generalizable conclusions that apply to diverse animal species, as well as human participants who vary in life stage, gender, class, and ethnicity. This book questions the validity of this ambitious idea. I hope to persuade investigators to question their resistance to acknowledging that the meaning of many measures on human participants varies as a function of the above categories.

Most measures have considerable inter-individual variation, partly because an individual's developmental stage, gender, class, and ethnicity affect the probability that a skill, action, belief, or emotion will be displayed. Not surprisingly, each of those four categories makes its most significant contributions to different outcomes. Life-stage influences cognitive skills and regulation of impulse. Gender affects variation in the desire for signs of potency, the establishment of close relationships, and the quality of feeling tone. Social class position contributes to a person's sense of agency along with physical and mental health. Ethnicity creates conceptions of self as an insider or outsider in a society and is associated with genes that create temperamental biases. The chapters that follow defend these claims.

My failure to devote separate chapters to the contributions of culture, historical era, and religion was pragmatic. Most research on human behavior necessarily relies on individuals who live in this historical era. Second, the vast majority of studies of psychological outcomes are conducted on North American or European white adults who are either Christian or agnostic. The November 6, 2018, issue of *Proceedings of the National Academy of Sciences* contains a series of papers pointing to the robust differences between these populations and individuals from other groups. The plea to accept this fact had been made before but has had minimal success in changing practices. Perhaps this time will be different.

An insufficient body of reliable facts is the reason for the failure to devote time to extensive discussions of culture, history, and religion, although their contributions are not ignored. The American Psychiatric Association's decision in 1973 to remove homosexuality from the DSM-II list of mental disorders had profound consequences for many gay adults.

Interest in psychology was high in 1950, because many Americans were curious about the experiences that led to crime and mental illness. The 1950s was a decade of economic growth, peace in Europe, low unemployment, 30-cents-a-gallon gasoline, lower income inequality in comparison to our own era, and climate change, pollution, cyberattacks, and radioactive waste were not yet regarded as problems. Historical events over the past seven decades have catapulted these concerns to an alpha position in the minds of many Americans.

I suspect that some readers will object to the suggestion that combinations of age, gender, class, and ethnicity can make qualitatively distinct contributions to an outcome. They will insist that it is more useful to regard all healthy humans as differing quantitatively on a variety of continuous dimensions. This claim is valid when one examines individuals on a single dimension rather than on a pattern. Mice and humans differ quantitatively on many measures, including number of genes, brain weight, and longevity. But the two species are qualitatively distinct when we focus on the pattern of features that defines each kind.

The silver foxes that were selectively bred for tame behavior with humans in the Institute for Genetics in Novosibirsk, Russia, appear to represent a distinct category. Tame, compared with aggressive, male foxes possess a pattern that includes more serotonin receptors in the brain and distinctive levels of expression of 146 genes in the prefrontal cortex (Wang et al., 2018). The frequencies of biting the hand of a human who tried to touch a tame or wild fox form two almost non-overlapping distributions.

Of course, only humans care about this controversy. No lion broods over whether hyenas and gazelles vary quantitively or qualitatively. Humans, however, want to understand the causes of phenomena and their likely consequences. Both are more easily obtained if agents are treated as members of discrete categories. For example, nineteenth-century European clinicians classified all adults who possessed retarded language skills, compromised reasoning ability, and a limited short-term memory as varying quantitively on a dimension called feeble-minded. Contemporary physicians and psychologists classify these individuals into different groups, based on etiology and age of onset, and often prescribe different treatments for the members of each group. College-educated white women in the United States in 2018 are more likely than any other combination of gender, class, and ethnicity to enjoy equal status with males in marriage and occupational opportunities.

Life stage, gender, class, and ethnicity combined with an investigator's measures form distinctive patterns. Removal of one component of a pattern usually alters the function of the entity in a major way. Removal of years of education from the pattern that defines social class changes the correlates of class. Removal of one of the sex hormones from the pattern that defines each gender has similar consequences. Although these differences affect the interpretations of evidence, they have minimal implications for social practices or legislation.

Few traits are adequately defined by a single measure. Nonetheless, some investigators classify individuals who make many errors on a single task as impulsive, independent of their developmental stage, gender, social class, or ethnicity. Others rely on the answers to one questionnaire to classify a person as depressed. The answer "Not satisfied" to the question, "All things considered, how satisfied are you with your life these days?"—given by adults residing in nations varying in wealth, democratic institutions, civil unrest, and health services—is unlikely to be the product of the same cascade of preceding conditions.

Others assume that the diagnostic label of attention-deficit/hyperactive disorder (ADHD) names a unitary mental illness with one major etiology. Huntington's disease is an example of such an illness because all its cases are due to more than 35 repeats of the nucleotides cytosine, adenine, and guanine (called a CAG triplet) in the normal huntingtin gene, which results in an abnormal protein in the brain. But a diagnosis of ADHD is given to individuals whose symptoms are the product of a large number of different causal cascades.

Readers may wonder why, given the stated purpose of this text, I devote three chapters to summaries of the critical features of developmental stage, gender, class, and ethnicity. These facts, although interesting, appear to be irrelevant to the book's theme. I did so because of the very few studies demonstrating that the contributions of these categories to predictor-outcome relations cannot be removed with statistics so that investigators can conclude that a relation between a favored predictor and outcome is independent of the influence of these categories.

My hope is that reflection on the unique properties of these four categories will persuade readers of the strong possibility that life stage, gender, class, and ethnicity affect the relations between predictor-outcome relations in complex, non-trivial ways. For example, African-American boys from working-class families in urban areas experience a pressure from peers to adopt a hyper-masculine persona that includes a resistance to teacher requests for conformity to school demands. This pressure is weaker in black girls and in African-American boys from working-class families living in a rural community in a Northern Plains state that has few black children. As a result, studies of national samples that remove the contributions of gender, class, and ethnicity are controlling for dissimilar contributions to a relation between parental encouragement of academic motivation during the preschool years and grades in high school.

Chapter 1 presents the argument for attending to kinds of agents and the reasons for the psychologist's celebration of measures that are indifferent to the subjects who provide the values. The chapter argues that it is a mistake to assume statistical procedures can remove the contributions of age, gender, class, or ethnicity in studies and allow investigators to conclude that a single predictor variable is related to an outcome. Despite the widespread use of these techniques, some of the world's most respected statisticians warn that no statistical procedure can accurately evaluate the contribution of a predictor to an outcome that is independent of the contributions of one or more of these categories. The psychologists who make such claims are often unaware of the fact that the statistics they used did not meet one or more of the requirements of the procedure, especially linear relations among measures.

Consider an investigator who controlled for the experience of early rearing by hired caretakers on later traits. This child-rearing practice was common on the kibbutz settlements established after Israel's nationhood and during Mao Zedong's reign in China. This form of rearing apparently had little effect on children's adaptation to their respective society, because the parents of these infants took responsibility for their children's development. The same rearing experience in orphanages in Greece or Romania impaired later adaptation because most of the children were the illegitimate offspring of less-well-educated young women who never visited their infants.

Why the Emphasis on Measures?

The salience of human thoughts and feelings motivated a small group of nineteenth-century scholars trained in the natural sciences or philosophy to probe the psychological phenomena that were being ignored by natural scientists because they were too difficult to quantify. These founders of psychology admired the physicist's measures of mass, charge, velocity, and temperature and assumed that reaction times, sensory thresholds, and percent of words recalled had the power to reveal basic truths about humans. They ignored the fact that none of the physicist's measures, considered alone, defined a particular kind of thing. Different kinds of objects can have the same mass or momentum. A reaction time of 500 msec on a match-to-sample task is equally ambiguous until other features of the behaving agent are specified. The need to perform experiments requiring manipulations that could not be used with humans rationalized the use of animals, usually mice or rats, to provide measures presumed to be relevant to humans. The fact that rats and humans were different kinds of animals was ignored. The spotlight was on the measure.

The threat of losing the opportunity to apply for research funds when Congress was establishing the National Institutes of Health and the National Science Foundation in the middle of the last century forced social scientists to defend their disciplines. Their representatives insisted that the members of these disciplines also gathered objective observations that could be assigned numbers. The plea worked. Psychologists were allowed to apply for funds, but this privilege biased them to reify single measures that could be quantified easily, rather than search for the patterns of values on multiple measures that defined a kind of individual. A recent paper defending this idea is a welcome sign (Buss, Jaffee, Wordsworth, & Kliewer, 2018).

Many single black women who did not graduate high school and are working for $12 an hour as health aides in the rural South report the same level of well-being as many happily married professional women with post-graduate degrees living on the coast of northern California. This fact implies that the meaning of a self-report of life satisfaction, which is easily gathered, is ambiguous. A Gallup poll of residents from many nations revealed that the variation in reports of well-being was minimally related to variation in household income, health, freedom to control one's life, or education (effect sizes ranged from 0.06 to 0.20; Graham, Laffan, & Pinto, 2018). Many investigators interested in the differential effectiveness of varied treatments for anxiety or depression pool patients from different gender, class, and ethnic groups, rather than try to find out whether one kind of patient—say, well-educated white men—profited more from a particular form of therapy (Bandelow et al., 2018).

Biologists are more likely than psychologists to search for the many reasons why a particular phenomenon was observed. A large number of psychologists, impatient to prove a hypothesis, assume that the measure they used is a sensitive index of the construct they want to affirm because a respected investigator said so.

One possible origin of the different research styles of the prototypical biologist and psychologist is traceable to the reason why these two kinds of young adults chose their respective careers. A majority of adults who pursue a career in a natural science are interested in solving challenging puzzles about an observable phenomenon that is amenable to a solution with a procedure that involves a complex apparatus. The specific problem is less important than its readiness for quantification and potential resolution. James Watson and Francis Crick chose the structure of DNA in the early 1950s because it was a challenging problem that appeared ready for solution. Had a different puzzle been dominant at the same time, I suspect they would have applied their talents and enthusiasm to that problem.

By contrast, many who choose psychology have a particular interest in the human mind. They wish to understand the origins of its complex products, even if a particular process is not yet amenable to accurate measurement. These scientists often have a favored outcome they would like to confirm. If the psychological study of children were forbidden in 1950, I might have chosen a different career.

Finally, psychologists are reluctant to devote a great deal time to develop a new technology or procedure that might facilitate their inquiry. The technologies psychologists use—EEG, fMRI, MEG, cameras, and computers—were invented by natural scientists or engineers who, in many cases, spent years developing them. New technologies usually produce new evidence, which, in turn, often requires new theory. These inventions explain major advances in physics and molecular biology. The invention and development of X-ray crystallography, which took more than five years, allowed scientists to infer the position of each atom in a molecule. Crick and Watson needed this information to discover the structure of the DNA molecule.

Many psychologists, by contrast, are less willing to invest many years developing a new, more sensitive procedure to assess an important phenomenon and continue to use procedures that have been popular for many years. This collection includes questionnaires, conditioning of a behavior, an autonomic response, recall and recognition memory, and response latencies. There are, of course, exceptions. Charles Osgood and colleagues devoted many years developing the semantic differential. Hill Goldsmith was willing to spend years perfecting a set of situations that would evoke in infants and young children responses that might reflect temperamental biases. Peter Lang and Margaret Bradley invested an equal number of years constructing a set of photos that investigators interested in emotion could use as incentives.

Although statisticians have invented methods to facilitate the discovery of kinds of participants, many psychologists are more interested in proving a particular relation between a predictor and an outcome that applies across gender, class, and ethnicity. That is why they rely on analyses of variance (ANOVA), rather than one of the new methods. Investigators also know that reviewers and editors prefer analyses of variance. Investigators believe that the interactions an ANOVA reveals allow discovery of kinds of subjects. I suggest, however, that interactions are less informative and less facilitating of theory than analyses that detect kinds directly.

An example helps to make this point. Imagine an investigator interested in the relation between the weight and cost of each item in the carts of 400 shoppers of women and men in 12 supermarkets. Suppose that an ANOVA revealed an interaction between weight and cost. Items that weighed less than a pound cost less than items weighing more than one pound. Had the scientists examined their data separately for women and men, they might have found that 80 percent of the items in the carts of the 320 female shoppers had a light weight and low cost compared with 50 percent of the items in the carts of the 80 male shoppers. The latter result is more informative than the interaction the analysis of variance revealed.

Chapters 2 through 4

The relevance of a person's developmental stage to many outcomes is the theme of the second chapter. I focus on the intervals between 6 and 12 months, 1 and 3 years, 4 and 10 years, and 11 to 15 years. Because an earlier book, *The Human Spark* (Kagan, 2013), contained a detailed account of the latter three stages, I devote more discussion to the first interval, which allows an examination of the controversial claim that young infants can add and subtract.

The next two chapters consider the reasons why gender, class of rearing, and ethnic identity are essential features in the patterns that define various kinds of humans. The evidence to be summarized implies that a person's gender, class of rearing, and ethnicity, within a particular society, are better predictors of health, arrest record, cognitive skills, and current life satisfaction than their genomes or answers to any personality questionnaire.

The chapter on gender acknowledges the male domination of females across time and place and applauds the current protest against this practice. The chapter documents some of the reasons for this state of affairs and summarizes the evidence implying that males and females make distinctive contributions to many psychological and biological measures. I insist, however, that these facts have no implications for legislation or for decisions by authorities to restrict opportunities for any educational degree or occupational role.

Gender identities develop as boys and girls, born with different biological properties, encounter their society's conceptions of the defining features of each gender. Although variation in the sex hormones affects the probability of developing select propensities in males and females, most youths and adults can subdue a host of behaviors that their biology favors. Physical fighting is typically more frequent among males than females in most species. Although adolescent boys from 21 of 25 countries admitted to more fighting than girls, the societal differences in fighting were far greater than the gender differences. Fighting was most common among males in sub-Saharan and eastern Mediterranean nations, but far lower in Asian and Middle Eastern Muslim societies (Swahn et al., 2013).

Most cultures socialize girls to nurture those in need, adopt an agreeable persona, cultivate attractiveness, and avoid excessively risky actions. The trio promoted in males emphasizes the ability to dominate others, control fear and anxiety, and prove the self's potency by risking danger. More females than males worry over losing a social relationship. More males worry over being the subordinate member of a dyad. Nineteenth-century American males were under greater pressure than contemporary men to develop hyper-masculine versions of these traits (Kimmel, 2012). Whether the biological differences between the sexes make a substantial contribution to this robust fact is a question that remains unresolved.

The asymmetric ratio of males to females in careers that require mastery of mathematics and the ability to mentally manipulate the spatial orientations of objects has become a focus of controversy. Earlier generations did not question the intuition that males were simply better at these tasks. Those who demand greater gender equality argue that men in elite positions in STEM disciplines (physics, chemistry, mathematics, and engineering) discourage women from seeking careers in these fields. Biology has nothing to do with it. The evidence implies that both sides are partially correct.

Although I suspect that most women are probably as capable as most men in the talents needed to master the skills STEM disciplines require, it is also true that more males attain unusually high levels of competence in these domains. It is possible that an equal number of females could attain equivalently high levels, but it would require more effort. Because no person likes to exert effort if they believe success is unlikely, fewer young women choose to become mathematicians or physicists and many who selected these fields initially decide later to pursue another discipline.

Ease of mastery of spatial and mathematical skills is not the only reason why more men choose a STEM career. The desire to assume a dominant posture plays a role. Because these fields have the reputation of being the most difficult to master, young men with the requisite talents often select math or physics because success in these domains allows them to announce their intellectual superiority over their peers.

Despite the recent increase in the proportion of women choosing a career in science, many more prefer biology or a social science to a STEM discipline partly because women find mathematics and theoretical physics arcane and unlikely to contribute to human welfare. Surveys of young scientists find that a large number want their research efforts to have an impact on society (Leeming, 2018).

Chapter 4 documents the fact that the education, occupation, and income of parents, across societies, predict their children's facility in language, academic competencies, IQ scores, careers, health, longevity, and the presence or absence of the symptoms of many mental illnesses. Adults occupying an elite class are apt to feel a sense of agency in many settings. By contrast, those in a disadvantaged class feel they are limited in the opportunity to alter their life circumstances. It is hard to find a psychological outcome a society cares about that is unrelated to class of rearing. The social class of the family in which children are reared exerts more influence than gender on the outcomes that facilitate or compromise adaptation to the local culture.

Even the consequences of an idea, invention, or book depend partly on those in privileged class positions who have the power to promote or stifle a novel product. No Irish or British publisher would print James Joyce's novel *Ulysses*. The novel's publication had to wait five years, until 1919, when an American magazine began to serialize it. A young Paul Cezanne raged against the hyper-conservative views of the French artists in the 1860s, who used their elite position to reject his paintings. Explorers and scientists who attained fame usually needed money from institutions, governments, or wealthy patrons to begin their missions.

Most infants born a few weeks before term eventually attain normal intellectual functions if born to parents with a college degree and an adequate income. This happy outcome is less likely if the parents did not graduate high school and live on a marginal income. Because class of rearing is always an element in the pattern linked to academic difficulties, it can be a mistake to statistically remove its contribution when studying the relation between prematurity and a cognitive talent or school achievement. This practice is analogous to removing the contribution of air temperature in order to assess the influence of humidity on the amount of snowfall.

Ethnic identity, also considered in chapter 4, is far more ambiguous than life stage, gender, or social class, because the latter three are marked by a few stable psychological features found in all cultures. This is not true of ethnicity, because the earlier reproductive isolation of populations is now limited to a small number of places. Humans who had migrated to the major regions of the planet by 15,000 years ago possessed unique genomes, languages, economies, and values. Therefore, it was not an error to claim that each population represented a distinct ethnic group. The rarity of isolated populations in 2018 renders the earlier definition of ethnicity obsolete. That is why social scientists prefer ethnic identity to ethnicity.

The development of an ethnic identity is facilitated by knowledge of shared bodily tissues combined with one or more distinctive physical features, a place where an ancestral population originated, the language they spoke, and their values. Those who hold such a belief possess psychological properties that can affect select psychological and biological measures. An ethnic identity is especially firm when the ethnic group is a minority in a society that has demeaned them for generations. The adolescent members of a victimized group find it difficult to ignore the beliefs held by the prejudiced majority, especially if minority status is combined with a compromised class rank. Some of these individuals turn against the society that rejects them. Others, who sense they have a talent, try to disprove their society's questioning of their desirability by trying to attain a sign of their virtue by pursuing a career in the clergy, medicine, science, humanities, or the arts. The journal *American Psychologist* devoted its September 2018 issue to this theme.

These facts have implications for the investigators who use statistics to remove the contribution of class and ethnicity to an outcome. Because the blend of beliefs, values, and motives of poor black males in Mississippi differs from the blend in poor, immigrant Vietnamese in Los Angeles, removing the contributions of class and ethnicity in a study of the relation between income and depression in a national sample controls for very different contributions to a bout of depression.

The brief Coda repeats the book's main ideas. The behaviors or talents that are due partly to biological differences between the sexes or among ethnic groups should not be used to restrict any individual from the opportunity to pursue the education, vocation, or position of authority they desire. Societies can simply ignore the distinctive biological features of males or females and allow women to be battle zone soldiers and men to serve as teachers of preschool children. The societies that have ignored biological variation among its healthy citizens have not suffered any obvious, undesirable consequences. A culture can safely ignore the contributions of biology to the different psychological patterns in males and females and among ethnic groups in order to implement an ethical value it wishes to honor.

Although the majority of statements are supported by cited studies, it is impossible to understand some robust facts without speculations that empirical data have not yet confirmed. If authors of articles in respected journals are allowed such speculations, surely book authors are entitled to the same privilege.

Since my last book, *Five Constraints on Predicting Behavior* (Kagan, 2017), was critical of psychologists and neuroscientists who believe that current brain measures can reveal and predict the origins of human thought, readers who do not know me are liable to decide that I am a dour sourpuss who enjoys being disagreeable. This conclusion is wildly inaccurate. I do not like being a squeaky wheel and would much rather support a majority position. Psychology is as important in 2018 as it was in 1950 when I chose it as my career. I ask readers to treat my criticisms as intra-family arguments offered with affection, not malice. I am an aging academic in my ninth decade who should have stopped trying to be a voice. However, I still feel a need to read and write. The theme this book addresses seemed to be a useful mission to fill each day until the time in late afternoon when a glass of wine replaced a pen. I hope a few readers agree.

Acknowledgments

I thank Lars Bergman, Dante Cicchetti, Nathan Fox, Marshall Haith, Ronald Kessler, Helena Kraemer, Eric Loken, Robert McCall, David Moore, Nora Newcombe, John Richards, Jay Schulkin, Nancy Snidman, Hal Stern, and Regina Yando for helpful comments.

1   The Core Argument

This book defends a central idea. Although all humans share a large number of biological and psychological properties, a person's developmental stage, gender, social class, and ethnicity add unique features that render those sharing all four classifications different from others. Seventeen-year-old Japanese girls from families in the bottom 20 percent of the income distribution possess a pattern of features that distinguish them from adolescent Welsh boys from wealthy families. If we assign every person to one of seven age groups, one of two genders, one of four social class ranks, and one of five ethnic groups, we should expect to see as many as 280 distinct patterns of biological and psychological measures in large representative samples.

Humans cannot suppress the urge to classify objects and events into distinctive kinds defined by their patterns of features and functions. Although each life form differs from every other in the number of nucleotides at specific locations, biologists parse these continuous distributions into three distinctive kinds of life: bacteria, archea, and eukaryotes that possess a nucleus. Humans possess a sufficiently large number of unique patterns of gene expression to qualify as a distinct kind of primate (Sousa et al., 2017). Investigators in many disciplines have found it useful to select a critical value on a continuous distribution that defines a small group with special features, whether a new particle, molecule, species, diabetes, or depression. The wavelengths that comprise the electromagnetic spectrum form a continuous distribution. But discrete wavelength ranges are given distinct category names, such as microwaves, visible light, and X-rays, because each range has unique properties. The psychologists who argue that all humans vary quantitatively on a variety of measures resist this idea.

Animals, too, parse continuous distributions into categories. Zebra finches trained to flip disks displaying two different colors fail to flip bicolored discs whose wavelengths correspond to our perception of two shades of red. But the birds do flip bicolored discs that differ at a boundary wavelength of 605 nanometers, which appears to humans as the border between red and orange. Infants show increased blood flow to occipitotemporal regions when a geometric form changed from green to blue or blue to green, but do not show a similar increase in blood flow to a change from one shade of green to another of the same hue (Yang, Kanazawa, Yamaguchi, & Kuriki, 2016). This phenomenon, called categorical perception, implies that life forms carve continuous sensory inputs into discrete kinds (Caves et al., 2018).

Patterns Define Things

The members of different categories differ in their patterns of features and functions. Ripe figs and marshmallows share the quality of sweetness but differ in other properties. Domesticated cats, dogs, horses, mink, and cattle share the property of tameness with humans, but each tame species possesses different patterns of alleles and brain profiles (Brusini et al., 2018). Tolstoy's novels *War and Peace* and *Anna Karenina* contain very few syllables that are unique to either book. It is the pattern of syllables in each novel that accounts for their different contents.

The era in which a person is born can be a significant element in a pattern of traits. Many Americans who reached adolescence between 1930 and 1940 developed an intense preoccupation with money because of painful memories of the family privations during the severe economic depression of that decade. If Abraham Lincoln, Theodore Roosevelt, John Kennedy, and Barack Obama had been born 50 years earlier than their actual birthdate the probability of their ascent to the presidency would have been very low. Analogously, the day of birth of pyramidal neurons in layers 5 or 6 of the mammalian neocortex, combined with the neuron's inputs, outputs, and neurochemistry, define the kind of neuron it will become (Baker et al., 2018).

Not surprisingly, animals respond to patterns. Five rhesus monkeys were trained to reach for and grab 36 objects. All the objects had the shape of a long rod, but the rod could be made of glass, ceramic, metal, stone, bark, wood, leather, or fur. The monkeys quickly learned to reach for smooth glass or metal rods but required more trials to reach consistently for objects made of leather, bark, or fur. One monkey never reached for any rod-shaped object made of fur (Yokoi et al., 2018).

Every observable, psychological phenomenon in humans is the product of at least two kinds of relations, each defined by patterns of features and functions. The first relation is between the pattern of brain activity and the pattern of possible psychological reactions, which can include feelings, thoughts, and/or actions. The second relation is between the pattern of likely psychological responses and the immediate conditions in the person's community during a historical era, which selects the particular feeling, thought, or action that will be actualized.

Had a person with Johann Sebastian Bach's talents, motivation, and family history been born in a developed society during the last 20 years of the twentieth century, for example, he probably would be a particle physicist or an expert on computer programs. A man with Max Planck's profile born in Germany in the seventeenth century would probably be composing organ fugues. It is difficult to predict the behavioral outcome of a brain pattern if one does not know the setting. The altered settings wrought by history rearrange patterns of psychological features. Industrialization, for example, changed the family relationships of those who left their natal homes for a job in the city.

Patterns of Symptoms in Mental Illness

The symptoms that define almost all the current mental illness categories require a pattern of at least three conditions. The first is a set of vulnerabilities associated with genes or events occurring during gestation or childhood that render a person susceptible to feelings or actions that interfere with adaptation. The second condition is a trigger, which can be a loss, frustration, illness, rejection, natural catastrophe, or war. The combination of the trigger and the vulnerabilities generates feelings and thoughts that are experienced as a form of unhappiness and/or lead to behaviors that compromise adaptation to the society. The person's immediate circumstances, the third condition, can mute or exacerbate the unhappiness or maladaptive actions and prevent or allow symptoms to appear. For example, the sudden rise in unemployment among young men in Italy between 2005 and 2013 was accompanied by an increase in self-reported symptoms of mental illness (Odone, Landsiscini, Amerio, & Costa, 2018).

For the sake of illustration, assume that most of the mental illnesses listed in DSM-5 can be precipitated by a pattern composed of 30 different vulnerabilities, eight kinds of triggers, and five kinds of circumstances. These conservative estimates imply that there can be 1,200 combinations of conditions capable of producing the symptoms that lead to the same diagnosis, whether depression, social anxiety disorder, or addiction. That is why patients given the same primary diagnosis often differ in their comorbid symptoms. One class of schizophrenics has rheumatoid arthritis, another has Crohn's disease (Wang, Yang, Gelernter, & Zhao, 2015).

Settings

Psychologists have repeatedly demonstrated the influence of the context, including the task demand, on an agent's response to an incentive (Magnusson, 1998; Magnusson & Torestad, 1993; Bergman, 1998; Hinde, 1998; Fox, Henderson, Rubin, Calkins, & Schmidt, 2001; Werner & Smith, 1982; Ainsworth, Blehar, Waters, & Wall, 1978). Each kind of setting lowers the threshold of a set of probable reactions selected from a larger collection: A forest primes a hiker to see trees. A dark alley at night in an unfamiliar city activates vigilance. The moment an investigator tells a subject what she or he will experience or be asked to do, the brain's threshold for one set of responses is lowered, and the thresholds for others raised. This process occurs before any stimulus or task has been presented (Dalton, Zeidman, McCormick, & Macguire, 2018). Because roads with few cars invite drivers to speed, it is not surprising that the incidence of fatal automobile accidents is highest in states with less dense populations, such as Wyoming and Montana, and low in the northeast.

Every participant older than 4 or 5 years knows that the examiner is judging their response. As a result, many adopt a mental set and accompanying brain state that may not resemble the ones actualized when they perform exactly the same behavior while alone. For example, the error-related waveform in the EEG that occurs about 100 msec after a person makes a mistake on a perceptual task might not occur if the person were performing the same task at home (See Herzog et al., 2019).

Although Hazda hunter-gatherers in Tanzania live in small camps that change residents regularly, the adults cooperate by sharing food, labor, and childcare. Surprisingly, however, most Hazda adults did not adopt a cooperative posture when an examiner administered one of the games popular with American psychologists studying cooperation. The response of a Hazda subject was determined by what the majority of the prior adults had done when they were tested, rather than by a stable cooperative habit (Smith, Larroucar, Mabulla, & Apicella, 2018). If laboratory settings induce states not realized outside the lab, the validity of an unknown number of current facts has to be treated as limited to the setting in which evidence was gathered.

The many investigators who spent hundreds of millions of tax dollars trying to prove that cognitive training of children improves diverse intellectual skills ignored the settings in which the training occurred and in which the skills were assessed or used (Katz, Shah, & Meyer, 2018). The psychologists' late recognition of the power of the setting is analogous to geneticists' recent recognition of the influence of varied epigenetic features on the expression of genes.

Although genes, gender, and social class are the best predictors of risk for an anxiety disorder or depression, urban environments increase the risk by a small amount in those susceptible to these symptoms. Large cities contain more incentives for these emotions than rural areas (McKenzie, Murray, & Booth, 2013). These incentives include noise, air pollution, difficulty making lasting friendships, feelings of anonymity, crime, and an impersonal style of social interaction.

The sister who leaves the small town in which she and her identical twin grew up in order to attend a university in a distant large city is at a higher risk for an anxiety disorder. John Wideman is a famous, respected writer who was born in 1941 in the poor, black Pittsburgh ghetto called Homewood. John became an adolescent in the late 1950s, a time of prosperity and conformity. His younger brother, Robert, entered adolescence a decade later when youths were rebelling against the Vietnam War and racism. Robert is in prison for being involved in an armed robbery that resulted in a murder. The different settings these brothers encountered contributed to their dramatically different lives.

Biologists know that local ecology selects which life forms will survive. Bold anole lizards who explore unfamiliar places are selected when the setting has few predators. More timid lizards are selected in contexts containing predators, because the timid lizards do not venture far from safe areas (Lapiedra, Schoener, Leal, Losos, & Kolbe, 2018). The grooming patterns of apes living in zoos differ from the patterns they display in their natural ecology (Rodrigues & Boeving, 2018).

Humans rarely encounter an object devoid of some context. Even a still-life painting of peaches has a museum gallery as a setting. It is odd, therefore, that many investigators measure brain activity to pictures of single objects without a background setting (Ward, Isik, & Chun, 2018). The few scientists who do present an object in one of its appropriate settings find a different brain pattern (Razavi, Martin, Pantazis, & Oliva, 2018). Infants treat a sequence of sounds as a source of symbolic meaning when they are uttered by a person interacting with another individual (Ferguson & Waxman, 2017). I invite readers to repeat an experience my wife and I had on a recent Thanksgiving afternoon when our daughter showed us photographs taken in various places more than 25 years ago. When the background was covered and only faces and bodies were visible we could not specify the place or time. But the full photo triggered a rush of associations that included both location and approximate year. (See Rubin, Deffler, & Umanath, 2019; Mirkovic & Altmann, 2019.)

A face of average attractiveness is judged unattractive when it follows a series of increasingly attractive faces but judged as attractive when it follows a sequence of increasingly unattractive faces (Goller, Leder, Cursiter, & Jenkins, 2018). These observations are inconsistent with the popular belief that the representation of an object is instantiated in a neuronal collection located in a particular place (Nitsch & Stabnisch, 2018).

The different contexts that societies present to their members over historical eras invite, require, or prohibit particular behaviors and beliefs. African-Americans and Hispanic-Americans living in ethnically homogeneous neighborhoods in one of America's 50 largest cities had far less contact with white or affluent residents than whites living in the same city (Wang, Phillips, Small, & Sampson, 2018). The serious increase in homicides in Latin American cities over the past decade was concentrated in only two percent of the streets in these large cities. The number of homicides committed by black males in the United States from 2008 to 2016 were highest in large, Midwestern cities with residential segregation and high levels of unemployment among the minorities in these neighborhoods. Chicago is an example (Legewie, 2018). The rates were lower among blacks living in the Deep South because many lived in rural areas that offered social support.

Settings have a profound effect on the probability of a significant discovery. Gregor Mendel went to the only monastery in his region that had a herbarium and an abbot interested in science. The discovery of penicillin required unique circumstances that could not be predicted. Equally unpredictable were the alterations in the shapes of the beaks of finches in the Galapagos Islands caused by climate changes that altered the available food supply (Grant & Grant, 2008).

Special circumstances in eighteenth-century Germany explain why this society established the first research universities. These included a competitive rivalry among the autonomous states, the desire among elite Protestant princes to reduce the influence of the Jesuit colleges, a meritocratic criterion for faculty appointments, generous state funding of research, and a favorable view of hard work. The latter value contrasts sharply with the disdain for work characteristic of French and British aristocracy.

New settings have altered the definition of a liberal. Eighteenth-century Englishmen defined a liberal as someone who favored free markets and minimal government intervention. Contemporary Americans regard liberals as favoring regulated markets and considerable government intervention because of changes in the size of businesses, globalization, the internet, and the demands by many for government restriction of monopolies and aid to those living on marginal incomes.

The historical era can affect the interpretation of evidence. In the late nineteenth century, Michelson and Morley discovered that the speed of light was constant in all directions, despite the fact that the earth, and therefore their laboratory, were moving in space. This result was interpreted as supporting Einstein's theory of relativity because all scientists by then agreed that the earth orbited the sun. If this same fact had been discovered in the fifteenth-century, a time when many believed the earth was still and the sun moved, the observations would have been interpreted as supporting this incorrect idea (Rees, 2018).

The category called autism provides a particularly persuasive example of the influence of historical contexts on mental illness diagnoses. The opening decades of the twentieth century were marked by an increased interest in children's development in Europe and North America. As a result, new institutions were created with staff who were sensitive to subtle behaviors that deviated from the norm and might require a new category of person.

Frye in the Netherlands, Asperger in Austria, and Kanner in the United States noticed that only a small proportion of seriously retarded children displayed unusual behaviors, such as pouring sand over their heads, head banging, and absence of interpersonal affect. The new term autism was invented to differentiate these children from the larger group, who also had severe intellectual deficiencies but did not display these odd behaviors. The smaller group of autistics had always existed, but earlier observers awarded exclusive emphasis to the cognitive deficiencies and ignored the odd behaviors (van Drenth, 2018).

The contemporary category of an autistic spectrum disorder is a regression, prompted partly by political pressures, because it lumps the children Frye, Asperger, and Kanner suspected had a distinctive etiology with a diverse collection of children who, a century ago, were classified as feebleminded owing to any one of a very large number of different genetic anomalies. The US Centers for Disease Control and Prevention announced that the prevalence of this disorder has risen from 1 in 68 in 2000 to 1 in 59 in 2018, only 18 years later. Since genes do not change that quickly, the increase means that more physicians are applying this diagnosis to more children. Retention of the concept of an autism spectrum misleads the public into thinking that there is an epidemic of a single disease.

Investigators who study animal altruism often ignore the critical fact that a solitary animal, for example a leopard or orangutan, is less altruistic than a member of a social species, such as a honeybee or baboon (Gilbert, 2018). Altruistic actions toward genetically unrelated adults over the course of a year are probably more common in small towns than in cities because the average resident in the former setting has established a larger number of close social relationships. It is not a coincidence that W. D. Hamilton, who gained fame by inventing an equation that was supposed to predict when altruism would occur, based his insight on the behaviors of honeybees, not spiders.

The extraordinary increase in the number of young adults pursuing a scientific career has created a work context marked by a competition for research funds and academic appointments that is far more fierce than it was in the years before the second World War. Three troublesome consequences of this historical change are the hyping of results, willful fraud, and seeking media publicity. These actions have been accompanied by a number of nonreplicable results in many disciplines (Brown, Kaiser, &

Allison, 2018). The pressure to publish many papers during a short interval has become so severe that many investigators, faced with the decision of whether to publish, have replaced their private belief in the validity of their conclusions with a statistically significant result.

The ambience in many laboratories in 2018 was captured in an essay in the March 6, 2018, issue of *Nature* magazine. The author advised young scientists to market themselves as if they were young entrepreneurs trying to build a business (Fiske, 2018). Most members of my generation chose science as a career because they were curious about an aspect of nature. Attempts to market one's talents were a serious violation of a consensual ethical norm. Newton, Darwin, Curie, Einstein, Bohr, Bridgman, Barr, McClintock, Franklin, and Rubin would be saddened by learning of behaviors they would have classified as distasteful.

Although Darwin, Marx, and Freud had an extraordinary influence between 1890 and 1930, Darwin's ideas on evolution have retained the highest level of validity. It may not be a coincidence that he was the only one of the three who, at age twenty-two, left his culture to sample other settings. The surprising observations he made during the five years on the Beagle voyage allowed him to compare what he knew with what he saw, and the resulting thoughts provoked a set of brilliant insights. Both Marx and Freud made the mistake of assuming that their interpretations of the temporary conditions in their societies were universal truths. A 25-year-old social scientist who spent one year in each of five isolated villages in New Guinea, Rwanda, Tibet, Patagonia, and Siberia would witness events that would provoke important changes in his or her parochial views of the determinants of psychological outcomes.

The suggestion to search for kinds of persons is not new (Fischer & Bidell, 2006; Nesselroade & Molenaar, 2016; Phares & Lamiell, 1977). Floyd Allport (1937), more than 80 years ago, argued for discovering categories of individuals defined by patterns of properties. Had the first few generations of psychologists gathered their measures on males and females from three age groups between 15 and 65, from three social classes, and three ethnic groups, instead of relying on convenience samples of middle-class, mainly white college students, the current indifference to kinds of persons might never have developed.

Critics of the suggestion to search for kinds argue that this strategy makes generalizations impossible because every individual possesses a unique pattern of features. However, those belonging to the same developmental stage, gender, class, and ethnic category often share select properties. More adolescent boys reared by economically stressed parents who belong to a minority group in a society share traits that are rare among girls from the majority ethnic group who grew up in wealthy families. These include failure to graduate high school, unprotected sex, gang membership, violence, and a feeling of marginalization. The history of psychology provides some insight into the reasons for the resistance to positing kinds of humans.

A Bit of History

The natural philosophers of the fourteenth and fifteenth centuries, whose observations led to the discipline of physics, claimed inanimate things as their territory. The scholars who came a little later took the material features and functions of living forms as their domain. This left the immaterial functions of living things without an owner, until the nineteenth century when a group of philosophers, physiologists, and physicists looking for a new challenge decided that the brain's emergent mental functions were ripe for quantification.

Because the physiologists and physicists were trained in and respectful of the natural sciences, they chose functions that could be quantified with measures that yielded continuous scales. They assumed that latencies to make a response, errors in remembering a list of words, and sensory thresholds were analogous to the physicist's measures of mass, velocity, and energy. They did not appreciate that the physicist's numbers formed ratio scales that rendered the magnitudes assigned to a phenomenon a faithful representation of the phenomenon. A stone weighing 8 kg is twice as heavy as one weighing 4 kg.

By contrast, the numbers generated by psychological measures form ordinal scales whose numbers do not correspond to the magnitudes of the processes that gave rise to the observations. A person who recalls 6 words from a 20-word list does not possess a retrieval memory that is twice as good as the person who remembers only 3 words. Nor is an adult who gives a rating of 4 on a 7-point scale of depression twice as depressed as one who offers a rating of 2 on the same scale.

Despite these problems, the reification of continuous measures remains popular. Two respected, influential psychologists suggested that all forms of psychopathology, whether schizophrenia, social anxiety, or gambling disorder, can be placed on a single continuous dimension, called *p*, which presumably reflects a fundamental process that renders a person vulnerable to the occurrence and severity of the symptoms of any mental illness (Caspi & Moffitt, 2018). This claim is silent on several issues.

First, it ignores the distinctive origins of varied symptom patterns. The conditions that precipitate bipolar disorder are dissimilar from those that precede an addiction to opioids. A brain tumor and too many glasses of wine can bring on a headache. Even Parkinson's disease has two distinct subtypes—tremor dominant or postural instability—that are associated with different neuronal patterns in the subthalamic nucleus (Telkes et al., 2018).

Second, clinicians use two different criteria in arriving at a diagnosis. One kind of illness is defined by infrequent traits that interfere with adaptation. Hallucinations, delusions, alternate states of severe depression and manic overconfidence, and an inability to complete a task because of an extreme level of perfectionism are examples. A second kind of mentally ill person possesses no obviously deviant traits and often functions adequately. This person visits a clinician because of recurrent bouts of worry and/ or depression.

An important reason to question the concept of *p* is that that membership in a less advantaged class increases the probability of symptoms in every society studied (Reiss, 2013; Castillejos, Martin-Perez, & Moreno-Kustner, 2018). This observation is not surprising. A less advantaged class position is correlated with more physical illnesses, envy of and anger at those who are more privileged, worry over having adequate resources, exposure to crime, and a compromised conception of self's sense of agency. These conditions generate the feelings that are often interpreted as a form of anxiety or depression. These emotions have the power to generate the number and severity of the symptoms that define the construct *p*.

The advocates of a general intelligence factor, *g*, also ignored the fact that the social class of the family of rearing is a consistently significant predictor of IQ scores (Carl, 2016). These observations do not deny the contribution of genes to both IQ and mental illness. Although genomes contribute to the heights of different species of trees across the world, the ecological conditions at different latitudes affect the heights of all trees, independent of their genes.

Restating the Theme

These facts affirm the primary theme of this narrative. Many psychologists and neuroscientists are not acknowledging the distinctive contributions of life stage, gender, class, and ethnicity to psychological and biological outcomes. A summary of papers on maladaptive behaviors presented by eminent scientists at a workshop at the University of Rochester described the brain measures that could mediate these outcomes without ever mentioning the effects of gender, class, or ethnicity (Diehl et al., 2018).

The increased reliance on data provided by online participants has been accompanied by a surprising indifference to the respondent's social class, ethnic identity, and the setting in which they provided the evidence (Grootswagers, Cicby, & Carlson, 2018). Many review papers that arrive at a broad conclusion based on meta-analyses are indifferent to the composition of the samples supplying the data. The average effect size for two dozen studies is misleading if the data do not come from the same distribution (Moreau & Corballis, 2018).

The same high score on a popular questionnaire measure of depression can be due to chronic poverty, a serious physical illness, chronic insomnia, recent loss of a close relative, or guilt over an action that harmed another (Carpenter et al., 2017). The number of deaths of Americans in 2015 owing to an opioid overdose was highest in non-Hispanic, white males from the bottom third of the income distribution who lived in the northeast. The lowest rate was found in advantaged white women living in Nebraska or one of the Dakotas (Rudd, Seth, David, & Scholl, 2016).

The committee that voted to support the development of the hydrogen bomb during Harry Truman's presidency consisted of two kinds of members. One group favored the bomb because they disliked James Conant and J. Robert Oppenheimer who opposed it. The same decision by other committee members was based on their fear that the United States would fall behind the Soviets in military power. The same outcome was mediated by different cascades of thoughts and emotion (Conant, 2017).

Some leading epidemiologists advocate replacing the popular practice of estimating the relatively small risk for a disease among the world's population with a search for the kinds of persons who are at high or low risk for a particular illness (Keyes & Galea, 2017). The fact that the increase in depressive disorder in the United States from 2000 to 2015 was largest among white female adolescents and smallest among blacks affirms the utility of this suggestion (Weinberger et al., 2018). The Australian psychologist Nick Haslam (2018) rejects the suggestion that one gender, class, or ethnic group could have many values on a measure that fell within a distinctive range (for example, the bottom or top quintile). He prefers to treat all humans as varying continuously on a number of personality traits.

Psychologists who analyze their data carefully often discover, to their surprise, the contribution of age, gender, class, or ethnicity to their measures (Barker et al., 2015; Davis & Buss, 2012; Pappa et al., 2014; Feng, Shaw, & Silk, 2008; Lahti et al., 2013; Cole, Zahn-Waxler, Fox, Usher, & Welsh, 1996; Viana, Palmer, Zvolensky, Alfano, Dixon, & Raines, 2017; Degnan et al., 2011; Sarkisian, Gerena, & Gerstel, 2007; Liu, Chen, Liu, Wang, & Jia, 2017; Goodyer, Ban, Croudace, & Herbert, 2009; McLaughlin, Rith-Najarian, Dirks, & Sheridan, 2015; Bruder, Tenke, Warner, & Weissman, 2007; Aslin, 2007; Reynolds, 2015; Reynolds, Guy, & Zhang, 2010; Braga & Buckner, 2017; Kagan & Snidman, 2004; Polevoy, Muckle, Seguin, Ouellet, & Saint-Amour, 2017).

A careful analysis was needed to discover that black females reared by a poor father in a city on the East or West Coast known for low levels of racial bias earned higher incomes in 2015 than any other category of African-American. Black males who grew up with a single parent in an equally poor family in a Midwestern city with high levels of racial prejudice had the lowest incomes (Banks, 2018). The best predictor of a suicide by an American adolescent during the first five years of this century combined a disadvantaged class, a rural region in a Western state, and a Monday between April and September (Berman, Jobes, & Silverman, 2006).

Categories often emerge when longitudinal data allow examination of varied trajectories over time (Degnan et al., 2014; Kagan, Reznick, & Snidman, 1988). This claim applies to children diagnosed with ADHD (Karalunas et al., 2017), victims of peer bullying (Ladd, Ettekal, & Kochenderfer-Ladd, 2017), the development of a preference for use of the right or left hand during infancy (Campbell, Marcinowski, & Michel, 2018), and styles of classification of objects or scenes (Kagan, Moss, & Sigel, 1963).

The popular practice of reporting only mean values and ignoring the proportion of subjects with low, moderate, or high values on each measure

can invite misleading conclusions. A study of the blood levels of 13 cytokines in 262 American, adolescent girls (62 percent Caucasian and 32 percent African-American) revealed that only 7 percent of the sample had high
levels on all 13 cytokines. This small group of girls contained many African-
Americans (Dorn et al., 2016). A significant correlation can be due to the
subjects whose values were in the top or bottom 15 percent of the distribution (Inman et al., 2018).

The mean values for limb activity, crying, and salivary cortisol were similar in four-month-old European and Chinese-American infants exposed
to unexpected visual and auditory events. But a small group of white boys
combined high levels of limb activity, crying, and salivary cortisol (Liu,
Snidman, & Kagan, 2016). Only 10 percent of middle-class, American,
4-month-old female infants displayed high levels of motor activity and crying to unexpected events, as well as extremely timid behavior during the
preschool years (Kagan, 1994; Kagan, Snidman, & Arcus, 1998).

Children with extreme values on a measure, say more than 1 standard
deviation from the mean, often represent a distinct kind with properties
that differ from those with less extreme scores (Robinson, Kagan, Reznick,
& Corley, 1992; Kagan, Snidman, McManis, Woodward, & Hardway, 2002).
Only three of 60 young, mainly middle-class, Caucasian American women
with blood injection phobia watching a surgical film combined feeling
faint, a large increase in heart rate variability, and withdrawal of sympathetic tone on the heart (Simon, Meuret, & Ritz, 2017).

Furthermore, groups with similar mean scores on a measure often differ
in the slope of change over time or over repetitions of an event. Members of
a gender, class, or ethnic group can differ in the slope of change of salivary
cortisol over the course of a day, or in the magnitude of an event-related
potential to a site over repeated presentations of a stimulus (Kuhlman,
Robles, Dickensen, Reynolds, & Repetti, 2018).

The absence of words describing categories of persons contributes to the
resistance to searching for them. It is easier, and more acceptable to reviewers, to compute the correlation between the frequency of being a victim of
bullying and later measures of anxiety or depression, controlling for class,
ethnicity, and gender statistically, than to combine frequent victimhood, a
disadvantaged class, male gender, white ethnicity, and presence of anxiety
or depression into a category for which no name exists.

I suggest that the second of the following two descriptions of an unpublished finding by Bergman and Andersson (2017) is more informative than the first.

1. After removing the contribution of social class, grades in mathematics and reading, aggressive behavior, and a stable or unstable family, the teacher ratings of 13-year-old Swedish boys on inability to maintain attention and activity level in the classroom predicted persistent criminal activity with an R^2 of 0.18.

2. A cluster analysis of data from a longitudinal study of Swedish males revealed that 37 percent of 13-year-old boys who were rated high on inability to maintain attention and activity level had a record of frequent criminal activity compared with three percent of boys who were rated as low on attention difficulties and activity.

Reifying Measures

A number of historical events are responsible for the love affair with single continuous measures whose values are presumed to have the same meaning across different kinds of agents. The possibility that social scientists would be deprived of research funds when Congress was establishing the National Institutes of Health and the National Science Foundation more than 65 years ago was one such event. The legislation initially excluded social scientists because natural scientists did not respect qualitative data and did not believe social scientists had reliable measures of significant phenomena. Psychologists argued that they did assign numbers to objectively gathered observations on important issues and promised to eschew qualitative evidence. The decision to allow psychologists to apply for research funds motivated them to emphasize continuous scales whose values could be assigned numbers. This commitment eventually led to the field of measurement theory, which is unconcerned with the kinds of agents measured (Aftanas & Solomon, 2018).

A research proposal to NIH that planned to administer a questionnaire to 500 adults who had recovered from a bout of depression has a higher probability of being funded than one that promised to conduct 12 hours of interviews with each of the 30 adults in remission. I suspect that William Styron's description of his recovery from depression in *Darkness Visible*

(1990) was far more illuminating than the answers to 25 questions by most samples of 500 adults recovering from a depression.

Investigators who are impatient to evaluate the validity of a favored a priori hypothesis about a hypothetical construct—perhaps attention, anxiety, depression, or impulsivity—provide a second reason for the attraction to measures. The desire among younger faculty seeking promotion to begin a study ASAP renders them receptive to any consensual declaration that a particular measure is a sensitive index of the favored construct.

This impatience leads some psychologists to replace observational measures of inattentiveness and restless movements, which had been the bases for diagnoses of ADHD, with parent or teacher reports, even though the latter are not highly correlated with the former across all populations. As a result, investigators eager to test hypotheses about ADHD are adopting the more convenient verbal report measure and assuming it is a proxy for the laboratory tests that have been the gold standard.

Natural scientists, by contrast, are more skeptical of claims about the meaning of a measure. They regularly probe the bases for a measure that a respected investigator has nominated as a useful index of a construct. The neuroscientists studying the conditions that affect blood flow in an fMRI scanner or the firing of place cells in the hippocampus are two examples (Kay & Frank, 2018). Many significant discoveries about genes are the result of careful empirical study of phenomena by scientists prepared for surprises. A skeptical attitude toward exaggerated claims about the meaning of a measure is less common in psychology. Reviewers for prestige journals accept papers that make bold claims about the psychological meaning of brain profiles, looking times, and response latencies based on experiments that lack the controls that might invalidate the claim.

A more serious interest in the adaptive consequences of a trait, state, or experience than in the causal cascade that generated it also drives an obsession with measures. A diagnosis of autism spectrum disorder ignores the fact that the defining symptoms can be due to a large number of different biological processes that include de novo mutations in the fetus and rarer, inherited mutations in promoter regions. The many, diverse causes of autism are accompanied by different patterns of compromised functions. A primary interest in the consequences of a set of symptoms, rather than its origin, obstructs the discovery of these patterns.

Happily, some investigators appreciate that the usefulness of a measure in one setting does not always mean that it will provide equally useful evidence in a different setting. One team found that the error-related waveform in the EEG that occurs when a person makes an error in a task requiring accurate perception of the direction of an arrowhead (flanker task) differs from the waveform recorded when a person errs in judging the duration of respiratory occlusion (Tan, Vandeput, Qiu, van den Bergh, & von Leupoldt, 2019).

Other problems plague the current faith in single measures. Every measure of an exemplar of a hypothetical construct is a choice among alternatives. For example, most investigators who quantify an event-related waveform in the EEG as an index of activation of a neuronal ensemble compute the average magnitude over many trials. The peak magnitude and the slope of the magnitudes over the first 50 or 100 trials are equally attractive measures of the same construct. Rarely do scientists measure all three variables.

Second, a majority of inferences are based on comparisons between two measures on the same individual or comparisons of the same measure on different groups of subjects. This practice makes the inference dependent on the specific comparison made. A dozen lemons weigh less than a dozen oranges, but more than a dozen grapes. Almost all inferences from fMRI values to varied sites are difference scores. Finally, although many psychological constructs imply that a property belongs to a person, most are dependent on a relation to another person. The trait of agreeableness, for example, concerns a style of interaction between a subject and others. Mary can be agreeable with three of her friends but disagreeable with a fourth. Too many social scientists are ignoring these caveats to their inferences from single measures.

The Influence of the English Language

Psychologists who study personality, mental illness, or social psychological phenomena often rely on answers to questionnaires as proxies for observed behaviors and experiences. This practice ignores several critical facts. First, the face, voice, and posture of a person affirming or denying a feeling, belief, or action in a direct interview provide information that contributes to the accuracy of an investigator's inferences. Second, self-reports of the emotion experienced in a situation are often an informant's judgment of how she or he ought to feel, rather than how they in fact feel.

The associations among the words in a question can evoke dissimilar semantic networks and lead to different replies from respondents with different cultural backgrounds (Arnulf, Larsen, Martinsen, & Egeland, 2018). For example, the answers to the NEO questionnaire given by adults living in one of a large number of different cultures invited the surprising conclusion that Norwegians were the most extraverted and Japanese the least conscientious (McRae, 2002). Behavioral observations invite the opposite inference.

Respondents who associate the word love with people, but not tasks, are less likely to affirm that they love their job but might affirm a question that asked whether they found their job enjoyable. The semantic networks of Swedish adults influenced their evaluations of personal health. Two questions that seem to ask the same question evoked different replies. One asked: "How would you assess your health in general—good, bad, or in-between?" The second question was comparative: "How would you assess your health compared with other people of your age—better, worse, or similar?" One reason for the modest correlation between the two replies is that the participants did not activate representations of the health of their friends when answering the first question. Older respondents judged their health to be better when answering the comparative compared with the first question (Waller, Thalen, Janiert, Hamberg, & Forssen, 2012).

Spanish-speaking Hispanic-Americans usually have less education than bilingual Hispanics who also speak English. As a result, when answering questions about their health, the former group profits from a semantic context that helps them understand the question. Spanish-speaking Hispanic-Americans rated their health far better when the question occurred in a context of other health-related questions (Lee & Schwarz. 2014).

Finally, the world's languages vary in the availability of words to describe sensory experiences, even though the adults asked to describe their experience may have very similar psychological and biological reactions to varied hues, shapes, sounds, textures, smells, and tastes (Majid et al., 2018). The answers to questionnaires reveal a person's surface persona but do not provide insight into many of the beliefs, motives, and values that guide action because the informant does not wish to reveal them or because they are not available to consciousness.

The Language of Scientific Papers

The language of published papers is an important reason for the psychologist's fondness for measures of constructs with broad generalizability that are indifferent to the agent and the context. A majority of the research psychologists who have published papers in the last 80 years wrote in English. English, along with many languages, usually places the subject before the verb so that listeners and readers can anticipate the intended meaning of the predicate. Very few languages place the subject after the verb or target, as in V-O-S or O-V-S grammars, because it leaves the listener unsure of the predicate's meaning. Sentences such as "Smelled carcass the hyena" or "Carcass smelled the hyena" are ambiguous until the speaker finally adds the noun hyena.

Social scientists, most of whom speak and write in the S-V-O language of English, are biased to assume that predicates possess a meaning that transcends agents, settings, and targets. The psychologists who believe that the English words *fear, sad, joy, anger,* and *disgust* name basic human emotions ignore the fact that many languages invented several terms for the same English emotional word in order to specify the experiencing agent and the origin of the feeling. Mandarin speakers use different words to describe an infant who is fearful of a stranger and an adult who is fearful of offending an authority figure (Wierzbicka, 1999). Japanese use the term *kashikoi* to name an infant's fear and *yuno* to describe fear in an adult. The Japanese have also invented different terms for the falling of rain depending on whether it occurred in the spring or autumn, as well as distinct words for raw compared with cooked rice.

One team saw no problem in asking adults to rate the intensity, salience, and valence of words such as *love, guilt, pride,* and *disappointed* that omitted any reference to the agent, the origin, or the target of the emotion (Nummenmaa, Hari, Hetanen, & Glerean, 2018). The agent performing an action is a salient feature of the older infant's representations of events, and preschool children are less likely than adults to extend a newly acquired verb linked to one kind of agent to a different noun agent (Cohen & Oakes, 1993; Tardif et al., 2008; Snape & Krott, 2018). The predicate *to reason* has different meanings when it is used to distinguish between humans and animals compared with distinguishing among humans.

English contains a number of words for events that implicitly assume a particular agent but name only the event. The term lullaby is an example.

This word is used to refer to a song with particular sound features but omits the fact that this pattern of sounds is usually sung by an adult, often a woman, to an infant. The same sequence of sounds sung by a daughter to her aging father in a hospital bed would not be called a lullaby. The same is true for the word trail, which implies a narrow space in a forest or meadow without grass or shrubs that humans traversed. If such a space were found in a location where no person or animal had ever walked it would not be called a trail.

The physical features of the actions named by many predicates often vary with the agent performing the action. Children, marathoners, and dogs *run* in different ways; *eating* is dissimilar in infants, bats, giraffes, and monkeys. The predicates *open, grab, give, learn, and kill* name actions with different features in worms, clams, frogs, birds, bats, monkeys, gorillas, and college students. The economist Paul Samuelson borrowed the concept of equilibrium in thermodynamics, which refers to inanimate entities, and assumed that it had a similar meaning in an economy in which human agents make choices.

Speakers of one of nine different languages slowed down more before uttering a noun compared with a verb (Seifert et al., 2018). This observation implies that a person wishing to communicate a thought needs a little more time to select the noun because it will determine the predicate chosen.

Despite these facts, one team of biologists described cooperation and cheating in a species of amoeba and implied that these predicates named processes that share features with the human forms of these acts (Madgwick, Stewart, Belcher, Thompson, & Wolf, 2018). I assume they would reject the suggestion that the predicate *destroy* refers to similar processes in sentences stating that the cells of the immune system destroy antigens, builders destroy old buildings, and fires destroy forests.

The late Stephen Hawking used the predicate *discover* when he wrote that black holes leaked radiation. Lay readers possessing the usual meaning of this predicate are apt to assume that Hawking actually made empirical observations of black holes. He did not. Hawking's discovery was a deduction from the equations of general relativity and quantum mechanics. This deduction is analogous to Pascal's deduction, from a set of sentences, that logic demanded humans acknowledge God's existence. By contrast, Newton's declaration that sunlight contained many colors was based on his observations of a rainbow of colors as light passed through a prism.

Some psychologists assume that the popular English predicate *stressed,* which is missing from many languages, has similar consequences independent of the agent stressed and the stressor (Marzi et al., 2018). The equally abstract predicate *uncertain* invites a similar skepticism because the feelings accompanying anticipation of the future, deciding on the optimal response to select from alternatives, and discerning the meaning of a sentence represent different psychological states.

Loneliness has become a popular psychological concept, but it, too, has multiple meanings because the nature of this state varies with the agent and its origin. A husband in his 70s who lost his wife after 50 years of marriage and whose grown children live far away experiences one kind of loneliness. A young woman who left her small town in Montana to work in Chicago and has not yet made close friends experiences a different kind of loneliness.

A third kind has dominated discussion over the past decade. Contemporary clinicians and the media have become concerned with the recent rise in complaints of loneliness among adolescents and young adults who enjoy sufficient food, shelter, protection from harm, and internet contacts. I suspect that a majority of these individuals have not found a life goal to pursue or a moral obligation they feel compelled to honor. Few writers, painters, or mathematicians who work alone for most of every day complain of loneliness because they are committed to a mission. A short story by the Swedish writer Par Lagerqvist, published in 1920 as part of a collection of stories titled *The Eternal Smile,* describes a number of dead professionals who are unhappy with their prior lives. After listening to many similar complaints, an older man stands and tells the group he does not understand why they are melancholic. He regarded his lifetime job of cleaning the urinals at the Stockholm railway station as an important assignment that allowed him to meet a large number of interesting men.

One of the unique properties of our species is the need to work for an outcome that the person regards as meaningful, significant, useful, or satisfies an ethical imperative. The individuals who cannot commit to a goal or moral standard experience a feeling they often interpret as boredom. Most try to mute this state by establishing social relationships. Failure to do so provides the person with a reason for their unpleasant state. They decide they are lonely. But the more important source of their state is the absence of a moral compass, not friends.

Jill Ker Conway, a writer and college president, grew up in an Australian family that owned a sheep farm many miles away from peers her age. But she does not remember feeling lonely because she had a surfeit of chores and many talents she wanted to perfect. Once again, an understanding of the meaning of a predicate requires knowing the agent and the causal sequence that leads persons to decide that lonely is the correct name for their state.

Most predicates in the world's languages require a noun to disambiguate their meaning. The language of a small population in New Guinea invented different words for the equivalent of the English predicate *give* in order to distinguish among the things that could be given—for example, giving water to a thirsty person versus giving advice to a friend (Foley, 2000). The Old English spoken prior to 1200 contained a few predicates that did specify the agent. The predicate *wrath* was usually reserved for God. Peasants became angry.

Because English allows some predicates to function as nouns, as in "Fear is unpleasant," it becomes easy to treat the term *fear* as if it were a natural kind. The same is true for the term *creative*. A fair number of adults and scientists assume that this word names a biological property, akin to eye color, that might be discovered with the methods of the natural scientist (Ivancovsky, Kleinmetz, Lee, Kurman, & Shamay-Tsoory, 2018). This assumption ignores the fact that a person has to first generate a product that many members of his or her society judge as creative.

Eminent geneticists initially failed to classify Barbara McClintock as creative when she claimed that the genes in maize could change their location. Mid-nineteenth-century readers did not judge Herman Melville, or his 1851 novel, *Moby Dick*, as creative. Nor did the nineteenth-century French public regard Paul Cezanne as a creative painter. The reassessments of these individuals as creative had to wait for the judgments of a later generation.

Although American and British intellectuals acclaimed Freud as creative during the early decades of the last century, continental Europeans, Africans, and Asians were skeptical. Far fewer Americans and British now regard Freud or his ideas as creative, while a growing number of contemporary, wealthy Chinese are becoming attracted to Freud's ideas.

Many neuroscientists are trying to find the neural correlates of English terms that were invented long before investigators could measure the brain. It is unlikely that the brain is tuned to respond in specific ways to the stimuli investigators treat as evocative of anxiety, anger, or consciousness (Buzsaki, 2018). Had fMRI been available a century ago, some scientists might be searching for the patterns of blood flow that represented the ego, id, and superego.

Many neuroscientists label neuronal patterns with psychological terms because they do not have a vocabulary able to describe the varied brain profiles they record. There are no biological words for a pattern of activation that includes the visual, temporal, and orbitofrontal cortex, amygdala, and central gray in college students looking at pictures of snakes and knives. A number of scientists do not seem to think this is a problem. They proceed directly from the brain data to the emergent psychological phase of the cascade. Other scientists (Richard Axel is an example) recognize the need for a vocabulary for brain evidence. Once that is accomplished, discovering the relations between these terms and psychological ones should be easier.

The neuroscientists Buzsaki and Llinas (2017) are suspicious of the popular practice of replacing a person or animal with the brain in sentences that have a psychological predicate. It is difficult to defend the assumption that the words speakers of different languages choose to achieve an optimal balance between accuracy and complexity in communications correspond to a specific brain profile (Francken & Slors, 2018).

One psychologist wrote, "The brain is continually scrambling to link together scraps of information" (Chater, 2018). Neither brains, neurons, nor circuits "scramble." Nor can they feel anxious, compute, or integrate. Neuronal collections respond selectively to inputs from the body or the outside world, transform these inputs, and send the product of these transformations to varied targets. Sentences declaring that brain sites "scramble" remind me of Noam Chomsky's (1957) famous sentence "Colorless green ideas sleep furiously." This grammatically correct sentence has no foundation in observation and, therefore, is empirically meaningless.

The English Word Consciousness

The biologist Donald Griffin argued that many animals possess a consciousness that shares features with the human state (Griffin & Speck, 2004). Griffin assumed a unitary phenomenon simply because there was only one frequently used English word referring to an awareness of varied psychological states. A majority of investigators in 2018 hold the same assumption, even though a word naming a single state of awareness is missing from the language of the ancient Greeks and did not appear in English until 1678.

Consciousness names diverse states that include an awareness of internal sensations and external events, the recognition that self has the freedom to select any one of a number of alternative responses, and an awareness of self's properties, location, and responsibilities. Searle (1998) suggested that the latter might be unique to humans.

Many neuroscientists favor a single conscious state because it makes easier the task of finding the brain profile that allows consciousness to emerge. That may be why no investigator, to my knowledge, has measured the brain profiles of adults when they are detecting a target in an array of distractors, reflecting on their feeling tone at the moment, remembering what they had for breakfast, and deciding which of five hand movements they will display on a signal. If the brain patterns for these four psychological states, all of which require consciousness, were different, neuroscientists and psychologists might alter their current view of consciousness as a single state.

Morrison and Reiss (2018) claimed that the behaviors of young dolphins in front of a mirror imply a self-awareness that shares features with human consciousness. It is not obvious, however, that dolphins who make bubbles in front of a mirror or orient to the location in a mirror where a body mark appears are aware of their gender, ability to inhibit an act, or feelings. These are the properties of consciousness in our species.

The Dissociation between Words and Phenomena
Francis Bacon, Johann von Goethe, Thomas Jefferson, and Alfred North Whitehead were among the many commentators on human nature who rejected the assumption that a frequently used word probably named a natural phenomenon. Whitehead (1916) did not believe that language was an accurate representation of experience.

Fanselow and Pennington (2018) ignored Whitehead's warning about the slipperiness of words when they suggested that the English word *fear* named a unitary state based on a distinctive pattern of neuronal activity. Another team of scientists labeled neurons in the mouse ventral hippocampus anxiety cells because they were activated by stimuli that signaled an aversive experience (Jimenez et al., 2018).

Many investigators assume that when a person uses the word *anxious,* he or she is *referring* to a single state with one representation in the brain. Unfortunately, this premise is flawed. A self-report of *anxious* is always a private interpretation of a feeling in a context. A majority of American youth during the first half of the last century were concerned with their family's economic security, getting a good job, and, if a member of the armed forces, being wounded or killed. Rather than tell a parent or doctor that they were anxious, they were apt to say that it was hard making money, difficult finding a job, and war was dangerous. Many of today's youth worry about getting into and paying for college, losing a friend, malicious gossip over the internet, nuclear war, and finding a meaningful life mission. These young adults are likely to say they are anxious, rather than describe the target of concern. It is not obvious that there has been a serious rise in the feelings that are the foundations of the varied forms anxiety can assume, although there is an increase in the tendency to use anxiety as a label for one's feelings.

The popular concepts of sensation-seeking and reward-dependence are silent on the particular novelties sought. There are different kinds of sensation seekers. Some look for new ideas, others want new friends, new scenery, or new body sensations. A similar diversity applies to the persons classified as reward dependent. Some require praise; others seek hedonic pleasures, recognition, or money. Yet most investigators fail to parse either concept into categories that are more homogeneous with respect to the event being sought.

The fact that the major psychological concepts are processes, rather than things, makes it easy for psychologists to celebrate predicates and implement research designed to discover the relations between the events the predicates represent. Two recent issues of psychology's premier research journal, *Psychological Science,* make this point. The titles of the papers in the September 2017 issue contain the predicates *prejudice, individualism, temptation, love, neuroticism,* and *late-life cognition.* The February 2018 issue has the terms *help-seeking, prosocial, learning, self-image, secure base,* and *optimism.* These words name heterogeneous processes.

Because it is difficult to generate an image of most psychological processes, psychologists are deprived of a source of insightful ideas. Bohr imagined a neutron deforming a uranium atom into the shape of a peanut. Einstein imagined himself riding a light wave. It is difficult to create an image of long-term memory and many psychologists continue to write about this abstract concept as if the kind of information registered in long-term memory were irrelevant (Unsworth, 2019).

The concept of engram, often used as a synonym for long-term memory, fails to acknowledge that every biological entity changes over time. The long-term memory of an event that occurred one week earlier is different from the memory two years after the event. The synapses that mediate the memories have also changed. Moreover, the separate features of the event vary in their level of preservation. Thus, there cannot be one place in the brain where the memory of my wedding ceremony is stored.

The attraction to abstract constructs that are indifferent to the class of information remains as strong as it was in earlier eras. The seven basic intellectual processes that L. L. Thurstone posited in 1938, which included reasoning and induction, failed to distinguish between the use of these talents to make money in financial markets, comprehend the data sent by the Hubble telescope, or understand another's motives. Frederick Mosteller, one of America's eminent twentieth-century statisticians, once told me that most statisticians are terrible poker players.

The concepts of natural scientists, by contrast, combine functions with a kind of entity. They appreciate that a predicate naming a function in one kind of thing does not always apply to other kinds. The processes that allow a molecule of water to separate into hydrogen and oxygen do not resemble those that occur when a pair of chromosomes separates.

Because psychologists theorize about processes, such as consciousness, memory, and learning, they assume, with insufficient proof, that each has a similar meaning across varied agents acting in different settings. As a result, they are prone to announce broad conclusions, such as "crows are intelligent," "fruit flies are aggressive," and "mice are anxious."

A Number Sense

The recent invention of the term *number sense* is another example of a broad construct applied to diverse agents. This concept is often called an *approximate number sense* for arrays with more than four or five objects, because neither infants nor animals can count the number of objects in arrays with six or more objects. Number sense was invented to explain why infants and animals usually look longer at an array of stimuli that differs from a prior array in physical features as well as quantity (Butterworth, Gallistel, & Vallortigara, 2018).

The advocates of a number sense claim that these subjects are responding to the change in number, even though the evidence implies that they are relying on changes in contour, spatial frequency, and locations of the objects. This controversy is analogous to the disagreements over interpretations of the activation of the amygdala to a face with a fearful expression. Does increased blood flow to the amygdala represent fear, or a reaction to the lower spatial frequency inputs to the amygdala from the superior colliculus and pulvinar nucleus of the thalamus (Gomes, Soares, Silva, & Silva, 2018)? Because the research on number sense provides an excellent example of an indifference to the agent and the kind of information, an extended discussion is appropriate.

I noted that number sense was invented to explain why many animals, including bees, fish, one-day-old chicks, chimps, and human infants, discriminate between visual arrays that differ in the quantity of bounded contours, usually black dots, by displaying an increase in attention to large alterations of a familiarized array. The advocates of a number sense claim that these agents are relying on processes that share some features with those of adolescents who have learned that numbers are discrete symbols representing a continuous sequence of increasing magnitude that transcends the specific objects in the collection. It is worth noting that the brain does not respond in the same way to all representations of number. For example, the adult brain generates different profiles to a subtraction involving numbers (e.g., 3 − 2) compared to number words (three minus two) (Baek, Daitch, Pinheiro-Chagas, & Parvizi, 2018).

Adults adding arrays of dots generate neuronal profiles in the medial temporal lobe and parahippocampal place area that differ from the profiles recorded when the same adults add Arabic numerals (Kutter et al., 2018). The use of dots rather than horizontal bars may be relevant. The cells in central vision (fovea and surrounding cells) have smaller receptive fields than peripheral cells. The former are tuned to shorter contours characteristic of dots (Ponce, Hartmann & Livingstone, 2017). I wonder if the results found with the curved contours of dots would be replicated if horizontal bars were the objects.

Sources of Evidence for a Construct

The investigators who posit a number sense assume that a change in look-ing time can replace the traditional measures of the understanding of num-ber, usually verbal reports or successful solution of arithmetic problems. Investigators who replace a measure that has consensual validity with a new one have to prove that the substitute is a valid index of the same con-struct (Bar-Anan & Nosek, 2014).

Estimates of the time of emergence of a species differ when the evidence comes from fossils compared with genes. The velocity of galaxy expansion, too, varies with the type of evidence. Cortisol from saliva, hair, and plasma furnish different indexes of the activity of the HPA axis. The pattern of blood flow to brain sites, as measured with fMRI, and changes in the mag-netic moments of neurons in the same sites, as measured with MEG, often yield different conclusions (Razavi, Martin, Pantazis, & Oliva, 2018). Parent reports of happiness or learning problems in their older children do not agree with the reports of the children describing their happiness or learning problems (Lopez-Perez & Wilson, 2015; Willard, Conklin, Huang, Zhang, & Kahalley, 2016). Three popular scales purporting to measure maternal sen-sitivity with infants were found to assess different aspects of this concept (Bohr, Potnick, Lee, & Bornstein, 2018). These results imply that investiga-tors cannot rely on intuition to defend a new measure of a construct.

Scientists who work with animals are accustomed to using different sources of evidence to evaluate a priori hypotheses about learning, forget-ting, stress, fear, or aggression in varied species. This premise is too permis-sive. There are no data supporting the belief that a rat's failure to explore a brightly lit alley, reluctance to venture into the center of an arena, and increased blood flow to the amygdala upon hearing a conditioned signal for shock are equally sensitive measures of the abstract concept of fear across different strains of rats.

These facts are relevant to the claim that changes in total time looking at altered arrays of dots is a valid proxy for statements about a number sense. Many investigators find no relation betweeen an approximate num-ber sense and arithmetic ability in school-age children (Anobile, Arrighi & Burr, 2019).

Aslin (2007) agrees that the meaning of total looking time is ambiguous. That is why a pattern of measures is needed to draw more valid inferences.

Changes in facial expression, a brief period of immobility, vocalization, and heart rate changes are candidates (Scherer, Zentner, & Stern, 2004). Indeed, total looking time often yields inferences that differ from those implied by duration of the first fixation (Kagan, 1971). Although the distribution of looking times is usually skewed to the right and a log transformation is appropriate, it is performed infrequently (Csibra, Hernik, Mascaro, Tatone, & Lengyel, 2016).

An increase in looking time to an alteration of a familiarized event can reflect either difficulty assimilating the event or attraction to it. Hence, longer looking times at 8 dots after seeing 4 dots could reflect the attractiveness of the increase in contour. Nonetheless, hundreds of studies designed to affirm a number sense rely only on total looking times at test events. The cascade that leads to prolonged looking at a change in the quantity of dots may not share any processes with the cascade of processes that allow 10-year-old children to say that a row of 10 marbles has a larger number than a row of 5 marbles.

The attractiveness of a number sense led one team to demonstrate a feature of this competence in an invertebrate. Honeybees were trained with a sucrose reward to alight on the one of two stimuli that had fewer black geometric shapes. After learning this association, which took about 45 trials, the test trials presented one stimulus containing no shapes and the other with one or more. The bees chose the former 64 percent of the time. This result led the investigators to conclude that bees understand the concept of zero as a number (Howard et al., 2018).

This is a bold claim for many reasons. The most damaging critique is that the property *less than*, which is the dimension the investigators used, is not the defining feature of or a synonym for zero. Second, the term zero passed through stages, beginning with its use as a symbol, as in the number 102, which the Babylonians invented about 4,000 years ago (Boyer, 1944). The concept of zero as a null set, which Howard et al. (2018) adopt, was invented many years later. Scholars from varied cultures altered the properties of zero across many centuries. This concept, like infinity, has more than one definition, depending on the mathematical system in which it is used. Zero in set theory is the symbol for an empty set. Zero in abstract algebra is the neutral number in addition. In lattice theory, zero is the bottom element of a bounded lattice.

Finally, the facts of evolution render the Howard et al. (2018) conclusion improbable. Had the set of unpredictable mutations that occurred after bees evolved proceeded in a different direction, modern humans would not have emerged to invent the concept of zero. It seems unlikely that bees, antedating humans by hundreds of millions of years, possess an understanding of a concept that did not yet exist. Unlike a stone, apple, or eye, zero is not a natural kind. Five-year-old children have great difficulty understanding that zero is a number because they assume a number refers to a quantity of some objects. It is difficult to accept the suggestion that bees understand an idea that is denied to many school-age children.

Critics of a Number Sense in Infants and Animals

The scientists skeptical of a number sense in animals and infants argue that these agents are relying on differences in the physical properties of the arrays, or parts of the arrays, to make the discriminations (Haith, 1998; Nunez, 2017). These features include changes in the locations, size, or densities of the dots, as well as the total amount of contour (Sophian, 2000). Alterations in one or more of these features would lead infants to increase their attention to a new array (Piazza, de Feo, Panzeri, & Dehaene, 2018; Bogartz, Shinskey, & Speaker, 1997; Rakison & Butterworth, 1998). Newborn infants respond differently to changes in the locations of three squares even though there was no change in the number of squares (Cassia, Valenza, Simion, & Leo, 2008).

No scientist would argue that a hawk, chimp, or infant who showed an increase in attention to the hands of a clock face corresponding to three o'clock, after seeing the position of the hands at noon, had a time sense. Because the physical features noted above are more salient to infants than the number of objects, children have to learn to ignore the physical features and attend selectively to the number of objects in a setting. School-age children are apt to do so when there are five cookies on a plate and six hungry children. They are less likely to do so when they see nine bushes with red blossoms on the side of a house.

Furthermore, infants and adults create averages of many experiences in a remarkably short time. These representations, called prototypes or ensembles, imply that infants presented with varying arrays of dots may be registering differences in the average magnitude of bounded contour in the familiarization and test arrays, rather than counting individual dots

(Whitney & Leib, 2018). Prototypes help infants acquire the elements of language in what Saffran and Kirkham (2018) call statistical learning.

Neurons in occipital and parietal sites are tuned to respond to changes in the physical features of the stimuli used in studies of a number sense (Leibovich & Henik, 2014; Leibovich, Katzin, Harel, & Henik, 2017; Mix, Levine, & Newcombe, 2016; Paul, Reeve & Forte, 2017; Ward, Isik, & Chun, 2018). The intraparietal sulcus (IPS) is usually activated when children or adults discriminate between different arrays of dots. The advocates of a number sense claim that the IPS is processing the number of dots (Kersey & Cantlon, 2017). This claim ignores the robust observation that the IPS and surrounding lateral intraparietal cortex are activated when a salient stimulus provokes one or more saccades, which would occur to arrays with more than three objects (van der Stigchel & Hollingworth, 2018; Chen, Snow, Culham, & Goodale, 2018; Weisberg, Marchette, & Chatterjee, 2018).

High-contrast visual stimuli, which characterize black dots on a light background, evoke a posterior-to-anterior traveling wave of synchronized neuronal firings over 100–200 msec that often follow a saccade (Muller, Chavane, Reynolds, & Sejnowski, 2018; Papadopoulos, Sforazzini, Egan, & Jamadar, 2018; Chen et al., 2016; Giannini, Alexander, Nikolaev, & van Leekuwen, 2018).

The Attraction to Abstract Ideas

Some scientists prefer explanations containing abstract constructs, even though less abstract interpretations are equally reasonable. Newborn human infants can discriminate between a woman speaking and white noise or music. That observation does not mean the infants understand language. Similarly, a 3-year-old who detects the only elliptical shape in an array of five circles does not understand a feature of geometry. Geometry is a branch of mathematics concerned with the properties and relations of points, lines, surfaces, solids, and higher-dimensional analogs. Perception of a physical difference between two forms is not a property of geometry. A British scientist once satirized the habit of attributing abstract ideas to infants based on simple behaviors. After observing that a sample of newborn infants reflexively brought their hand to their mouth when they burped, he concluded that they understood the concept of politeness.

Constructs Imply Causal Cascades

The construct invented to explain a set of observations often implies its probable origins. The advocates of a number sense have not described its origins. Many years ago, Robert Tryon (1939) bred strains of rats that learned a maze easily or with difficulty. He chose the concepts "maze bright" and "maze dull" to describe the two strains, because he believed that the mechanisms that mediated the performances were related to human intelligence. Later scientists discovered that the "maze dull" rats had been bred for poor visual acuity. Tryon chose a misleading concept to account for the evidence. Zhao (2018) notes that rats and humans utilize different mechanisms when they navigate.

An inborn sense of beauty is another node of controversy. Young infants look longer at highly attractive female faces than unattractive ones because the former faces contain greater symmetry and are less frequently encountered. This attentional preference does not mean that infants understand the concept of beauty (Langlois et al., 1987). The ornithologist Richard Prum (2017) suggested that the females in most bird species rely on a subjective appreciation of beauty when they select a mate. This bold hypothesis assumes that birds share essential features with the idiosyncratic human judgment of beauty, which requires a judgment of an object in a setting. A violin broken into two pieces lying in an attic is not a beautiful sight. Yet I had an immediate aesthetic response to a broken violin mounted on a wall in a Danish art museum because, as a novel object in that setting, it provoked an appreciation of the creativity of the artist who detected a metaphorical relation between a broken violin and the state of contemporary societies.

I suggest that a male bird's plumage, beak colors, contour contrasts, song, and/or extravagant behavioral displays make two contributions to the female's arousal and subsequent receptivity to mating. Select sites in her brain are tuned to respond to some of the physical features of the male and, as a result, recruit her attention. A second, equally necessary, contribution to the female's preference for certain males originates in the discrepant qualities of the features of attractive males. If the male's features deviate from the female's schemata for most of the male birds she has encountered, she is likely to attend to him and become receptive to his sexual advances.

If red roses grew everywhere but deep green grass was seen rarely, lovers would send a dozen tufts of grass to their beloved on Valentine's Day.

The Balance between Evidence and Theory

The controversy surrounding a number sense in animals and infants has analogues in all scientific disciplines. Each discipline tries to maintain a balance between the empiricists who gather evidence and the theorists who synthesize their data into general principles. The history of the sciences reveals that, prior to the twentieth century, most theorists were dependent on the empiricists. Kepler needed the observations of Tycho Brahe's many assistants to discover that the planetary orbits were elliptical and not circular.

The physicists working in the domain of quantum mechanics are altering the complementary relation between empiricists and theoreticians. Most physicists studying quantum phenomena agree on the validity of the Standard Model of the late 1970s. The mathematics of this model, containing only 27 concepts (space, time and 25 particles), fit many observations with extraordinary precision. However, the model fails to explain gravity and contains too many mathematical concepts that can assume a large range of values.

Because the machines that might provide the data needed to resolve these puzzles are not available or cannot not be built with current technology, physicists with advanced mathematical skills are turning their energy to developing new mathematical models that might solve these problems. Their proposed equations predict phenomena that have never been observed, for example multiple universes and tiny strings vibrating in many dimensions.

Although a few eminent physicists are critical of theoretical entities that cannot be subjected to experimental test, the theorists dominate the experimentalists in particle physics. These theorists realized they needed a criterion to separate the more from the less fruitful mathematical models. They chose beauty, whose criteria were simplicity, naturalness, and elegance. Simplicity implies ease of understanding. Naturalness is more ambiguous, but one feature is the absence of very small and very large dimensionless numbers, such as the ratios of the masses of two particles. Ratios close to

1, the theorists declared, were the most natural. Elegance is a gut feeling the scientists cannot describe (Hossenfelder, 2018). Many mechanisms that control gene expression and protein production by ribosomes are neither simple nor elegant.

This digression into particle physics is relevant to the controversy over a number sense in animals and infants. I suggest that the advocates of this idea are relying, implicitly or explicitly, on the beauty of continuity. Continuity in evolution assumes a seamless set of changes from the first life forms to modern humans. This premise implies that many species should possess some components of properties that had been assumed to be unique to humans, such as morality, language, and mathematics. This premise is the basis for psychology's adoption of the albino rat as a model of an organism that was supposed to supply insights into the psychology of humans.

Developmental continuity implies that properties appearing during later stages of development contain components present during an earlier stage. Many young Americans born in the decades between the two world wars were attracted to Erik Erikson's description of the eight stages of life, which promised that infants who acquired a trust in adults were on their way to an adolescence marked by a feeling of ego integrity and an old age of contentment (Erikson, 1959). Continuities are more beautiful than discontinuities because the latter events appear to have no obvious cause. The observation that infants detect the difference between arrays of 4 and 8 dots makes it easier to understand why school-age children can add numbers.

Strategies to Find Categories of Persons

The statistical procedures of latent class, latent profile, cluster, or network analysis can reveal theoretically important categories of individuals (Loken, 2004; Christensen, Taylor, & Zubrick, 2017; McElroy, Shevlin, & Murphy, 2017; Bruno et al., 2017; Goldberg & Halpern, 2017; von Eye, Mun, & Bogat, 2008; Qu & Leerkes, 2018).

These statistical methods are not applied more frequently because they require large samples. Samples of 200 are too small to reveal significant differences in outcomes among the members of categories defined by combinations of gender, social class, and ethnicity. In addition, these methods have stringent requirements that are difficult to meet, and faculty teaching statistics and journal reviewers prefer analyses that compute ANOVA,

MANOVA, and regression on continuous variables (Pervin, 1978). Investigators prefer to write that they found a significant interaction among gender, class of rearing, and ethnicity with respect to use of illegal drugs. Had they performed a careful analysis of the evidence they might have discovered several categories of drug-abusing youths that differed in gender, class, and ethnicity.

The application of one of these methods to the performances of college students on a navigation task that required learning two different routes within the same virtual environment revealed three distinct groups (Weisberg & Newcombe, 2016). A latent class analysis of the performance of third-grade children on tests of arithmetic, reading, general intelligence, problem solving, and working memory separated the small proportion who were deficient only in arithmetic from those who performed poorly on many tests (Swanson, Olide, & Kong, 2018). A latent profile analysis of performances on varied tasks yielded four groups of children who had received the same diagnosis of ADHD (Lambeck et al., 2018).

A latent class analysis of the answers of Dutch college students to the standard questionnaire measure of intolerance of uncertainty revealed four groups. The largest group had low scores on all questions. Twenty-seven percent admitted to uncertainty over whether or when an undesirable event might occur. A third group experienced uncertainty when forced to choose one behavior from a set of alternatives. The smallest group, about 20 percent of the sample, experienced both kinds of uncertainty in many situations. These individuals are most likely to report the high levels of anxiety that invite a diagnosis of GAD, or general anxiety disorder (Boelen & Lenferink, 2018).

A small, but growing, number of scientists are documenting the value of searching for networks of genes, physiology, past history, culture, and current life conditions that represent a risk for a mental illness (Guloksuz, Pries, & van Os, 2017; Boorsboom, Cramer, & Kalis, 2018). For example, the middle-aged member of an American monozygotic twin pair who suffered from depression was more likely than his or her healthy sibling to have had less gratifying love relationships, experienced a trauma (e.g., a car accident), or had a poor job history (Kendler & Halberstadt, 2013). The unmarried or divorced member of a Danish twin pair was more likely than his or her married sibling to possess poor health (Osler, McGue, Lund, & Christensen, 2008). This evidence implies the protective qualities of a satisfying relationship with a partner in the individualistic and isolating conditions that penetrate contemporary developed societies.

These and other studies imply that many samples contain different kinds of participants who can have similar mean values on a measure (Fisher, Reeves, Lawyer, Medaglia, & Rubel, 2017). It is common for the relation between two variables measured at one point in time to differ from the relation between the same variables measured on the same individuals on two occasions. For example, the relation between typing speed and errors is usually negative in a random sample of adults, because experienced typists, who type rapidly, make fewer errors than less experienced typists, who type more slowly. But the relation is positive when the average person is asked to type at their usual speed on one occasion and more rapidly on another (Fisher, Medaglia, & Jeronimus, 2018).

Statistical Control for the Contributions of Correlated Variables

The common practice of using statistical procedures to remove the contribution of age, gender, social class, or ethnicity from a relation between independent and dependent measures often violates two critical requirements. The relationships between the predictor and the outcome are the same across all levels of the controlled variables, and their impacts on an outcome are additive. If one or both of these requirements are not met, the investigator cannot be confident in inferences drawn about causal relations (Gelman & Hill, 2007).

These assumptions are violated when the contributions of social class are removed from the relation between a predictor, say childhood abuse, and an outcome measure of social anxiety, depression, antisocial behavior, marital status, or academic achievement, because the influence of the experiences linked to class is usually not the same for members belonging to different class groups (Knutson, 1995; Sasser, Bierman, Heinrichs & Nix, 2017; Temby & Smith, 2014).

Polygenic risk scores estimate the probability of developing a disease by examining the differences between patients and controls in the positions of millions of bases in the genome. The score assumes that the contributions of all the risk genes are additive and there are no gene-by-environment interactions (Conley & Zhang, 2018). This assumption is obviously flawed in many instances. For example, disadvantaged Americans are more prone to depression than the affluent, and blacks and Hispanics are overrepresented among the disadvantaged. Because these two ethnic groups possess some alleles that are unique to their group, an unknown number of bases in the polygenic risk score make no biological contribution to depression.

Investigators who remove the contribution of social class to a measure of health ignore the fact that, among middle-age Americans, the relation of education to telomere length in leukocytes (white blood cells) is nonlinear (Needham et al., 2013). Telomeres are repetitions of six bases (TTAGGG) at the ends of each chromosome that protect genes from mutations and protect the chromosome from fusing with others. The number of repetitions declines with age. Healthy newborns have the largest number of repetitions. The typical adult has 400 repetitions of the six-base sequence, but the number is only 250 in old age.

Many psychologists violate the requirements of the statistical procedures used most often to control for gender, class, or ethnicity. The decision to control for these categories requires investigators to assume, often without proof, that they are not required for the outcome. It is easy to arrive at a questionable inference when the scientist ignores conditions that are required for the outcome. One pair of social scientists wanted to find out whether the state where a person lived made an important contribution to their life satisfaction. They removed the contributions of income, age, gender, ethnicity, amount of education, and employment from a sample of 1.3 million Americans. Because many of the controlled variables contribute to a feeling of satisfaction, the statistical analysis revealed that Louisiana residents were the most satisfied Americans (Oswald & Wu, 2010). This conclusion rubs against the brute fact that few Americans move to Louisiana. A March 6, 2011, poll conducted by the *New York Times* indicated that Louisiana residents were among the least happy Americans. This example should persuade investigators who rely on statistics to control for "nuisance" variables of the likelihood of arriving at bizarre inferences.

A number of respected statisticians have criticized the practice of controlling for sources of heterogeneity in order to evaluate the contribution of a variable of interest to an outcome (Rohrer, 2018; Achen, 2005; Spector & Brannick, 2011; Torrey & Yolken, 2018; Kraemer, 2015). Donald Rubin, in a personal communication, wrote, "Very few social scientists . . . understand the geometry behind regression, and many interpret their results without a clear comprehension of what the method did with their data." Helena

Kraemer, also in a personal communication, was blunt: "Removing (controlling for) certain variables is just crazy. . . . I really do think that quite generally the conclusions based on removing sources of heterogeneity are more likely to be false than conclusions in which this is not done."

Judea Pearl, a computer scientist with a deep knowledge of statistics, is more optimistic in *The Book of Why* (Pearl & Mackenzie, 2018). The authors note that there are statistical procedures that deal with nonlinear relations among variables, although psychologists use them infrequently. The book's boldest claim is that causal inferences are possible from structural equation modeling as long as the investigator is willing to posit a priori hypotheses. This strategy is easier to implement in the natural than in the social sciences. Few a priori, cause-effect hypotheses for mental illness, personality, or cognitive skills enjoy a consensus among a majority of psychologists.

Statistical methods that control for gender, class, or ethnicity remove the contribution of these categories to the mean values on the outcome measures. However, the same mean value on an outcome can be the result of different causal cascades. Hence, the relations between the controlled variable and the outcome can differ among a sample of participants. Youths who have grown up in poverty differ in the possession of conditions that are more common among the disadvantaged in every society. These include frequent infections, a chronic pro-inflammatory state, compromised language skills, attendance at poor schools, shame over their class position, and anger at those who are more privileged. Because most poor youths do not possess all six properties, investigators who control for social class in a study of the relation between a predictor and a psychological outcome are removing dissimilar contributions of class membership across the sample (Bleakley et al., 2017).

No biologist would pool animals from different species or strains and use statistics to remove the contribution of species or strain to an outcome, because they appreciate that this strategy cannot remove all the important features that belong to a particular category. Social scientists, too, should appreciate that no statistical manipulation can remove all the contributions of a person's developmental stage, gender, class, or ethnicity to an outcome measure so that they can conclude that one particular condition contributed to an outcome, independent of the variables whose contributions were removed with statistics.

The largest decrease in abortion rates in the United States between 2008 and 2014 occurred among women between 15 and 19 years who used a long-acting contraceptive and lived in states in which the number of clinics performing the procedure had declined (Foster, 2017). This statement is more meaningful than one that claimed there was a 10 percent decline in abortions between 2008 and 2014 after controlling for age and contraceptive use.

The reliance on statistics to control for class is a problem in long-term longitudinal studies because the less well-educated participants are more likely than the better educated to drop out of the study. Investigators who use statistics to impute the missing values for these individuals will exaggerate the effect of education on the outcome (Lewin, Brandeer, Benmarhnia, Frederique, & Basile, 2018).

The self-reports of internalizing symptoms by adolescents from one of seven nations (France, Germany, Turkey, Greece, Peru, Pakistan, and Poland) revealed the danger of controlling for the contribution of variables that are correlated with the outcome. In this case, the outcome was a self-report of internalizing symptoms. The two measures that were controlled, which were correlated with the outcome, were self-reports of both stress level and maternal behaviors that promoted anxiety. As a result, the data revealed that boys had more internalizing symptoms than girls in five of the seven nations (Seiffge-Krenke et al., 2018). This result is inconsistent with the hundreds of investigations of diverse samples that found girls displaying and reporting more behaviors indicative of an internalizing personality.

Equally important, individuals vary in their interpretation of the meaning of the norms for their gender, class, or ethnic category. Not all males assume they ought to suppress the emotions of fear or empathy. Not all women receiving food stamps feel ashamed when they use them at a store. Not all Hispanic-Americans oppose legislation restricting immigration. However, the statistics used to remove the contributions of gender, class, or ethnicity ignore this variation and treat all members of a category as making the same contribution to the outcome measures.

Finally, nonlinear relations, often S-shaped functions, are common in psychological studies (Looser & Wheatley, 2010). A few individuals with extreme values on a measure can tempt investigators to arrive at misleading inferences when they use statistical manipulations that seek least squares minimization, which is a feature of structural equation modeling (Breckler, 1990; Judd, McClelland, & Culhane, 1995; MacCallum & Austin, 2000). There are many examples of nonlinear functions in which a new outcome appears discontinuously when a critical "tipping point" is reached. These include the symptoms of shingles when a weakened immune system reaches a critical level of compromise.

Despite the advice by John Tukey, one of the world's most respected twentieth-century statisticians, to examine data carefully before implementing any formal statistical procedure, many investigators do not consistently check to see if the relations among variables are roughly linear, distributions are close to normal, and there are no outliers (Cox, 2017).

Other Sources of Invalid Inferences

Most significant correlations between a predictor and an outcome in psychological research are modest (less than 0.30) and due to the 10 to 20 percent of the sample who were low or high on both measures. However, investigators usually imply a linear relation between the variables instead of examining the distinctive properties of the small proportion with low or high values on both variables (see Beaty et al., 2018; Jeffery et al., 2018). If most psychologists examined the distributions produced by different kinds of participants in their studies, some would discover different distributions for young and old, males and females, poor and rich, and members of different ethnic groups.

When an analysis of variance implies that two groups are significantly different, the result is occasionally due to the fact that the groups are of unequal size and the ratio of the variance of the smaller group over the variance of the larger group is five or larger. Under these conditions, the investigators are susceptible to assuming, incorrectly, that they found a significant result. This mistake is likely to occur when a large, healthy control group is compared with a smaller, mentally ill group whose symptoms have heterogeneous etiologies.

Consider a study of the N400 event-related waveform to incongruous semantic endings to sentences gathered on 300 healthy controls and 80 individuals with autism. If 20 percent of the patients were seriously compromised intellectually, due to a de novo mutation that altered the development of the temporal and frontal lobes, their waveforms might be very much lower than all the other patients. If the variance of the waveform values for the autistics were five times larger than the variance of the 300 controls, the analysis of variance would yield a significant F value. But the investigators would be at risk for a type 1 error if they concluded that autistics, as a group, were impaired in the detection of incongruity (Blanca, Alarcan, Arnau, Bono, & Bandayan, 2018).

Infrequent outcomes, like suicides and homicides, are difficult to predict from any prior set of properties. There were 45,000 suicides in America in 2016, which represents 1 of every 6,000 Americans between 10 and 80 years of age. A majority of victims were white. Homicides were rarer. The average rate in the United States between 2010 and 2015 was only 4 per 100,000 (Griffin, Richardson, Kerby, & McGwin, 2017). A disproportionate number of murders occurred in only 15 large cities: nine in the South, five in the Midwest, and Oakland, California.

An African-American male between 17 and 35 who did not attend college was more likely than any other age-gender-ethnic combination to commit a homicide. Homicides committed by a black male were highest in Missouri, Michigan, Illinois, Indiana, and Pennsylvania. These are states in which young blacks live in ethnically segregated sections of large cities and find it difficult to find a well-paying job. Rates were lower in New England and the Upper Plains states. But even this knowledge does not permit a confident prediction of who will commit a murder on any particular day, because the act depends on many events that defy accurate prediction.

When an analysis reveals a significant relation between a predictor and outcome measure, social scientists are usually reluctant to probe further to see if one category of person might be responsible for the result. Consider a social scientist hoping to prove the effectiveness of a new curriculum designed to improve the vocabularies of preschool children who removed the contributions of age, gender, and pre-intervention vocabulary to the outcome. If the result implied that the intervention worked, the investigator is unlikely to examine the data to see if the result was due to the scores of one category of child, perhaps older girls who had high pre-intervention vocabularies. Moreover, in a large number of studies, the results imply a Bayes factor less than 10 and an effect size less than 0.3. These values are too small to generate a high level of confidence in the replicability of the study (Aczel, Palfi, & Szaszi, 2017).

Reasons for Current Practices

Most social scientists, including the author, favor an egalitarian ethic. This premise does not mean that males and females and members of different ethnic groups are basically similar in their physiologies, abilities, and emotional responses. This belief is an important reason why investigators assume that most psychological measures have the same meaning across all kinds of individuals. The evidence does not support that premise. For example, individuals with an Asian, African, Hispanic, or European pedigree often possess DNA sequences with implications for psychological functions (Ackerman et al., 2012).

The egalitarian premise allows the authors of papers in prestige journals to fail to tell readers the ethnic composition of their sample (Kim et al., 2017). Some are indifferent to both ethnicity and social class (Kosinski, 2017). A paper in the January 2018 issue of *Psychophysiology* reviewing the many studies of the correlates of frontal asymmetry in alpha band power in the EEG never mentioned the influence of gender, class, or ethnicity. A paper in *Human Brain Mapping* examined the relations between single point mutations (SPMs) and EEG power bands in samples from three nations (Netherlands, Australia, and United States) varying in both class and ethnic composition. The authors did not report analyses that might have revealed distinct relations for blends of gender, class, and ethnicity (Smit et al., 2018). These omissions assume that these categories are irrelevant to the outcome measures. This is unwise. A small number of African-American college students in a multi-ethnic sample were the only participants who failed to show conditioned skin conductance response to a conditioned stimulus when the unconditioned stimulus consisted of an electric shock (Kredlow, Orr, & Otto, 2018).

One social scientist concluded that there was no relation between self-reported anxiety over mathematics, based on answers to two questions, and choosing a STEM career in a national sample of American 11- and 13-year-olds followed to high school graduation (Ahmed, 2018). However, the investigator ignored the fact that 70 percent of the children studied grew up with parents who did not attend college and, therefore, were unlikely to select a STEM career independent of anxiety over mathematics. An elegant study of the stability of salivary cortisol across days, weeks, and years in a multi-ethnic sample with less than 50 percent white participants

failed to search for differences due to ethnicity (Kuhlman, Robles, Dickensen, Reynolds, & Repetti, 2018). Developmental scientists active during
the 1930s, by contrast, often examined variation associated with gender,
class, or ethnicity (Flory, 1935; Fales, 1937; Hattwick, 1937; Rhodes, 1937).

Ignoring Biology Need Not Exact a Cost

Most of the biological features of those belonging to one gender or ethnic
group should not be used to restrict that person from an educational degree,
occupation, political position, or social role in contemporary society. Yet
many worry that the prejudiced members of a society will exploit the discovery of a statistically significant difference between genders or ethnic
groups as a reason for imposing such restrictions. A society is neither fool-
ish nor irrational if it chooses to ignore the biological differences between
the genders or ethnic groups in order to promote an ethical value held by
a majority of the population. Scientific facts need not be the basis for all
laws or court judgments when the issues touch on the moral sentiments
of a community. Most men can throw a grenade farther and with greater
accuracy than most women, but Americans have decided that women in
the armed forces can serve in battle zones.

Judges are supposed to use common sense when deciding on the relevance of a scientific fact to a particular case (Jasanoff, 2018). A judge's
common sense usually matches the belief held by a majority in that society.
Although a three-month-old fetus could be regarded as alive because its
heart is beating, oxygen is being metabolized, and it is capable of movement, survival is totally dependent on its mother. An elderly patient on a
respirator receiving intravenous feeding is alive but is dependent on the
hospital's technology and staff. A society can decide that aborting the fetus
is legal, but euthanizing the patient is not. We shall see in chapter 4 that
chronic poverty has seriously detrimental effects on health. Yet a majority
of Americans in 2018 are unwilling to vote for representatives who would
raise taxes on the affluent in order to reduce the number of chronic poor.
This observation confirms my claim that a society can ignore facts that are
inconsistent with the premises they wish to honor.

Although the egalitarian ethic that motivates a reluctance to study or
acknowledge biological variation between genders or among ethnic groups
is praiseworthy, it can lead to an indifference toward sources of variation

that could illuminate an important theoretical puzzle (Lonigan et al., 2015; Kagan, Kearsley, & Zelazo, 1978). No treatment or intervention has the same effect on all persons. Rather than assume that this variation is due to error variance, it will prove useful to look for the variation attributable to different categories of persons.

The next three chapters present the evidence pointing to the value of looking for categories of individuals based on patterns of measures that include developmental stage, gender, class of rearing, and ethnicity.

2   Developmental Stage

The influence of a person's developmental stage on both biological and psychological functions is well documented for the interval from birth to adolescence and is beginning to be described for the years after 65 when compromises in sensory, motor, and cognitive abilities become more common. This chapter does not summarize this extensive corpus. Instead I describe, for our species, the major changes that occur from early infancy to puberty to illustrate the effects of maturation on psychological properties.

The new or expanded psychological functions that occur during the transitions between birth and 4 months, 5 and 12 months, and between 1 and 3, 4 and 10, and 11 to 18 years have been described by others. Although there is variation in the age when exemplars of a new function emerge, partly due to experiences, there is a limit to the range because of brain maturation (Piaget, 1950; Kagan & Herschkowitz, 2005; Sabuncu et al., 2016; Ullman & Klingberg, 2017; Schmitt, Giedd, Raznahan, & Neale, 2018). The age when impairments in cognitive functions and motor coordination occur in the elderly is far more variable because of differences in genes, diet, exercise, and lifestyle.

The Second Year

I begin with the second year and postpone a more extended discussion of the first year. A quartet of psychological functions unique to *Homo sapiens* emerges in an early form during the second year. The big four are the comprehension and production of a symbolic language, the ability to infer thoughts and feelings in others, the recognition that some actions are bad and punishable and some good and praiseworthy, and, finally, a conscious awareness of the self as a source of feelings, thoughts, and actions (Kagan, 2012).

The brains of all species are biologically prepared to respond to particular sensory events. Human infants treat the sounds spoken by others as salient because select neurons in auditory cortex are tuned to respond to the formant frequencies in human speech. Neurons in the visual cortex are tuned to react to the spatial frequencies in the symmetrically placed eyes in a human face. Thus, when a parent speaks to an infant, the latter naturally attends to the sounds and links them to the object or event that is salient in the infant's perceptual field. The result is an association between the schema for the object and the word spoken.

All languages invent words to name different exemplars of objects or actions that share some features. All apples share a particular shape and the quality of edibility. As a result, children during the second year begin to acquire words for object categories that possess the few critical features. By the second birthday, nouns naming objects, animals, or people outnumber verbs for actions and adjectives for qualities in most, but not all, languages (Ferguson & Waxman, 2017).

The capacity for inference that appears during the second year is necessary for language, because the child has to infer when an adult utterance refers to an object or event that is or is not in the perceptual field, and whether the comment is addressed to the child. Inference is also needed to acquire the rules that apply to behavior. Local female examiners in Boston, an island in the Fiji chain, and a Vietnam village modeled three distinctive actions with different toys and then said to each child, who was between 18 and 30 months, "Now it's your turn to play." She did not say "Can you do what I did?" or imply that the child had an obligation to imitate what she had done. More than half the children older than 21 months in each of the three settings cried in response to the simple statement, "Now it's your turn to play." This observation implies that as children approach their second birthday, they begin to infer what adults expect of them. The children who cried sensed their inability to imitate the adult and understood that their failure violated an inferred obligation to imitate the adult (Kagan, 1981).

An inferential talent is also revealed when children want to understand the reason for an observation. Why do only some plants produce a flower? Why do dogs and cats move spontaneously but not toy soldiers? Why does water boil when put on a lit stove but sand does not? These and other experiences lead the child to infer that many kinds of objects possess invisible properties that are necessary features of their category. This idea makes it easy for children to assume that some things possess an inherent property that is an essential component of their category. Young children, for example, insist that a dog who had no ears, tail, legs, or bark was still a dog. Scholars call this frame of mind essentialism.

Two-year-olds have learned that certain actions are followed by punishment. This knowledge, combined with an initial understanding of the meanings of the words *bad* and *good*, allow the emergence of the first stage of a moral sense. This novel set of representations builds on the earlier habit of attending to unexpected events. A parent who suddenly yells, "No, don't do that" when her 12-month-old is about to topple a vase evokes uncertainty and links the action with the salient parental utterance.

By the end of the second year, most children have created prototypes representing the behaviors that are apt to evoke a form of punishment. These prototypes extend to actions never committed. Few 2-year-olds have poured cranberry juice on a white tablecloth and, therefore, have never been punished for this response. Nonetheless, they are unlikely to display this behavior if their mother gives them a glass of cranberry juice in a laboratory setting and asks them to pour the juice on the clean white cloth.

Two-year-olds will point to broken dolls or trucks and say "Yukky," but do not do so to unfamiliar toys that are not damaged (Kagan, 1981). These comments imply that the child inferred that someone damaged the objects in an action that is punishable. The ability to infer another's likely thoughts and behaviors following certain actions is a crucial component of the moral sense and necessary for the emotion of shame, which usually appears early in the third year (Kagan, 2018; Lewis, 2014).

Finally, 2-year-olds are aware of the fact that they are agents capable of thinking, feeling, and acting in ways that they label good or bad. I suspect that the composers of *Genesis* intended to describe this uniquely human property when they wrote that after Adam and Eve had eaten the apple, "the eyes of both of them were opened and they knew that they were naked." The psychologist Fritz Heider remembered the moment he first became aware of his selfhood. While watching his father read to his older brother, he suddenly became conscious of a feeling of frustration because he had been excluded (Sabbagh, 2009). No ape possesses these properties in the forms they assume in 2-year-olds across all cultural settings.

Although these four competences have distinctive features, their emergence during the second year implies a shared origin in brain maturation. An increase in the connectivity between the right and left hemispheres is one possible component of this maturational advance. The neurons in layer 3 of the prefrontal cortex, which connect the hemispheres through the corpus callosum, elongate and grow spines during the second year (Mrzljak, Uylings, van Eden, & Judas, 1990).

From Age 4 to Puberty

The transition between the fourth birthday and the onset of puberty is marked by an improved ability to: (1) maintain a schema or semantic form in working memory for a longer interval; (2) integrate events in the distant past with the present; (3) anticipate the future and plan for its demands; (4) understand the concept of causality; (5) rely more consistently on semantic networks, rather than schemata, to register experience; (6) consider more than one dimension in classifying unfamiliar events; (7) detect a shared relation between different events or categories; (8) adopt the perspective of another in settings that do not involve strong feelings; (9) activate strategies to aid memory; (10) appreciate the advantage of inhibiting an impulsive response; and (11) understand that the words bigger, heavier, or smarter depend on the specific objects being compared.

These changes occur earlier in children from developed societies who enter school at age 5, but can appear as late as the adolescent years in unschooled children from isolated cultures (Kim, Moon, Han, & Choi, 2017; Long, Benischek, Dewey, & Lebel, 2017; Wu, Muentener, & Schulz, 2017; Moffett, Moll, & FitzGibbon, 2018; Boudreau, Dempsey, Smith, & Garon, 2017; Liu, Su, Yu, & Pei, 2018; Worle & Paulus, 2018; Gao, Su, Tomonaga, & Matsuzawa, 2018; Siegler, 1996; Sameroff & Haith, 1996).

Although most 4- to 6-year-olds can inhibit a simple motor response to an infrequent stimulus in a go/no-go task most of the time, they fail on about 5 percent of the no-go trials. This failure is correlated with less blood flow to the right frontal lobe and less functional connectivity between the frontal and parietal lobes in the right hemisphere (Mehnert et al., 2013). These facts imply that the few errors might be due to a failure to maintain in working memory a schema of the no-go signal during the several minutes of the task.

A study of 3- and 4-year-olds who experienced a sequence of events over an eight-day interval in their day care center illustrates the improved ability to integrate past and present. On the first day the adult examiner showed each child a puppet named Clem who liked to eat frogs. After displaying a bright orange toy frog, the adult asked the child to feed it to Clem. The next day, the examiner led the child to a corner of a large room where a toy house was located. The examiner then showed the child how a red key could open one of three doors of the house where the orange frog seen the previous day was located. On the third day, the child was led to a different part of the room where a set of three keys, one of which was red, was resting.

Five days later—there was no contact during days 4 through 8—the examiner returned, presented Clem and announced, "Clem is hungry. Can you give Clem something to eat?" More than two-thirds of the 4-year-olds, but only one-fourth of the 3-year-olds, remembered the sequence of past events. They went first to the location where the keys were located, proceeded to the house, opened the door with the red key, retrieved the frog, and fed it to Clem. The 3-year-olds could perform this sequence when all the events were presented within the same session, but had difficulty when they had to retrieve their memories of these events presented on separate days (Loken, Leichtman, & Kagan, 2002).

The ability to recall and reflect on a past action that violated a family norm renders 4- and 5-year-olds susceptible to guilt. Signs of guilt are missing in 2-year-olds, even though they appreciate the difference between right and wrong and display signs of shame to violations because they infer the critical thought of others. But 2-year-olds do not yet feel responsible for an act that violated a moral standard and, therefore, do not feel guilty. The fact that the capacity for guilt does not appear until the later childhood years helps explain why the Catholic Church does not require confession before age 7 and English common law did not regard a child younger than 7 responsible for a criminal act.

School-age children can evaluate the difficulty of a task and activate strategies to aid performance. These include silent rehearsal of a string of numbers or words they have to recall. I noted that the child's culture affects the age when these abilities emerge. Children reared in an isolated Mayan Indian village in northwest Guatemala, most of whom did not attend a school, did not perform well on difficult working memory problems until they were 13 years old, compared with 7 years for children from Boston (Kagan, Klein, Finley, Rogoff, & Nolan, 1979).

This interval is also marked by a more automatic search for the cause of an event and a reflective strategy in problem situations. Children who appreciate that the error they just made on a task was due to their impulsivity are apt to slow down on the next trial. Three-year-olds are less likely to attribute an error to their impulsivity and, therefore, usually do not slow down after making a mistake on an unfamiliar problem.

The expanded reliance on semantic networks alters cognitive functions in a major way. Children younger than 4 register more experiences with schemata than with words. Seven-year-olds who had been frightened by a dog on a street add semantic networks to their schemata for the event and the place where it occurred. The average adult asked to describe their earliest memory usually recalls an event that occurred after the fourth or fifth birthday because they search for events that had been labeled with words (White & Pillemer, 1979). Many years ago I saw an Ingmar Bergman film about 10 years after seeing it for the first time; I tried to anticipate certain scenes before they appeared, but was unsuccessful for most scenes because I had registered them with words.

Semantic networks are more likely than schemata to imply the origin of an event. The sentence "The leaf is on the ground" evokes associations to the knowledge that leaves are usually on trees. Therefore, the wind must have blown this leaf from a tree. The schema of a leaf on the ground does not contain that information. Moreover, semantic metaphors, such as "Max's smiling face is like a pumpkin," do not evoke the cognitive dissonance that would be generated by seeing Max with a pumpkin replacing his head.

Semantic networks and schemata imply different relations between or among events. Some nouns belong to a hierarchically nested set of categories, as in Rex, dog, animal, and living thing. A child's schema for his pet dog Rex does not contain that knowledge. Maturation makes a critical contribution to the way younger and older children describe their feelings. Children older than age 5 will often name more than one emotion, as in "I felt happy when I received the gift of a book but angry because it was not the gift I wanted." Younger children will use one word for the feeling experienced in a situation.

Most children younger than 5 years do not understand the idea of relative size. If they affirm that dog A is smaller than dog B and are then shown dog A alongside an even smaller dog C and asked which dog is smaller, they become confused. Older children immediately appreciate that size can be relative to the objects compared. This appreciation of the influence of the context on the relations between things affects their self-descriptions. Four-year-olds asked to describe themselves name their possessions, family name, and personal traits. Seven-year-olds name traits, such as popularity, academic ability, and strength, that involve a comparison between self and others (Harter, 1996).

The rapid detection of relations between or among semantic concepts becomes more common after age 6 or 7. Younger children have no problem detecting the observable physical feature or functions shared by a set of objects. However, they have difficulty recognizing shared abstract properties, such as "the best member of a category." Seven-year-olds, but not 4-year-olds, are able to detect the similarity between the gentlest dog, the tastiest food, and the smartest child.

Girls and boys feel obligated to adopt the features and functions that represent the best examples of the gender stereotype promoted by their society. Children and adults possess representations of the perfect member of each semantic kind, whether an apple, a speech, or a girl, and wish to be the best member of the categories they accept as self-defining.

Children older than 5 are prepared to identify with a parent, relative, or the family's social class, religion, or ethnic group. Children who know that their parents are poor, or members of a victimized minority, are susceptible to an uncomfortable feeling of shame. On the other hand, those who know that a parent is famous, skilled, or unusually popular enjoy a self-enhancing pride. The brilliant eighteenth-century polymath Johann Wolfgang Goethe persuaded himself that he came from an elite pedigree by inventing the idea that his grandfather was a member of German nobility (Safranski, 2015).

Finally, most children by their fifth or sixth birthday are able to appreciate that another person can possess a belief or a perspective that differs from their own. This new talent allows children to appreciate that someone who killed another may have done so because of mitigating circumstances (Pnevmatikos, 2018). Apes can possess a representation of what another ape sees or has seen recently, but they seem unable to create complementary representations of their understanding of a situation as well as that of another (Tomasello, 2018). This competence requires an acceptance of equally valid, but different, representations of the same event.

The Influence of Brain Maturation

These additions to the child's cognitive functions are preceded by a number of maturational changes that attain values close to those of adults by the seventh birthday. These include brain weight; a balance between adding and pruning synapses that favors the latter; receptor densities for glutamate, GABA, and serotonin; concentrations of dopamine in the prefrontal cortex; rate of axon myelinization and functional connectivity between the superior temporal gyrus and distant sites; and greater blood flow to the left hemisphere (Giedd et al., 1996; Chugani, 1991, 1994, 1998; Young, Fox, & Zahn-Waxler, 1999).

Tomasello (2018) suggested that brain maturation alone cannot account for the 4-year-old's ability to recognize that a person can hold a false belief. The biology must be supplemented with social experiences, especially cooperation with others and possession of language. The need for language is obvious in the standard procedure for false belief, because the examiner asks a question and the child has to give a verbal answer. However, it is not unreasonable to speculate that this talent, like the bird's ability to fly, will develop in every child with an intact brain, independent of the opportunities to cooperate with others or possession of a language.

All children will eventually be able to throw a ball, pick up a stone, and yell even if they have never expressed these actions before. I was surprised one afternoon in 1972 when I gave Play-doh to a 6-year-old Mayan child living in an isolated village in northwest Guatemala. Although the child had never seen Play-doh or a similar substance, he was able, on request, to sculpt excellent replicas of a person, pig, and bowl. The first human who drew an animal on a cave wall could not have learned this skill from another. The first human who spoke a meaningful communication to another had not been exposed to a language.

Puberty

The cognitive talents that emerge with puberty include the ability to apply logical rules to hypothetical or impossible events. Most 15-year-olds, but few 10-year-olds, would affirm the conclusion that "Watermelons can fly" when it follows the premises stating that "All fruits can fly" and "Watermelons are fruits." Adolescents can separate the facts and logic of a problem from their understanding of reality. Adolescents from the isolated Mayan village mentioned earlier, which borders Lake Atitlan, were able to generate a number of reasonable consequences that would follow the drying up of the lake, despite having never considered that possibility.

Post-pubertal youths become troubled when they detect a semantic inconsistency in their beliefs. For example, youths who believe that their father is affectionate with them but cruel with their mother feel the need to resolve this inconsistency and decide whether the father is a good or a bad man. Similarly, youth who have been socialized to regard premarital sexual activity as morally repugnant must resolve the inconsistency between this imperative and the fact that consensual sex provides pleasure without harming anyone. They also grapple with the inconsistency between the scientific explanation of life and religious accounts.

Youths who were victims of poverty, harsh parenting, bullies, or prejudicial comments are susceptible to classifying those in positions of power as bad. As a result, they try to avoid positions of power, even when they are deserved. Some who attain such roles feel they are "faking it." The eminent British literary critic Frank Kermode, who grew up in poverty, confessed to a feeling of "not belonging" after he had been accepted by elite British society.

The experiences of late childhood and adolescence can create emotions that form the bases of desires that are never satisfied. An unknown proportion of youths who grew up in poor families with harsh parents who deprived them of the belief that they were valued live with a persistent motive for wealth, acceptability, fame, or power. No one understands why only some adults who had depriving childhoods live for years with a feeling they describe as "a hole that cannot be filled." Although these adults may have inherited a neurochemistry that made the childhood experiences salient, it is likely that this bias has to be combined with the belief that they possessed the talents needed to gratify their wishes for wealth and fame.

This assessment motivated them to invest great effort to attain high grades and positions of honor during the adolescent years. The actions required to attain these goals muted the unpleasant emotions and, therefore, functioned as rewards for thoughts and behaviors that become increasingly strong, especially if they led to more honors and acceptability. By the time they are middle-age they have become addicted to days devoted to working for additional victories. These men and women are never satisfied because there is always a more desirable goal to command. This set of habits remains strong because the goal states these adults seek are not the ones they needed as children, whether a sign that they were valued, forgiveness for a moral violation, or vicarious pride in their family pedigree. Neither wealth, fame, power, friends, nor sexual conquests can satisfy the wish for experiences that can no longer be had. Luis Bunuel's 1977 film *The Obscure Object of Desire* captured the cost this dynamic exacts on its victims. The Buddhists understood the dangers of deciding that one must possess a particular object, position, or feeling.

Adolescents believe that they are able to consider all the possible solutions to a personal problem. This belief renders them vulnerable to bouts of depression when they decide there is no solution. A 16-year-old, unmarried pregnant girl rehearses the possible solutions to her plight. She could get an abortion but has no money and the nearest clinic is 300 miles away. She could ask the father to take her to the clinic and pay the fee, but she does not know where he is. In addition, the girl cannot tell her parents because they would become extremely angry. Because she believes all reasonable actions have been considered, and none is possible, a bout of depression may occur. Younger children are protected from this mood because they are never sure that they have considered all the solutions to a problem.

Finally, youths can analyze an unfamiliar phenomenon into its relevant and irrelevant causes (Inhelder & Piaget, 1958). Youth are able to separate, often quickly, the possible from the less likely cascades that preceded an event—say, a friend's anger, a rash, or a fallen tree. The ability to analyze the many factors contributing to a state of affairs one at a time renders adolescents better able to cope with a personal problem. These new competences are accompanied by enhanced connectivity among varied brain sites and a balance between excitation and inhibition that favors the latter (Blakemore, 2012; Larsen & Luna, 2018). The cognitive skills gained at puberty allow many youths who had been diagnosed with ADHD as children to control their symptoms without the need for medicines (Schweren et al., 2019).

The cognitive processes that emerge between the first birthday and adolescence represent a hierarchy of distinct contributions to psychological outcomes. The functions of the second year are necessary for the later talents. Older children add semantic networks for kinds of things and the ability to integrate acquired knowledge with a present challenge. An understanding of the demands of logical rules, which emerges at puberty, provides youths with an armamentarium that can handle many situations.

The Second Half of the First Year

The changes that occur between 5 and 12 months are not only less well known, but they are also relevant to a controversy surrounding the claims that young infants possess early forms of knowledge that a majority assume are reserved for older children. For these reasons, I present a more detailed discussion of this transition.

During the second half of the first year, but especially after 7 to 8 months, most infants begin to crawl; reach for objects more consistently with their right hand; play with two or more objects for a longer time; imitate the complex actions of another; acquire prototypes for the phonemes of the language to which they are exposed; generate different brain responses to native versus non-native speech sounds; devote more attention to events that are moderate, rather than minimal or extreme, violations of their knowledge; integrate information from two modalities (visual and auditory or tactile and auditory); avoid the deep side of the visual cliff; cry upon the departure of their caretaker in an unfamiliar setting and when an unfamiliar adult approaches quickly without a smile; coordinate the rhythm of body movements with the rhythm in the music they are hearing; and, most important, display an enhanced working memory. These advances are accompanied by increased synchronization of theta band oscillations across large sections of the brain and increased functional connectivity between sites in the parietal and frontal cortex (Fenson, Kagan, Kearsley, & Zelazo, 1976; Fox, Kagan, & Weiskopf, 1979; Kagan, 1971; Diamond, 1988; Pelphrey et al., 2004; Zentner & Eerola, 2010; Oakes, 1994; Campbell, Marcinowski, & Michel, 2018; Kobayashi, Macchi-Cassia, Kanazawa, Yamagichi, & Kakigi, 2016; Kuhl, Ramirez, Bosseler, Lin, & Imada, 2014; Hochmann, Benavides-Varela, Flo, Nespar, & Mehler, 2018; de Boisferon et al., 2015; Quinn, Cummins, Kase, Martin & Weissman, 1996; Ortiz-Mantilla, Hamalainen, Realpe-Bonilla, & Benasich, 2016; Richards & Rader, 1981; Damaraju et al., 2014; Choe et al., 2013; Webb, Long, & Nelson, 2005; Jacobsohn, Rodrigues, Vasomolos, Corbetta, & Barreiros, 2014; Cuevas, Bell, Marcovitch, & Calkins, 2012; Kuhl & Rivera-Gaxiola, 2008; Super,

Guldan, Ahmed, & Zeitlin, 2012; Moding & Stifter, 2016; Scherer, Zentner, & Stern, 2004; Kidd, Piantdosi, & Aslin, 2014; Scott, 2006; Courage, Reynolds, & Richards, 2006; Reynolds & Richards, 2017; Xie, Mallin, & Richards, 2017; Schmidt, Trainor, & Santesso, 2003; Gartstein et al., 2017; Otsuka, Ichikawa, Kanazawa, Yamaguchi, & Spehar, 2014; Helo, Rama, Pannasch, & Meary, 2016; Ziv & Sommerville, 2017; Barry-Anwar, Hadley, Comte, Keil & Scott, 2017; Kaiser, Crespo-Llado, Turati, & Geangu, 2017; Geangu et al., 2016; Mireault et al., 2018; McDonald & Perdue, 2018; Gratch, 1982; Langsdorf, Izard, Rayias, & Hembree, 1983; MacTurk, McCarthy, Vietze, & Yarrow, 1987; Vouloumanos, 2018; Thomas, Misra, Akkunt, Ho, & Spence, 2018).

The responses to the classic A not B task by 28 infants observed monthly from 6 to 12 months of age reveal the gradual improvement in working memory during this interval. In the A not B procedure, infants first see an examiner hide an object at location A several times and are allowed to reach for it. The examiner then hides the object at location B, and, after a varying delay, the infant is allowed to reach for the object.

No 6-month-old, but every 12-month-old, reached to location B when the delay was as brief as 2 seconds. All 28 infants showed their greatest improvement in successful retrievals of the object between 6 and 8 months (Fox, Kagan, & Weiskopf, 1979). Moreover, the infants who had better working memories at 6 months displayed less 6 to 12 Hz power at occipital sites during a baseline period. This fact implies the replacement of the lower frequencies with neural oscillations at the higher frequencies that accompany the mental effort working memory requires (MacNeill, Ram, Bell, Fox, & Perez-Edgar, 2018).

The Ambiguous Meaning of "Infants Know"

Most scholars claiming that infants younger than 6 months possess elements of the talents older children possess rely on changes in looking times to alterations of a prior event as the only source of evidence. I noted in the earlier chapter that this measure requires infants to maintain the prior event in working memory for several seconds and to relate it to the subsequent test event. The fragile working memory of young infants implies that this requirement may not always be met (Powell & Spelke, 2017; Kagan, 2017).

The frequent dissociations between duration of attention to a physically impossible event and behavior challenge the assumption that prolonged attention to a violation of an expectation is a sensitive index of what infants know. For example, 2.5-year-old children who displayed prolonged attention when an object appeared to pass through a solid wall, implying that they "knew" that objects cannot do this, failed to search for an object at the place where a wall prevented an object from moving beyond it (Hood, Cole-Davies, & Dias, 2003). Infants as old as 18 months who showed prolonged attention to a novel object alongside a familiar one did not reach toward the novel object in a delayed-nonmatch-to-sample paradigm (Diamond, Lee, & Hayden, 2003).

These observations imply that the meaning of the phrase "infants know" depends on the measure used. Looking times and reaching do not reflect the same understanding. Prolonged looking at unexpected events is not a proxy for the performances and verbal reports that are the measures of abstract knowledge in older children. I automatically orient to a change in illumination or motion in my peripheral vision without having any idea of the event that caused the change.

It is worth repeating that the validity of every statement depends on the source of evidence. The validity of the statement, "Snow is white" offered by a congenitally blind adult who did not know the color of snow and explained her answer by saying that the cold temperature was the basis for her reply, differs from the validity of the same statement by a sighted person. The validity of statements about an infant's knowledge based on longer looking times at unexpected events is limited to that source of evidence.

Can Infants Add and Subtract?

This discussion is relevant to the claim that 5-month-old infants can add and subtract (Wynn, 1992). The evidence for this statement was based on data generated by the following procedure. One group of infants initially saw one doll on a stage, followed by the raising of a screen that blocked their view of the doll and the stage. The infants then saw a human hand holding a doll at one end of the stage move the doll to the approximate center of the invisible stage and then withdraw. A few seconds later some infants saw a stage containing a single doll, while others saw a stage with two dolls. The former group looked longer than those who saw two dolls. The author argued that the infants had mentally "added" their representation of the doll on the stage to the representation of the second doll added to the stage. Hence, they expected to see two dolls. Their surprise on seeing one doll led to prolonged attention to this event.

In order to demonstrate the process of subtraction, a separate group of infants initially saw two dolls on a stage, followed by the raising of the screen and a hand removing one doll. On the test trial some infants saw a stage with one doll while others saw a stage with two dolls. This time the infants who saw two dolls on the test trial looked longer than those who saw one doll. The explanation was that the infants mentally subtracted one doll from the stage after seeing the hand remove a doll. Hence, they expected to see one doll and the appearance of two dolls recruited longer looking times.

This explanation requires 5-month-olds to be able to hold three sequential events in working memory for at least 4 to 5 seconds and relate them to the test event—the initial perception of the doll(s) on the stage, the movement of the screen hiding the stage, and the hand's movements with a doll. The evidence implies that most 5-month-olds cannot retain a firm schema of the first event for several seconds, especially when it is followed by an event with a similar feature (Gratch, 1982; Fagan, 1977; Xie & Richards, 2016). Furthermore, the physical salience of an element in a scene has a greater influence on the looking times of 5-month-olds than 6- or 8-month-old infants (Kwon, Setoodehnia, Baek, Luck, & Oakes, 2016).

The evidence implies that the longer looking times at one object in the addition procedure and at two objects in the subtraction episode could be interpreted as the expected outcomes if 5-month-olds were comparing the test event with their degraded schema of the first event they saw several seconds earlier (Piantadosi, Palmeri, & Aslin. 2018; Cohen & Marks, 2002). Infants look longest at events that share some features with their existing schemata and less at events that share too many or too few features with their representations. That is, there is an inverted U-shaped function relating duration of attention and magnitude of discrepancy between the current event and the representation it evokes (Kagan, 1971; Piantadosi, Kidd, & Aslin, 2014).

Replications of Wynn's original study on 26 samples revealed that only 12 of the 26 samples replicated the original result. These 12 studies used three dimensional dolls or puppets, as Wynn did. The data from studies using computer displays were not significant. However, the use of dolls or puppets is vulnerable to experimenter bias because the examiner knows how many dolls to put on the stage at each phase of the procedure. The 14 non-significant studies relying on computer displays are immune to examiner bias (Christodoulou, Lac, & Moore, 2017). Moore and Cocas (2006), using a computer display, found that the girls' looking times, but not that of boys, affirmed Wynn.

Wynn (1992) provided one reason to question the notion that the 5-month-olds were engaged in a form of addition or subtraction. Infants looked longer on a test trial displaying three dolls on the stage than one or two dolls. Cohen and Marks (2002) reported a similar result. This observation implies that the total amount of bounded contour affects looking times (Rogers, Franklin, & Knoblauch, 2018).

It is also relevant that the infants had to infer that the hand at one end of the stage was actually adding or taking away a doll from a stage they could not see. Both visual working memory and inference are precisely the abilities that mature between 5 and 12 months (Rose, Feldman, & Jankowski, 2001; Buss, Ross-Sheehy, & Reynolds, 2018). Both advances are due, partly, to increased myelination of tracts linking anterior and posterior brain sites between 5 and 12 months (Diamond, 1988, 1990; Geangu, Senna, Croci, & Turati, 2015; Reynolds & Romano, 2016; Short et al., 2013; Fox, Kagan, & Weiskopf, 1979; Cuevas & Bell, 2011; Kaldy & Leslie, 2005; Oakes, Ross-Sheehy, & Luck, 2006; Pruett et al., 2015; Xie, Mallin & Richards, 2019).

A control procedure might have revealed a flaw in the original conclusion. Imagine a group of infants seeing an empty human hand at the edge of the stage that neither added nor took away a doll. If the infants' looking times were similar to those found in the original study, we would be forced to conclude that 5-month-olds were not engaging in addition or subtraction. Six-month-olds have difficulty inferring that a desired toy just beyond their reach can be seized by pulling in the cloth on which the toy rested. Hence, it is reasonable to question the assumption that 5-month-olds inferred that the hand was adding or taking away a doll from a stage they could not see (Willetts, 1999). Studies by Andersen, Hespos, and Rips (2018) and van Loesbroek and Smitsman (1990) are relevant to this claim.

Uller, Carey, Huntley-Fenner, & Klatt (1999) provide some indirect support for this argument. When 10-month-old infants saw all the objects being lowered on to a stage from behind a screen, instead of seeing one or two dolls on the stage initially, their looking times implied the ability to hold the sequence of events in working memory and to recognize that an object had been added or taken away. But 5-month-olds did not show this competence.

Finally, it is relevant that the looking times of infants who saw either zero, one, two, or three puppets on the addition or subtraction test trials were shortest when the stage had no puppets, even though this event is just as impossible as one doll in the addition or two dolls in the subtraction procedure (Cohen & Marks, 2002). I suspect that 1-year-olds, who have a firmer working memory and are beginning to show an inferential talent, would display long looking times to test trials with no objects (Andersen & Lundqvist, 2019).

The complete corpus of evidence implies that the pattern of looking times Wynn found is replicable when three-dimensional forms resembling humans are the objects. But there are reasonable, alternative interpretations of this result that do not require any computation. The most likely is that 5-month-old infants are responding to the fading schema of the first scene they saw, which was one doll for addition and two dolls for subtraction. It is not certain, therefore, that the infants were performing a cognitive process resembling addition or subtraction, no matter how these words are defined.

This close examination of the second half of the first year was intended to illustrate the significance of developmental stage in patterns that define kinds of individuals. There are life stage discontinuities in many processes. I noted, for example, that no 1- or- 2-year-old can experience the emotion of guilt. The results of statistical procedures that remove the contribution of age to a relation between a predictor and an outcome in samples that include subjects from dissimilar life stages are difficult to interpret. That is why investigators should restrict their analyses to subjects from the same developmental stage.

Relevance for Artificial Intelligence

The fact that children rely on more than one kind of code to represent experience has implications for those who hope that the products of artificial intelligence (AI) programs will eventually provide a sensitive measure of human thoughts and problem solving. This wish fails to acknowledge that computer programs and brains arrive at their products through different cascades. AI relies only on a digital code that requires a yes or no answer to every decision. Humans exploit three kinds of representations and solve many problems by evaluating a sequence of probabilities none of which informs the person if each decision in a series is correct.

Schemata represent the patterns of physical features of an event. Semantic forms include collections of words organized into networks, often called concepts. A familiar scene simultaneously evokes nonverbal schemata for the functions and locations of the objects in a setting along with one or more semantic networks (Hurely et al., 2018). A third kind of mental representation consists of the average of a collection of schemata, called prototypes or ensembles. A glance at a stand of trees creates a representation of the average height of the trees.

No current AI program is a faithful representation of the processes a monkey and human activate when recognizing a familiar object, say a banana, in different contexts (Rajalingham et al., 2018). Nor are AI programs able to recognize highly abstract representations of familiar objects. Although humans have no problem recognizing a stylized glass sculpture of a rabbit, one AI program classified this object as an hourglass, ladle, or washbasin (Baker & Kellman, 2018).

Humans and AI programs acquiring the rules for classifying two kinds of trees (many leaves vs. many branches) profit from different learning conditions. Humans make fewer errors on test trials if the leafy and branchy trees were presented in separate blocks during learning. The AI programs made more errors under this condition (Flesch, Balaguer, Dekker, Nili, & Summerfield, 2018). Humans establish stronger associations between events when a feeling accompanies the events. AI programs do not code for feelings.

Scientists regularly create novel schemata to represent possible events. I suspect that no AI program fed all the facts of physics and mathematics in 1920 would generate Einstein's image of riding a light wave or Schrodinger's wave equations. No program exposed to 100,000 famous paintings by nineteenth-century European artists would generate Picasso's *Guernica*.

Stuart Russell, an AI expert, noted that no current program implementing a sequence of algorithms "knows whether it is on the right track" toward a solution (cited in Rees, 2018, p. 103). These observations imply that, at present, AI programs do not simulate the ways humans classify objects, learn abstract principles, or solve complex problems. AI will produce better robots, more accurate rockets, and more profitable investment choices, but the simulation of human mental processes seems less likely.

AI scholars accept Alan Turing's claim that if observers cannot tell the difference between a product created by two distinct mechanisms it is acceptable to conclude that the two outcomes are the same. This principle has serious problems. Oil, coal sunlight, water, or wind could be the source of energy that lights a lamp. Contemporary experts on climate change care deeply about the mechanism that lights lamps, even though no observer can detect the origin of the energy that lights a room.

3 Sex and Gender

The controversies surrounding the reasons for the psychological differences between the females and males of our species have become more strident. Many societies are challenging assumptions that have dominated minds and social practices for thousands of years. The fact that 88 percent of current medical students in France are women represents a dramatic break with the past. Hence, two declarations should facilitate an unbiased reading of this chapter. First, every conclusion applies to differing proportions of males or females, because there are exceptions to every inference. Second, documented gender differences, including biological properties, have no necessary implications for a society's laws or restrictions on opportunities to obtain whatever life goals an individual desires. Societies can ignore these differences without exacting a serious cost to their economy, strength, or stability, as long as a majority of the citizens advocate this ethical standard. Women can serve as front-line soldiers in wartime and men can be aides to the sick and elderly.

The argument for treating sex or gender as a component of the patterns that define kinds of humans is persuasive. Males and females in every known culture, past and present, possess distinctive patterns of psychological and biological features that influence outcome measures in different ways. Although complex blends of experiences and biology create the phenomena to be described, I deal first with the consequences of socialization and societal values because I suspect they exert a greater influence than biology on more of the psychological traits that differentiate the genders.

Gender Identity

Sex is defined by the possession of two X chromosomes or an X and a Y chromosome. The genes on these chromosomes make a major contribution to genital anatomy and the ability to carry out the reproductive functions of a female or male. Most social scientists are more interested in the complementary concept of gender identity, which is a personal choice. This concept is being discussed by the media because of the debates over transgender individuals and same-sex marriage.

Humans automatically detect the features that distinguish between two kinds of things. Women and men in all cultures differ in primary sexual characteristics, ability to conceive and give birth to a new life, menstrual cycles, size, and strength (Ellemers, 2018; Roberts, Ho, Rhodes, & Gelman, 2017). This small collection of distinguishing features invites different socialization practices that gradually establish distinctive gender identities in children from all societies. Some of the products of these family practices appear by the second birthday (Zosuls et al., 2009; Fiske, 2017; Serbin, Poulis-Dubois, & Eichstedt, 2002).

Features Associated with Gender

Older children and adults from diverse cultures associate the concept of female with events that have a gradual quality and associate male with more punctate events (Kagan, 2013). Turkish college students possess symbolic networks that link femaleness with curved shapes, sweet tastes, and smooth textures, and maleness with angular shapes, sour tastes, and rough textures (Blazhenkova & Kumar, 2018). A 4-year-old in one of my studies asked why he chose the angular shape of the tops of picket fences as more like his father than his mother replied, "Because sharp things can hurt you."

Children in many cultures associate maleness with the lower-pitch, more punctate sound of a trumpet and drums, and femaleness with the higher-pitch, more fluid sound of a clarinet or a flute (Elliott & Yoder-White, 1997). More American girls choose to play the flute, clarinet, or violin while more boys play a trumpet, drums, or trombone (Conway, 2000; Abeles, 2009).

Listeners evaluating single words whose pitch contours were manipulated judged words with a high or increasing pitch as trustworthy and those with a low or decreasing pitch as dominant (Ponsot, Burred, Belin, & Aucouturier, 2018). The popular seventeenth-century violins made by the

Stradivari family had a brilliant sound whose frequencies generated a sound that resembled a woman singing a vowel that ascended in frequency across the notes of a scale. Violins made by others at the same time were tuned to the qualities of male voices (Tai, Shen, Lin, & Chung, 2018).

The first names contemporary Americans give their infants differ on a continuum from gradual to punctate. Names given to girls often have two or more syllables that possess a gradual quality, such as Maria, Sophia, and Jennifer. The single-syllable names given more often to boys, such as Carl, Marc, and George, have a punctate quality. American youth treat boys with multi-syllable names, such as Alexander or Frederick, as possessing feminine traits and are likely to tease them (Mehrabian, 2001).

The messages of Facebook users across the world reveal a gendered pattern of communication. The females were more likely to use words that were affiliative and compassionate. Male messages contained more hostile, impersonal language (Park et al., 2016). When men wrote about their wife or female partner, they were more likely than women describing a male partner to precede the noun with the word *my,* implying that many males regard their female companion as a possession (Schwartz et al., 2013).

Not surprisingly, the ads posted by American firms seeking new employees have a gender bias. The ads recruiting men emphasize words such as leader, competitive, and dominant. The ads for women employees more often contained the terms support, understanding, and interpersonal (Gaucher, Friesen, & Kay, 2011). Children as young as 6 assume that females help others while males promote themselves (Block, Gonzalez, Schmader, & Baron, 2018). Juvenile female chimpanzees usually travel in large same-sex groups, while males typically travel alone or in small groups of males (Lonsdorf et al., 2014; Furichi, 2011).

Beatrice and John Whiting sent their anthropology students to six different cultures to observe 3- to 11-year-old children in their usual settings (Whiting & Whiting, 1975). Five of the sites were farming villages in Okinawa, Philippines, India, Kenya, or Mexico. The sixth site was a New England town of 5,000 residents. Although physical aggression was rare in all settings, boys displayed this class of behavior more often than girls in all six sites. By contrast girls in the five farming villages displayed actions that helped another more frequently than boys.

Boys are more likely than girls to engage in games characterized by a single winner. These experiences shape a competitive style that is less common among females. Women can maintain a love relationship, birth a healthy child, and be sexually attractive without being the best example of these properties. Although contemporary Sweden is among the most gender equal nations, Swedish women say it is important to be attractive to men (Albanesi, 2009).

Variation in Gender Identity

Some features in a society's definition of gender identity change with history. Women who came of age before 1950 did not regard a male's comment on their attractiveness as demeaning. Many contemporary women resent such comments. The ability to engage in mutually pleasurable sex is becoming as important as the capacity to conceive a child as a fundamental requirement for a confident female identity among a small, but growing, proportion of educated women in developed societies. The presence of upscale sex toy stores for women interested in purchasing vibrators was unimaginable only 60 years ago. These observations do not mean that the ability to conceive and give birth to an infant has been eliminated as a critical node in the semantic network for female. This competence is too distinctive to be vulnerable to the vicissitudes of history.

Cultures vary in the traits they assign to each gender. Although most ancient societies placed men in the dominant role, Egypt, India, Athens, and Rome celebrated female goddesses. The Egyptians even allowed the wife of the pharaoh to ascend to that role if her husband died and the male heir was too young to be pharaoh. The ancient Chinese were far more misogynous than most societies. They did not give their daughters a name, bound their feet, and practiced female infanticide. The Mandarin character for woman is a person kneeling with hands folded implying a submissive posture. Women were seen as cunning, weak, timid, and deceitful. The ancient Japanese, by contrast, attributed to women the more desirable qualities of purity and beauty (Fan, 1996). These older stereotypes are muted in contemporary China and Japan.

The citizens in small villages in South India believe that the distinctive psychological properties of males and females are the product of a blend of semen and menstrual blood at the moment of conception. The Melanesians, on the other hand, believe that behaviors are the bases of gender identity. Women cook, care for children, and assume a submissive posture. Men fish, fight, and are dominant (Busby, 1997).

Occupations

Occupations acquire a gender stereotype when one sex dominates a particular job category. Fewer men than women apply to nursing school, despite the reasonably high salaries of registered nurses, because this profession is dominated by women. Fewer women apply for jobs in the local police force. The recent decrease in the number of African-American males applying to and graduating from a medical school may be due, in part, to the rising number of black women physicians.

The increased proportion of American women in professional occupations from 1960 to 2015 has been accompanied by a decline in the salary attached to these jobs (Mandel, 2018). The annual incomes of neurosurgeons, portfolio managers, and computer programmers, occupations that have remained dominated by men, have risen by a larger amount than the salary increases for pediatricians, school principals, and manuscript editors, which recruit a disproportionate number of women. This asymmetry implies a prejudiced view of the monetary value of a woman's talents.

The men who are executives in male-dominated jobs deny being prejudiced against females. They claim that many women are reluctant to study or apply for occupations with very high salaries because a majority of these occupations are either technically difficult, require long hours on unpredictable schedules, or pose the risk of causing serious harm should an error occur. A large number of experienced female nurse practitioners in Florida who had made a medical error confessed to intense anxiety over their future career, somatic symptoms, and guilt (Delacroix, 2017). Although there are many successful woman executives, few women have been as willing as Jeff Bezos of Amazon to ignore the high probability of failure that was present when he began this business.

Although females are risk averse when a decision might lead to a loss of money, a taint on one's reputation, harsh criticism, or physical harm (Sapienza, Zingales, & Maestripieri, 2009), females are not risk averse when a child, husband, or parent is in danger. Nor are women risk averse when they agree to have unprotected sex in order to please their partner. Moreover, there is evidence suggesting that women are less risk averse during the few days before, during, and after ovulation, when estrogen is at its highest level in brain sites that contribute to risky behavior (Lazzaro, Rutledge, Burghart, & Glimcher, 2016). Naked predicates, such as risk averse, are ambiguous until an agent, target, and setting are specified.

Mary Beard, a brilliant British classicist, did not consider the effects of voluntary choice in her brief book *Women & Power* (Beard, 2017). She argued that women are as eager as men to assume a position of power over others, but males have frustrated them. Beard did not entertain the possibility that many women do not have an irrepressible desire to occupy a position of power.

Men have not used their power to prevent women from choosing to master the trumpet, earning extra money plowing snow from driveways, or owning lumber companies. Some gender differences are the result of a preference rather than male prejudice. This suggestion is supported by a study of gender differences on a number of self-reported personality traits in 76 nations varying in gross national product and degree of gender equality. The gender differences in traits related to dominance and power were larger in the richer, more gender-equal societies where women have the greatest opportunity to pursue any career (Falk & Hermle, 2018).

This fact has a perfect parallel in research indicating that the heritability of IQ scores (defined by the degree of similarity in IQ among genetically related members of a family) are close to zero for children growing up in poor families, but substantial in children from affluent families (Turkheimer, Haley, Waldron, D'Onofrio, & Gottesman, 2003). This observation and the former on gender can be understood by recognizing that the genes that contribute to IQ or personality traits have more influence when the experiential bases for the property are minimal. Many children from poor families go to less adequate schools and are not encouraged to develop language skills or a desire to acquire the knowledge tapped on IQ tests. These influences swamp the power of genes that affect IQ. By contrast, many children from affluent homes are exposed to the conditions that facilitate IQ. Hence, the genes that influence this measure are allowed to be expressed.

The same logic explains why the gender differences in risk-taking in business and positions of power are larger in richer, more egalitarian societies that allow many adults to choose the traits they find compatible with their biology. Under these conditions, the genes that make small contributions to these traits can exert their influence. Males and females living in poor nations are burdened with the need to survive, which makes it harder to develop preferred traits. Moreover, the barriers to women in gender-biased societies deny females the sense of agency that would allow them to choose the kind of person they wish to become. These observations imply that some of the gender differences in personality traits and occupation in the rich, egalitarian nations of North America and western Europe are due to free choice rather than male prejudice. The balance between male prejudice and female dislike of the demands of many high-paying jobs remains unclear. I suspect that both are relevant.

The Significance of Comparisons

Children automatically compare their traits with those of their peers. The comparisons each child makes with members of the other gender have a profound effect on the traits each child adopts. If children in a hypothetical society spent their first 18 years with members of their own sex, adult gender identities would be different. But some differences would not disappear because biology guarantees sex differences in strength, vigor of motor actions, speed of locomotion, and daring (Giles & Heyman, 2005; Miller, Dancher, & Forbes, 1986).

The comparisons children make with those of the other gender usually magnify the differences that biology favors. A majority of girls across cultures believe that because boys are stronger, more aggressive, and more willing to take risks that could lead to injury, they assume it will be difficult to outperform males in these domains. Most individuals are reluctant to invest the effort needed to attain a goal if the probability of success is low.

Many females, therefore, decide to master other traits, such as physical attractiveness, cooperativeness, kindness, and agreeableness. Mid-level female managers in companies located in one of 27 countries were more likely than male managers to report that cooperating with the members of a team facilitated their advancement (Paris, Howell, Dorfman, & Hanges, 2009). The communications among the members of 200 surgical teams at three urban hospitals confirmed the female's tendency to be cooperative. Cooperative comments were more frequent when the teams consisted of many women but conflictful comments were more common when most of the team consisted of men (Jones, Jennings, Higgins, & de Waal, 2018).

The ability to dominate another in some contexts is a critical feature of a male identity. Adolescent boys who always play a subordinate role are susceptible to an uncomfortable feeling provoked by the sense that they have violated an obligation linked to their gender. Many women devalue a dominant posture and avoid roles that award the occupant a position of power over others because these qualities are associated with maleness.

After examining the concept of manliness across diverse cultures, Gilmore (1990) concluded that most societies demand that males demonstrate their ability to be outstanding in some domain the society celebrates, whether wealth, a position of authority, capacity to dominate a social situation, athletic prowess, bravery, fighting ability, or sexual conquests. Children and adults rely on a person's height, muscle mass, and facial width to estimate the likelihood that they will assume a dominant posture (Toscano, Schubert, Dotsch, Falvello, & Todorov, 2016).

The average male face is broader than the typical female face. A popular measure is the ratio formed by the width of the face at the zygomatic bone located on each upper cheek divided by the distance between the eyebrow and upper lip. The men who were CEOs of Britain's leading firms had broader faces than the typical British male (Alrajih & Ward, 2014). The females from two species of monkeys from the genus Macaca that display a strict, linear dominance hierarchy had broader faces than the females from the nine other species of macaques (Borgi & Majolo, 2016).

Because television allows voters to view the faces of candidates running for public office, men with broader faces are a little more likely to be elected. Apparently, voters believe they will be more effective. Ninety percent of American homes had a television set in 1960. Voters elected 10 presidents over the interval from 1960 to 2016. Eight of those 10 men had broader faces than the average male. Because there are more broad faced men in government, a broad faced man is more likely to be accused of corrupt behavior and pictures of these men are likely to appear in the media. Thus, it is not surprising that Americans looking at photos of unfamiliar elected officials judged the men with broader faces as more corruptible (Lin, Adolphs, & Alvarez. 2018).

The Concept of Potency

Close to 50 years ago, adults from societies speaking one of 21 languages rated, on a 7-step scale, a long list of nouns on 50 pairs of antonyms that included big-small, nice-mean, deep-shallow, strong-weak, active-passive, and good-bad (Osgood, May, & Miron, 1975). Factor analyses of the ratings revealed that the first factor, which accounted for the largest proportion of variance (45 percent), reflected an evaluative dimension in which the antonyms good-bad, nice-awful, pleasant-unpleasant, and comfortable-uncomfortable had the highest loadings. This result is not surprising in light of the centrality of morality in human functioning. Humans automatically categorize their experiences on this dimension (Kurdi & Banaji, 2017). The terms girl, woman, and female were given a higher rating on the good side of this factor than boy, man, and male.

The second factor reflected the contrast between potent and less potent things, with the antonym pairs large-small, strong-weak, and heavy-light having high loadings. The third factor was defined by the antonyms active-inactive, fast-slow, and exciting-spiritless. The terms boy and male had higher ratings on the potent and active ends of each of these two factors than girl and female (see also Langford & Mackinnon, 2000; Chi & Baldwin, 2004).

Because strength and courage are needed in times of danger, diverse societies assumed that males were more likely than females to display resilience in time of threat (Leslie, Cimpian, Meyer, & Freeland, 2015; Bian, Leslie, & Cimpian, 207). This belief made it likely that men would assume leadership of the first human groups and, millennia later, write the legends that made males—Zeus, God, the Jade Emperor, Itzamn, Moses, Jesus, and Mohammed—the heroes youths were to admire. When boys learn that the majority of idealistic heroes have been men they find it easy to accept an imperative to reach for the stars. I remember an afternoon in 1958 when my 4-year-old daughter rejected my suggestion that God might be a woman.

Had women assumed leadership roles when our species emerged, they would have been the authors of the legends, and contemporary females might feel an obligation to become their nation's smartest, wisest, bravest, and most virtuous heroes. The fact that only females can conceive and birth a new life made this outcome a little less likely. Societies socialize their girls to accept the notion that females possess a special capacity to care for those in need. The Buddhist goddess Kuan Yin is known for her compassion, the Egyptian goddess Isis for the ability to heal, and the Hindu goddess Shakti for fertility.

Nineteenth-century American Protestants argued that women were especially sensitive to another's distress because they felt a vicarious suffering with victims. A capacity for empathy with the pain of others made it easier for women to identify with Christ's suffering and to heal the sick (Curtis, 2007). German noblewomen from the twelfth to the sixteenth centuries were often consulted about a cure for an illness because it was known that these women continually gathered information on the natural products that had proven effective with different illnesses, (Rankin, 2013). When men assume a healing role, it usually takes the form of expert knowledge characteristic of shamans or physicians. Women healers are more likely to implement actions that involve touching, helping with bodily functions, and administering medicines.

Because the men in most societies fight its wars, their moral culpability for killing is diluted and their guilt muted. The daily dairies of a sample of Canadian college students offers some support for this idea. Each student reported for 12 consecutive evenings the number of times they were rude, failed to meet an obligation, or inconvenienced another and whether they apologized for the violation of proper behavior. There were no gender differences in frequency of offenses, but the women were more likely than the men to apologize for causing distress to another (Schumann & Ross, 2010).

The Gender Bias in Languages

Although there are exceptions, a majority of the languages spoken by small, isolated populations that use a grammatical mark to designate the gender of a noun use a feminine form for smaller, flatter, wider objects and a masculine form for bigger, taller, narrower things. For example, the Cantabrian language, spoken by a small group living in the mountains of northern Spain, treats a large stone and a narrow river as masculine and a small stone and wide river as feminine (Holmquist, 1991). The Manambu language, spoken in a region of Papua, New Guinea, treats size and shape as salient marks of the gender of objects, plants, and animals. Things that are large or long and slender are male. Things that are small or round are female. As a result, the language of the Manambu marks the sun as female because of its shape. By contrast, the sun is male in Mayan languages because heat, rather than shape, is regarded as the sun's salient property, and hot things are male (Aikhenvald, 2012).

The semantic associations to male and female are not necessarily predictive of a person's behaviors or attitudes. A number of older girls who have acquired the normative associations between femaleness and the assumption of a subordinate role dominate boys and regard their mother as more dominant than their father. This fact invites a deeper examination of the relevance of automatic semantic associations to behaviors and conscious attitudes.

Semantic associations to female or male generate an initial expectation about the probable behavior of an unfamiliar male or female in an unfamiliar setting. An adolescent girl offered help by an unfamiliar man in a sparsely populated section of a city is more likely to feel uncertain than if the stranger were a woman. The contemporary companies that advertise medicines on American television apparently assume that their product is more likely to be purchased if viewers believe the claims about its efficacy. These ads often feature a woman describing the drug because the current gender stereotype suggests that females are more trustworthy than males. This was not the case 60 years ago.

However, a person's actions and attitudes toward a person or object are not linked to a single feature, but to a pattern of features in a context. If attitudes toward an object were mediated only by its color, no one would buy brown-skinned potatoes. Humans eat raspberries and strawberries, but not red candles or ribbons, despite their similar surface colors. Red has a pleasant valence when associated with an apple, but an unpleasant valence when it generates an association with blood.

Biology and Gender

Few scientists question the extraordinary power of cultural values to create different behavioral and belief profiles in each gender. Nonetheless, the biological differences between the sexes cannot be ignored when interpreting data (Lonsdorf, 2017; Zaruli et al., 2018). This issue has become so tendentious, it is necessary to repeat the earlier declaration that the known biological differences between females and males have relevance for scientists trying to understand their evidence. A society, however, can decide that admission committees for universities, personnel hiring executives, judges, and legislators are to ignore these differences.

The sexes differ in genomes, telomere lengths, epigenetic marks, DNA recombination at meiosis, parental origin of single nucleotide polymorphisms (SNPs), body and brain anatomy, neurochemistry, timing of puberty, immune responsivity, left-handedness, violent behavior, binge eating, prevalence of select diseases, ease of acquiring select cognitive processes, susceptibility to distress over possible harm or loss of a close relationship, rumination over personal problems, and a host of other properties (McCarthy, de Vries, & Forge, 2017; Ardekani, Figarsky, & Sidtis, 2013; Brick et al., 2018; Tomasi & Volkow, 2012; Pavlova, Sokolov, & Bidet-Ildei, 2015; Satterthwaite et al., 2015; Boo, Matsubayashi, & Ueda, 2019; Zhan et al., 2017; ; Chung & Auger, 2013; Reizel et al., 2015; Ecuyer-Dab & Robert, 2004; Needham et al., 2014).

Many physical features are significantly more variable in males. The male's possession of only one X chromosome, compared with two in females, is one reason why more males than females have either very high or very low values on many biological and psychological measures. This biological feature implies that the risks accompanying a deleterious mutation in a gene on the male's single X chromosome is likely to have an effect. Symptoms of autism caused by a de novo mutation are far more common in males than females (Wierenga et al., 2018b). Although older women report more illnesses than men, most are not life-threatening. Men have a shorter lifespan due partly to the more serious symptoms that accompany a compromise in the immune system, cancer, or cardiovascular system (Abelionsky & Strulik, 2018).

Sex Hormones: Testosterone

The male and female sex hormones have different effects on brain structure and function. The secretion of testosterone by the male fetus, during the first three post-natal months, and again at puberty, have a profound effect on genital anatomy and a host of other outcomes. Male brains take a little longer to transfer information between hemispheres (Moes, Brown, & Minnema, 2007); have a stronger response to blue light (Cowan et al., 2000); possess a firmer functional connection between the amygdala and the orbitofrontal cortex (Spielberg et al., 2015); and a larger medial preoptic nucleus and bed nucleus of the stria terminalis (Greenberg & Trainor, 2016; Allen & Gorski, 199).

These phenomena may help explain why boys are slower to acquire language (Redmond & Ash, 2017), and why males have a higher threshold for pain (Aloisi & Bonifazi, 2006; Verriotis et al., 2018), display fewer spontaneous smiles (Ellis, 2006), possess a less effective immune system (Neigh,

Nemeth, & Rowson, 2016), and inherit a different skeleton and pattern of musculature (Lombardo & Deaner, 2018).

The surge of testosterone at puberty is accompanied by changes in brain anatomy and function that include axon myelination and declines in delta and theta power in non-REM sleep. This hormone reaches peak values at 17 to 19 years, remains high until the fourth decade, and then declines by about 1 percent a year (see McIntyre, Cohn, & Ellison, 2005; Federman, 2006; Koscik, O'Leary, Moser, Andreasen, & Nopoulos, 2008; Amunts et al., 2007; Fischer, Hess, & Rosler, 2005; Salinas et al., 2012; Keller & Menon, 2009; Lombardo et al., 2012; Shiino et al., 2017; Campbell, Grimm, de Bie, & Feinberg, 2012; Hertig, Maxwell, Irvine, & Nagel, 2012; Culbert, Sinclair, Hildebrandt, Klump, & Sisk, 2018; Harden et al., 2018; Gagliano, Nadal, & Armario, 2014; Long, Sadler, & Kolber, 2016; Genc, Malpes, Ball, Silk, & Seal, 2018; Wierenga et al., 2018a; Satterthwaite et al., 2014, for relevant papers).

A majority of males possess both the primary sex features of a penis and testes and the secondary features of a broad, angular face, thin lips, a muscular body, and a smaller ratio of the lengths of the index and ring fingers (called the 2D:4D ratio). A smaller 2D:4D ratio is associated with greater endurance and elite athletic performance in older boys and men (Ranson, Stratton, & Taylor, 2015; Weinberg, Parsons, Raffensperger, & Marazita, 2015).

A small number of men who possess a penis have the rounder face, thicker lips, larger 2D:4D ratio, and less muscular build characteristic of most females. Possession of a less responsive receptor to male sex hormone, which results in failure to defeminize the male, is one reason for this pattern (Schwarz & McCarthy, 2008). The gene for the androgen receptor on the X chromosome has more than 500 alleles, most of which reduce the responsivity of the receptor to male sex hormone.

Male bonobo fetuses (a chimpanzee species called Pan paniscus) secrete less testosterone than males from the more common chimpanzee species (Pan troglodytes; Oetjens, Shen, Emery, Zou, & Kidd, 2016). Male bonobo adults are less aggressive and have a larger, feminine 2D:4D ratio (Hare & Yamamoto, 2017). Female rat fetuses developing between a pair of males acquire some male biological and behavioral features that are missing from female fetuses who are not next to a male (Vandenbergh, 2003).

In the rare cases in which receptor insensitivity is present in many bodily sites, called androgen insensitivity syndrome, a genetic male newborn

might lack a penis and be raised as a girl. However, the secretion of testosterone at puberty by these genetic males creates feelings that persuade
these youths that they are boys (Imperato-McGinley, Petersen, Gautier, &
Sturla, 1979). This fact provides the most persuasive support for the claim
that, for a small number of outcomes, biology can overcome many years
of socialization.

Men and women even differ in the reasons for the impairments in memory and reasoning that are signs of dementia in the elderly. Alzheimer's
disease, the most prevalent cause, is more frequent in women. Dementia in
older men is more often due to a stroke or Parkinson's disease (Podcasy &
Epperson, 2016; Satterthwaite et al., 2014).

The adrenal glands of both sexes secrete an androgen related to testosterone, called dehydroepiandrosterone (DHEA), beginning around 4 years of
age. This hormone binds to different receptors and has some consequences
that are different in males and females (Nguyen, 2018; Sano et al., 2016).
This evidence implies that the patterns of biological activity in males and
females do not lie on a continuum (Salvatore et al., 2018).

Functions of Estradiol

The secretion of estradiol (the most important member of the estrogen
family) by human females at puberty is accompanied by a variety of consequences that are mediated by receptors called alpha, beta, and G-protein
(Paletta, Sheppard, Matta, Ervin, & Choleris, 2018). Estradiol protects dopamine neurons in the substantia nigra and ventral tegmental area from cell
death and slows the degradation of dopamine in the synapse by downreg-
ulating the two forms of monoamine oxidase (MAO-A and B; Harro et al.,
2001). As a result, more females than males have a high concentration of
dopamine in the striatum and frontal cortex (Watson et al., 2006). This phenomenon implies that post-pubertal females ought to have a smaller phasic
increase in dopamine to an unexpected, but desired, event. If so, females
should experience an unexpected, desired event as a little less hedonically
pleasant than males (Dluzen, 2005; Becker, 1999; McCarthy, 2008; Kelly &
Goodson, 2015).

The larger number of dopamine neurons in the substantia nigra of
females that project to the tail of the striatum implies that girls and women
should be more likely to avoid or retreat from unfamiliar events and settings
(Menegas, Akiti, Amo, Uchida, & Watabe-Uchida, 2018). Cholens, Galea,

Sohrabji, and Frick (2018) and McEwen and Milner (2017) have published useful reviews of sex differences in brain-behavior relations in animals.

Some post-pubertal, pre-menopausal females are aware of subtle changes in bodily feelings during each menstrual cycle because of fluctuating estradiol and progesterone levels over the 28-day interval (Kiesner, 2011). The concentration of estradiol is lowest during the first nine and last two days of the cycle. The level begins to rise on day 10, reaches a peak a day or two before ovulation, and is moderately high from day 17 to 26. Progesterone remains low until days 16 or 17, peaks during days 18 to 24, the luteal phase, and then gradually declines.

Most women dismiss the subtle change in feeling tone during the luteal phase. Some women, however, cannot ignore the sensations and ruminate on the possible psychological reasons for their dysphoric feelings (Jacobs et al., 2015). It is easy to remember a prior act that is a basis for guilt or a sign of rejection that is cause for anxiety. About five percent of women experience a more severe dysphoria because a derivative of progesterone potentiates GABA-ergic activity which leads to a feeling of lethargy (Bixo et al., 2018).

The changing levels of estradiol and progesterone also affect eating habits, body dissatisfaction, memory for unpleasant stimuli, regulation of emotion, subjective reports of distress following failure in a lab setting, and performance on language and spatial tasks (Albert, Pruessner, & Newhouse, 2015; Bayer, Schultz, Gamer, & Sommer, 2014; Cacioppo et al., 2013; Hildebrandt et al., 2015; Kiesner, 2011; Racine et al., 2012; Kimura & Hampson, 1994; Wu, Zhou, & Huang, 2014).

The changing estradiol concentrations affect activity in the medial and central nuclei of the amygdala which, in turn, send projections to targets of the autonomic nervous system, ventral striatum, and central gray. These targets generate changes in the cardiovascular system, gut, and striated muscles. When these changes in visceral activity accompany a salient experience, long-term memory for that experience is improved. That is why an unusual event that excites the amygdala is remembered for a longer time. Because females possess higher tonic concentrations of estradiol than males, it is possible that women have a more faithful long-term memory for traumatic experiences than men (Paletta, Sheppard, Matta, Ervin, & Choleris, 2018).

Females are especially prone to bouts of rumination, worry, and depression. The insula receives sensations that originate in the gut, heart, and muscles and contributes to the conscious feelings that are interpreted as emotions. Most neuroscientists believe that the anterior insula makes a significant contribution to an awareness of one's feeling tone (Nieuwen-huys, 2012).

The insula in the right hemisphere receives inputs from the thalamus, reflecting sympathetic activity in the cardiovascular system. Female fetuses have a slightly higher heart rate and slightly lower heart rate variability than males, which implies that females have greater sympathetic tone on the heart before they are born (DiPietro, Costigan, & Voegtline, 2015).

Female college students watching two-minute film clips of high arousal-unpleasant scenes displayed larger rises in heart rate, larger reductions in heart rate variability, and shorter latencies between the contraction of the left ventricle and the ejection of blood than most men (Wilhelm et al., 2017). These sex differences in cardiovascular function are influenced, partly, by the sex hormones (Barnes, 2017; de Zambotti et al., 2018).

The sexes vary in the ease with which intrusive feelings are muted or reg-ulated. Women possess a weaker functional connectivity between the left insula and sites in the prefrontal cortex that regulate feelings (Kann, Zhang, Manza, Leung, & Li, 2016; Duerden, Arsalidou, Lee, & Taylor, 2013). The anterior cingulate, too, contributes to the regulation of intrusive feelings. Although variation in the size and connectivity of the anterior cingulate could have been inherited and contributed to a cascade that led to effective or deficient regulation, it is equally likely that the variation is due to many years of exercising, or failing to exercise, regulation of feelings and the sup-pression of inappropriate acts (Lee et al., 2016).

These data imply that the female's susceptibility to bouts of anxiety, guilt, or depression rests partly on her biology (Williams et al., 2018). One out of four American adolescent girls in 2015 admitted to at least one act of non-suicidal self-harm, compared to only one of 10 boys (Monto, McRee, & Dercyk, 2018). Guilt over casual sex, a rude comment to a friend, or anger at a parent that cannot be rationalized may contribute to the high self-harm rate among American girls, especially among those with a European ancestry.

College-age women appear to be more anxious than men when they have to interact with an authority figure. American undergraduate women who contacted a faculty member usually relied on an e-mail to inquire about a grade or an assignment. The men, by contrast, more often asked to meet with a faculty member in order to discuss ideas or volunteer for research (Cohen, 2018). This observation implies that the males felt more relaxed when talking with an older adult holding an authority position, even if the faculty member was a woman.

Biology, Uncertainty, and Mental Illness

Hundreds of studies across varied cultures affirm that more men than women display the symptoms of schizophrenia, autism, severe intellectual delay, or psychopathy (Lundh, Wangby-Lundh, & Bjarehed, 2008; Almeida & Kessler, 1998; Crocq, 2017). Twice as many females as males, however, are diagnosed with anxiety or depressive disorder (Carnevali, Thayer, Brosschot, & Ottaviani, 2017).

More than 5,000 residents of Sao Paolo, Brazil, recalled their childhood adversities. Reports of neglect and family violence yielded the largest gender difference favoring females (Coelho et al., 2018). Hong Kong women who knew of an epidemic of a respiratory illness (Moran & Del Valle, 2016), and female emergency physicians in Germany were more likely than males to report feeling anxious (Sand et al., 2016). A latent class analysis of the health of more than 28,000 Swedish twins between ages 41 and 64 revealed five classes. The largest contained those with no serious health problems. Classes 2 through 5, which accounted for 34 percent of the variance, had more women than men complaining of chronic pain, anxiety, or depression. The female vulnerability to pain is due, partly, to the presence of estrogen, which reduces the ability of endogenous opioids to mute pain (Kato, Sullivan, & Pedersen, 2010). Four weeks after Hurricane Sandy in October 2012, women living in the New York metropolitan area were more likely than men to report fear of another catastrophe (Hamama-Raz et al., 2015).

The higher heart rates of women may contribute to the female's susceptibility to interpret an event as a threat. A signal sent from the heart, which arrives in the brain a fifth of a second after each heartbeat, resets the phase of the oscillatory patterns of neuronal collections and activates the insular cortex. This phenomenon is called a heartbeat-evoked potential, or HEP (Park et al., 2018). The average woman has about three heartbeats every two seconds, compared with two beats for the average man. The more frequent interruption of brain activity by the HEP may render females more vulnerable to a conscious state they occasionally interpret as anxiety. Those who arrive at that interpretation should regard an accelerating heart rate as an aversive signal. American women with social anxiety showed a larger HEP than controls when told that their heart rates were rising (Judah et al., 2018).

Female reports of worry over possible future threats implies a susceptibility to feelings of uncertainty. This suggestion is supported by the more frequent retreat from and crying to unfamiliar objects or situations among 2-year-old girls than boys (Robinson, Kagan, Reznick, & Corley, 2008). Women are even more cautious in a laboratory setting navigating a large virtual environment searching for objects (Blume et al., 2017; Panno, Donati, Millioni, Chiesi, & Primi, 2018; Gagnon, Cashdan, Stefanucci, & Creem-Regher, 2016).

An unexpected change in the loudness or pitch of a tone typically evokes uncertainty and an EEG waveform in the posterior cortex about 300 msec after hearing the tone. This neural response is called the auditory P300. A review of gender differences in the amplitude of the P300 found that females had a larger waveform than males in 42 percent of the studies, while males had a larger P300 in only 6 percent of the papers (Melynyte, Wang, & Griskova-Bulanova, 2018).

The evidence invites a speculative, but reasonable, hypothesis that begins with the assumption that the typical female brain, compared with that of the male, more often generates unpleasant sensations to mildly threatening or infrequent events. When these sensations are interpreted as anxiety, shame, or guilt, the person searches for the origin of the feeling. A childhood marked by these feelings, combined with stressful current circumstances, can precipitate a level of anxiety or depression that interferes with the ability to cope with the day's responsibilities. Failure to meet personal standards governing the proper reaction to sexual overtures are common sources of shame or guilt in girls who display breast growth earlier than their peers (Wichstram, 1999).

The reasons for a sex difference in the timing of puberty remain unknown. The timing of the release of the gonadotropins that stimulate the growth of the testis or ovary is not due solely to the age when 10- to 14-year-olds experience a spurt in height and weight. The age of the spurt, which is partly heritable, is predictable from the child's height during the preschool years (German, Shmoish, & Hochberg, 2015). This fact implies that biological factors, and perhaps psychological experiences as well, contribute to body growth many years before the onset of puberty.

These facts explain why the National Institutes of Health require all investigators studying a phenomenon in an animal species that has relevance to human health to include both sexes. This decision was motivated by the extensive evidence revealing significant sex differences in multiple domains in many species (McCarthy, Woolley, & Arnold, 2017; Gillies, Virdee, Pienaar, Al-Zaid, & Dalley, 2016).

Biology and Early Behavioral Differences

More male than female infants, humans as well as monkeys, prefer to play with objects that move (Hassett, Siebert, & Wallen, 2008; Alexander & Hines, 2002). Male, but not female, infants devoted a longer bout of attention to a change in the point light display of a man walking. One possible reason is that the displays of men walking contained more motion than the women's displays (Tsang, Ogren, Peng, Nguyen, & Johnson, 2018).

About one-third of American mothers living in an East Coast community reported that their young child had an intense interest in a particular activity or object. More than 75 percent of these children were boys who were interested in cars, trains, or machines (DeLoache, Simcock, & Macari, 2007). The gender differences in detection of and attention to moving objects are not surprising. Both processes require tracking the changing spatial location of a target. Sites in the parietal cortex of males appear to be more biologically prepared to process this information. Although many women have made significant discoveries in diverse fields in engineering and the natural sciences, far fewer females than males made major advances in domains that require imagining how the many small parts of a machine—a steam engine, clock, car, computer—move together in precise ways to generate an appropriate function.

More 7-month-old male than female infants who saw an adult cradle a balloon in one video and punch the balloon in a simultaneous video imitated the punching action, which involves a more vigorous motor response (Benenson, Tennyson, & Wrangham, 2011). This observation is in accord with the replicable finding that boys from varied cultures engage in more vigorous motor activity than girls, due partly to the effect of male sex hormone on the substantia nigra and dopamine pathways in the basal ganglia (Prioreschi et al., 2017; Veldman et al., 2017; Purves-Tyson et al., 2014). Even the activity in leg muscles while running is dissimilar in boys and girls (Zavrsnik, Pisot, Simunic, Kokol, & Blazun-Vosner, 2017).

It is not surprising that girls born with high levels of adrenal androgens (DHEA), resulting from a rare recessive disorder called congenital adrenal hyperplasia, played with masculine toys more often than typical girls, reported an interest in masculine careers, were likely to have a male as their best friend, and were vulnerable to gender identity problems (Servin, Nordenstrom, Larsson, & Bohlin, 2003; Nordenstrom, Servin, Bohlin, Larsson, & Wedell, 2002; Berenbaum, Beltz, Bryk, & McHale, 2018; Walia, Singla, Vaiphei, Kumar, & Bhansali, 2018). Many of these women have an enlarged clitoris resembling a penis, a smaller vagina that resists penetration, bodily hair, a deep voice, and are ashamed of their bodies (Meyer-Bahlburg, Khuri, Reyes-Portillo, Ehrhardt, & New, 2018).

Home videos recorded during the childhoods of heterosexual and bisexual or gay adults revealed that the childhood play of the latter group conformed less to sex role stereotypes (Rieger, Linsenmeier, Gygax, & Bailey, 2008). Transgender men (genetic females with a male gender identity) reported being tomboys as children (Burke et al., 2018). Although uncommon, some monozygotic twin pairs consist of one heterosexual and one gay adult (Timmins, Rimes, & Rahman, 2018).

Far more boys than girls, ages 4 to 9, from the Boston area told an examiner that they enjoy engaging in physical aggression in their play activities. Even before the second birthday, displays of kicking or hitting another are more frequent in boys than in girls (Baillargeon et al., 2007). These facts are relevant to the robust fact that more males than females commit acts of physical aggression as children, youths, and adults (Pedersen & Bell, 1970; Benenson, Carder, & Geib-Cole, 2008). Caucasian boys from Great Britain who displayed high levels of sex-typed masculine play at 3.5 years reported the highest levels of physical aggression when they were 13 years old (Kung, Golding, & Hines, 2018).

Even when the desired resources in a game are plentiful, and there is no need for any child in a quartet of same-sex 10-year-olds to be competitive, more boys than girls tried to reduce the winnings of the others in their group (Roy & Benenson, 2002). This observation implies that more males than females possess an urge to display a superiority over others. Both male and female members of American university crew teams experienced a rise in cortisol before a competitive race. The men with large increases said that winning the race would satisfy their desire to be a member of the best crew. The women reported that they did not want to disappoint the other members of the team (Kivlighan, Granger, & Booth, 2005).

Spatial Skills

Gender stereotypes imply that males are more proficient in mathematics. American children as young as age 7 have already acquired an association between maleness and the symbols of mathematics, even if the father's occupation has nothing to do with numbers (Cvencek, Meltzoff, & Greenwald, 2011). This stereotype is inconsistent with the fact that school-age boys and girls in developed nations typically obtain similar average scores on tests of mathematical skills (Hyde, 2005; Hyde & Mertz, 2009; Zell, Krizan, & Teeter, 2015; Spelke, 2005). However, it is equally true that twice as many males as females attain scores in the top 5 percent of the distribution (Raymond & Benbow, 1986). The ratio of males to females participating in International Mathematical Olympiads, which are limited to those with an extremely high level of mathematical talent, approaches 9 to 1 (Hyde & Mertz, 2009). However, the ratio of males to females with perfect scores on the mathematics section of the SAT has been dropping steadily over the past 10 years.

Males also attain very high scores on tests requiring the mental rotation of three-dimensional geometric forms, although the gender difference is smaller when the forms are familiar bottles, dresses, or cups. Success on mental rotation tasks requires the ability to hold schemata of an object, usually a geometric shape, in visual working memory long enough to decide whether a spatial transformation is the same as or different from the original form (Machin & Pekkarinen, 2008; Heil & Jansen-Osmann, 2008; Handa & McGivern, 2015; Nowell & Hedges, 1998; Bergold, Wendt, Kasper, & Steinmayr, 2017; Ehrlich, Levine, & Goldin-Meadow, 2006).

Male infants and preschool boys also display high levels of competence in these skills (Constantinescu, Moore, Johnson, & Hines, 2018; Lauer, Udelson, Jeon, & Lourenco, 2015; Levine, Huttenlocher, Taylor, & Langrock, 1999). Five-year-old boys performed better than girls when they had to select the one of four geometric forms that combined two complementary shapes (Ehrlich, Levine, & Goldin-Meadow, 2006). First- and second-grade boys performed better than girls when they had to recognize the correspondence between an adult's location in a room and on a map of the room (Liben & Downs, 1993). Three-year-old boys were more successful than girls in opening the one of four doors that was the place where a toy, moving from right to left, had been stopped by a visible wall (Hood, Cole-Davies, & Dias, 2003). Many analyses of children's drawings reveal either that boys spontaneously include features implying more sophisticated spatial skills or no gender difference (Brown, 1992; Tuman, 1999).

Because chess requires spatial skills, it is not surprising that more boys than girls select chess as a hobby and the select group of women who play in tournaments have lower ratings than the men (Stafford, 2018). Males are more accurate than females in localizing the source of a familiar sound in a collection of familiar sounds coming from other locations (Zundorf, Kamath, & Lewald, 2011), integrating two different routes in the same virtual environment (Weisberg & Newcombe, 2016), and tracking the trajectory in space of a single moving object embedded in an array of moving objects across an age span from adolescence to old age (Kenneth Nakayama, personal communication, July 2018).

Finally, the speech of boys observed at home from 14 to 46 months contained more words relevant to space, such as *in, on, behind,* and *between,* than the girls. Although the speech of the mothers of sons also contained more space words, the investigators could not rule out the possibility that the nature of the boys' play invited the mother's use of space words (Pruden & Levine, 2017). This observation is in accord with the male superiority in geometry, but not in arithmetic, in societies that promote gender equality (Guiso, Monte, Sapienza, & Zingales, 2008) and with a bias among 4-year-old boys, but not girls, to use visual cues to judge the spatial position of their invisible hand (Livesay & Itili, 1996).

The Brain and Spatial Skills
The ability to mentally rotate the forms on tests of spatial ability depends on sites in the occipital and parietal cortices, especially in the right hemisphere (Lamp, Alexander, Laycock, Crewther, & Crewther, 2016). Testosterone affects cortical sites in the right hemisphere, especially in the parietal region (Koscik et al., 2008; Levman et al., 2017). Individuals processing

mathematical symbols typically activate the intraparietal sulcus, which is longer and deeper in males than in females (Fish et al., 2017).

These observations invite the speculation that male sex hormone acting on parietal sites makes a contribution to male superiority in mental rotation problems (Wong et al., 2018). The male superiority in learning the names of several landmarks in two virtual routes and the connections between the routes is small before puberty. But after the surge of testosterone at puberty boys perform better than girls (Nazareth, Weisberg, & Newcombe, 2018). Men with androgen insensitivity syndrome solving mental rotation problems displayed blood flow profiles to the parietal cortex that were characteristic of women (van Hemmen et al., 2016). In addition, women between 20 and 38 who had low levels of estradiol when they took a mental rotations test did better than women who had high levels (Hampson, Levy-Cooperman, & Kalman, 2014; Chai & Jacobs, 2012). Finally, 15-year-old Dutch boys displayed higher blood-velocity levels than girls in the right hemisphere during a mental rotations task, but not on a language test. The Dutch boys in this study who had high prenatal testosterone levels in the amniotic fluid had higher scores on the mental rotations task than those with low levels (Beking et al., 2017).

The sex difference in human spatial skills is present in animals. Male rats require fewer trials than females to learn the location of a platform hidden in opaque water (Choleris, Galea, Sohrabji, & Frick, 2018). Equally relevant is the fact that male rats with a smaller 2D:4D ratio were better at finding the location of an object (Muller et al., 2018).

Training and Motivation Help

Although biology appears to make a contribution to the very high scores that males obtain on tests of spatial abilities, biology is not destiny. When first-grade Israeli children were trained in the solution of mental rotation problems, the mean scores of girls improved (Tzuriel & Egozi, 2010). In addition, when adults had to manipulate human figures, rather than geometric forms, the gender difference in average score disappeared (Tarampi, Heydari, & Hegarty, 2016).

These results imply that males and females may differ in the strategy they adopt with spatial problems, rather than in a fixed, biologically based compromise in the cognitive abilities required to solve these tasks (Speth

& Parent, 2006). This suggestion finds support in a sample of American college students tested in a virtual environment who had to find the place where each of many objects was located. The females were more cautious than the males on the early trials and revisited the same place more than males. However, they abandoned this initially conservative strategy on later trials (Gagnon et al., 2018).

Variation in the ease of acquiring and exploiting a talent appears to be a useful way to explain the gender differences in spatial abilities. Although a sample of men and women performed similarly on a task requiring rotation of cubes, the females showed larger increases in pupil diameter, which implies more mental effort during the task (Campbell, Toth, & Brady, 2018). The need to invest more effort may help explain why Canadian college-age women report more anxiety over tests of spatial and mathematical ability than men (Sokolowski, Hawes, & Lyons, 2019).

The excess of males over females in careers that require math and spatial skills makes it easy for boys to assume that they should be proficient in these fields. Furthermore, youths of both genders agree that these disciplines are the hardest to master. Douglas Hofstadter remembers, as a 15-year-old, perusing the pages of Rudolf Carnap's *The Logical Syntax of Language* in a bookstore. Although he did not understand the prose, Hofstadter recalls that the ideas in the book set his "brain on fire" because they promised to uncover the deep secrets that only geniuses understood (Sigmund, 2017).

A feeling of intellectual superiority over others, which Hofstadter assumed geniuses feel, is a more pressing concern for males than females. Young men who sense they possess a talent in math or physics know that many of their peers will regard them as having superior intellectual abilities. Hence, the choice of a STEM career promises a feeling of superiority. This feeling renders the study of these topics especially appealing, and its mastery is accompanied by a special kind of pleasure. Motivation and the pleasure that accompanies involvement in and solution of mathematical and spatial tasks appear to be as, or more, significant than biology in explaining the gender differences in these domains (Hausmann, Schoofs, Rosenthal, & Jordan, 2009). I knew five Harvard undergraduate women majoring in mathematics or physics who were receiving A grades in these courses. All five decided as juniors to drop their concentrations in these fields, despite their ability to do the work. When I asked why, all five agreed that they did not find the work satisfying.

This anecdote finds support in a study of older Americans born in the 1960s who, at age 13, had scores on mathematical tests in the top 1 percent of the distribution. Despite the fact that the females in this select group had exceptional mathematical ability, they were less likely than the males to pursue careers in a STEM science (Benbow, Lubinski, Shea, & Effekhari-Sanjani, 2000). The ratio of men to women choosing a STEM career is largest in nations with the greatest gender equality, such as Norway, Iceland, Sweden, Germany, and the Netherlands. Although there was no gender difference in the number of PhDs in the Netherlands from 2008 to 2012, far fewer women than men chose a STEM discipline, partly because they regarded these fields as too difficult or too arcane (Waaijer, Sonneveld, Buitendijk, van Bochove, & van der Weijden, 2016; Wong et al., 2018). These facts support my earlier claim that a woman's conscious choice, not male prejudice, often explains the decision to avoid a career in one of the STEM disciplines.

The results of a decision by the German government in 2003 to require all German high school students to take a course in advanced mathematics did not support the popular belief that if adolescent girls took more math courses, they would have more confidence in their talent and would consider a STEM field for a career. A measure of mathematical knowledge, confidence in one's mathematical ability, and vocational aims of 4,730 males and females attending one of large number of high schools in the state of Baden-Wurttenberg were gathered before and after the requirement. The females required to take the advanced course had, as expected, a higher score on the index of mathematical knowledge than the high school females who were not required to take the advanced course. But, to the surprise of many, the former group of females had less confidence in their mathematical talent and were less likely to favor a STEM career.

The authors' interpretation was that the females who took the advanced course were exposed to many boys who were more competent than they in the classroom. Hence, their prior self-confidence was compromised. Girls with reasonable confidence in their math ability who were protected from interacting with many proficient boys were able to retain a belief in their talent and willing to consider a STEM career (Hubner et al., 2017).

This observation shares features with the greater self-confidence of talented youths living in small towns, compared with equally talented adolescents living in a large city who encounter many more talented peers. This phenomenon is called "the big fish in a small pond" effect. It is worth noting that 14 of the 20 American presidents who served since 1900 spent their early childhood years in a small community, rather than in one of America's major cities or one of its suburbs.

Of course, many males do not find STEM fields interesting, and many females, such as Rosalind Franklin, Lisa Randall, and Vera Rubin, do. Two women working in a STEM science shared Nobel prizes in 2018. Nonetheless, more American and European males than females reported a greater interest in manipulating objects than in interacting with people; more females than males reported the opposite preference (Su, Rounds, & Armstrong, 2009; Vock, Koller, & Nagy, 2013; Morris, 2016).

A Summary

The facts summarized invite two summary statements. The first, which is less controversial, suggests that each gender makes different contributions to a variety of measures. Investigators cannot remove these contributions with statistics. It will prove more profitable to treat gender as one element in a pattern of factors that leads to a set of outcomes. The documented sex differences in many domains warrant examination of all data sets for gender differences in the shape of the distributions and correlational patterns before pooling male and female participants because of similar mean values on the major measures (Barth, Villringer, & Sacher, 2015; Borkenau, Hrebickova, Kuppens, Realo, & Allik, 2013; Huynh, Willemsen, & Holstege, 2013; Ahl & Keil, 2017; Geary, 2016, 2017; Nystrom & Bengtsson, 2017; Carrel & Brown, 2017; Greenberg, Lengua, Coie, & Pinderhughes, 1999).

The scientists who prefer conclusions that apply to both genders rationalize pooling the data from males and females when the means are not significantly different. A recent paper on the stability of alpha band asymmetry at F7/8 to an approaching stranger in infants seen at both 6 and 12 months reported a significant level of stability for the entire sample (Brooker, Canen, Davidson, & Goldsmith, 2017). My examination of the data, sent to me by one of the authors, revealed that the stability was only significant for girls. This is not the only occasion when my examination of requested raw data from a published paper revealed that the report of a significant effect for the entire sample held for only one gender.

The second conclusion is more nuanced. Although few scientists deny that the sexes of all mammalian species differ in biological properties that affect behavior, some argue persuasively that the sex differences in human behaviors require socialization by cultural agents. This perspective assumes that most youths and adults can suppress the actions generated by the distinctive biology of males and females. The cultural values are the only important determinants of the gender differences in psychological traits observed in every society. This is not an unreasonable position. Although infants are born with a biological bias to reject the bitter taste of alcohol, many adults acquire a desire for this liquid. Cancer experts believe that lifestyle can prevent many kinds of cancers (Song, Vogelstein, Giovannucci, Willett, & Tomasetti, 2018).

On the other hand, investigators who have studied this issue in depth believe that culture cannot suppress all of the outcomes that biology favors. These include the urge to engage in sexual behavior, persistent attempts to dominate others, unusually high levels of talent in spatial skills, and, most important, genetic males raised as girls who feel uncomfortable with their female identity when they secrete testosterone at puberty.

Jill Ker Conway (1999) examined themes in the autobiographies of men and women who grew up in a Western democracy, excluding the memoirs of slaves. The men's memoirs usually described a solitary hero battling forces arrayed against him in order to achieve fame, wealth, or political power for its own sake, free of guilt over the selfishness of the endeavor. Most of the memoirs by the women emphasized the satisfaction of helping and cooperating with others. These women lived in societies that were far less denigrating of females than Asian, African, or Middle Eastern Arab societies.

Nonetheless, the existing evidence is not sufficiently free of ambiguity to allow complete confidence in the belief that biology contributes to gender differences in ways that transcend a society's socialization and stereotypes. One reason is that most cultures, past and present, promoted the same traits that the biology favors. Until the corpus of data is more complete, a tolerant attitude toward those who advocate either point of view is appropriate. Even if future investigators prove that biology makes a contribution to gender differences in select behaviors and feelings that transcend socialization, those facts have no necessary implications for a society's laws, ethics, or opportunities for self-enhancement.

4 Social Class and Ethnicity

The need to include social class and ethnicity as components in patterns of measures gathered on human subjects is as persuasive as the case for gender. Because the members of a particular class or ethnic group vary on a host of psychological traits, statistical procedures that control for these categories run the risk of removing different contributions to an outcome.

Class and ethnicity are considered in the same chapter because the consequences of ethnicity often depend on the person's social class, which in most contemporary societies is defined by income, education, and occupation. African-Americans are the only ethnic group in the United States in which more women than men from a disadvantaged class obtain careers with high salaries. Dark-skinned African-Americans who grew up in poor families report less self-confidence than equally dark adults who had the advantages of an affluent family (Thompson & Keith, 2001). Finally, short telomere lengths on white blood cells were more frequent in European-Caucasian immigrants to the United States who did not graduate high school than in black or Hispanic immigrants with similar levels of education (Needham et al., 2013).

Class Rank in a Society

The concept of class is discussed first because of the large corpus of evidence linking class position with variation in a host of significant outcomes. The social class in which a person is raised is, at the moment, the best predictor of outcomes that are of concern to parents, social scientists, and physicians. These outcomes include illnesses, years of schooling, achievement levels in reading, science, and mathematics, asocial behavior, cooperation, likelihood of being a bully or a victim of bullying, depression, anxiety, marital status, and inflammatory states. Class of rearing exerts far more influence on the above outcomes than the person's genes or class position as an adult (Johnson, Riis, & Noble, 2016; Sasser et al., 2017; van den Akker, 2015; Turkheimer, Haley, Waldron, D'Onofrio, & Gottesman, 2003; von Kanel, Malan, Hamer, & Malan, 2015; Lovden, Karalija, Andersson, Wahlin, & Axelsson, 2018).

Many working-class American mothers believe that their daughter's chances of a better life depend on exploiting their physical attractiveness in order to marry a man with a higher, more secure income. Some of these mothers spend more money than they can afford, occasionally as high as $10,000, on expensive costumes their daughter needs to compete in one or more of the 3,000 annual beauty contests held mainly in California, Florida, and New York (Giroux, 1998).

A compromised class rank is correlated with decreased functional connectivity during cognitive work (Perry et al., 2017), less cerebellar gray matter (Cavanagh et al., 2013), less surface area in cortical sites involved in language and executive functions (Noble et al., 2015), and less white tract integrity (Gianaros, Marsland, Sheu, Erickson, & Verstynen, 2013; Farah, 2017; Chan et al., 2018). Adults who grew up in less advantaged families are more likely to have infections of *Helicobacter pylori* bacteria, which pose a risk for stomach cancer (Malaty & Graham, 1994; Sitas, Yarnell, & Forman, 1991).

Preschool children from extremely disadvantaged families were the only children who displayed a linear decrease in scores on tests of executive functioning over a five-year interval, despite a yearlong intervention designed to improve their abilities (Sasser et al., 2017). The observation that disadvantaged children show decreases over time in the volume of the left inferior frontal gyrus, while advantaged children display an increase, may be relevant to the above observation (Foulkes & Blakemore, 2018).

A physiological pattern called the metabolic syndrome is present in a third to one-half of American adults who grew up in a disadvantaged family. These adults have abnormally high concentrations of interleukins, cytokines, triglycerides, fasting glucose levels, and stress hormones (Manuck, Phillips, Gianaros, Flory, & Muldoon, 2010; Miller, Chen, & Parker, 2011; Hawkley, Lavelle, Bernston, & Cacioppo, 2011). This profile, which predicts many chronic diseases, is the product of more untreated infections, irregular medical care, an unhealthy diet, uncertainties over finances, crime, unemployment, and, for those who are members of a minority group, exposure to prejudice. The Americans reared by parents who did not graduate high school who possessed few signs of the metabolic syndrome reported a more nurturant family environment during their childhood (Miller et al., 2011).

A chronic illness is a risk for a bout of depression, and such illnesses are more common among the poor. Across 53 different nations, women who had little education and lived on a marginal income were at the highest risk for a depressed mood (Rai, Zitko, Jones, Lynch, & Araya, 2013). Clinicians invented a new childhood diagnosis called "sluggish cognitive tempo," defined by low motivation, drowsiness, and boredom. Children from economically stressed families comprised the majority given this diagnosis. These children are often hungry, sleepy, and spend many hours in front of a television screen. These symptoms should have been classified as a poverty syndrome.

Failure to graduate high school was a better predictor of an intracerebral hemorrhage in a multi-ethnic sample of Americans than alleles that are known risk factors for this dangerous event. Many of the 10 percent of Americans who did not have a high school diploma in 2017 eat less healthy foods, drink too much alcohol, and have a lifestyle that contributes to high blood pressure and hemorrhages (Sawyer et al., 2018). Class can even affect the probability that a pregnant mother will contract the flu. College-educated American women usually plan the month of conception so that the birth will occur in the warm spring or summer months. Women who never attended college are less planful. As a result, many conceive in the summer and give birth during February or March, when the odds of coming down with a flu infection that can harm the unborn child are higher.

Because infections activate the immune system and their products can enter the brain, individuals who suffer from more infections for longer times should have brain states that differ from those possessed by healthier persons (Reardon, Murray, & Lomax, 2018). Americans serving in the army who grew up in less advantaged families were more likely than more advantaged soldiers to have made a suicide attempt while in the service (Ursano, Kessler, & Naifeh, 2018).

A person's class is correlated with the kind of neighborhood in which they live and, therefore, the settings that children and adults encounter. Although close to half of an urban Midwestern sample of disadvantaged white and minority women who had been abused or neglected as children were arrested for a crime, an equal proportion of women with the same high-risk profile had no arrest record (Trauffer & Widom, 2017). More of the latter lived in more cohesive neighborhoods with less criminal activity that protected them from frequent threats (Chauhan, Schuck, & Widom, 2017).

Two Definitions of Class

Class has two correlated meanings in most of the contemporary world. A majority of social scientists, and especially economists, prefer an objective index that combines income, education, and occupation. Social scientists prefer to use each person's subjective evaluation of their class position because it is a better predictor of a few interesting outcomes. Europeans with the incomes and occupations that define a working-class rank favor progressive, leftist candidates when their subjective class matches the objective one, but are likely to vote for conservative candidates when they say they belong to the middle class (D'Hooge, Achterberg, & Reeskens, 2018). The correlations between objective and subjective class among contemporary Americans are modest, with a value of 0.40 for whites but only 0.10 for African-Americans (Cundiff & Matthews, 2017).

Although income, years of education, and occupational prestige are usually correlated, many adults do not possess similar values on all three features. Many athletes with high incomes do not have a college degree. The small proportion of sex workers who earn high incomes do not enjoy the class position of professors of poetry living on a far lower annual income. Thornton Wilder, the author of the popular play *Our Town*, was aware that his family was poor and in debt in 1911 when 14-year-old Thornton was attending a private school in China on a scholarship. But Thornton believed he belonged to a privileged class because his father came from an elite family, was a graduate of Yale University, had owned a Wisconsin newspaper, and was the American consul in Shanghai.

Many years ago, my wife and I, along with four other professional couples, were guests at a New Year's Eve party. As midnight grew near, the hostess, who had had too many drinks, asked each of us to confess our deepest disappointment. The last person to reply was the wealthiest and best-known Bostonian in the room. He surprised the group by confessing that he has always regretted not having a college degree. George Washington might have felt that his privileged class position, first as a general and later as America's first president, rested on a less than perfect foundation because he did not have a college degree (Chernow, 2010).

Nonetheless, objective measures of income, education, and/or occupation have become the primary indexes of class over the past two centuries as family pedigree, race, and religion lost their significance as signs of social privilege. T.S Eliot (1949) mourned this change because he believed a culture needed a dominant religion in order to preserve its vitality. Religion and family pedigree still count as indexes of class in India. Adults born to Muslim parents or those who were formerly called Untouchables comprise more than 80 percent of those in the lowest class positions (Shah et al., 2018). Colonial Americans, too, used religion for assigning class rank. Most Puritans, who were reformed English Protestants, had a higher class rank than Catholics or Jews (Pyle & Davidson, 2003).

I spent most of 1972–73 observing families in the small village of San Marcos, population 850, located on the shore of Lake Atitlan in northwest Guatemala. All the adobe homes were small, had dirt floors, and lacked running water and electricity. But the children of the families who owned the tiny plot of land on which their home rested attained higher scores on a battery of cognitive tests than the children of parents who rented the land. Har Gobind Khorana, who shared the 1998 Nobel Prize in Medicine, grew up in a family with a modest income in a small village in India's Punjab region. However, his parents enjoyed a privileged class position because they were the only literate adults in the village.

When a person's ethnicity, religion, or family pedigree had a determining influence on their class position, as they did in medieval Europe, the less advantaged were protected from intense shame or guilt because they could rationalize their compromised position as due to conditions that were not under their control. The less advantaged members in developed societies in 2018 are told that anyone with average ability who is willing to work hard can acquire a college education, a career with a secure income, and enhanced class rank. American schoolchildren are reminded of Andrew Jackson, Abraham Lincoln, Henry Ford, and Thomas Edison, who grew up in families of modest means in communities lacking special advantages.

A number of Americans who did not attend a college and live on modest incomes in jobs that do not require a technical skill attribute their circumstances to bad decisions made earlier. This conclusion renders them vulnerable to an uncomfortable feeling of shame or guilt. Sarah Smarsh (2018), who grew up in a poor white family in Kansas, described the shame she felt over being poor and white in a country where whites were supposed to be financially secure. Older Dutch citizens who grew up in poor families and remained poor as adults reported feeling inadequate and ashamed (Bosma, Brandts, Simons, Groffen, & van den Akker, 2015).

Some Americans blame professional elites and members of Congress for their inability to earn more money and rise in class position. The decision to blame those who are the sources of one's guilt is a common dynamic in human affairs (Chase & Walker, 2012; Gould, 2003). This idea is the theme of Khaled Hosseini's popular 2003 novel *The Kite Runner,* which became a film.

The Need for Fairness

A demand for fairness in the distribution of material comforts, justice, and respect is a fundamental property of our species. Three-year-olds protest an unfair distribution of cookies that ignored the larger contribution of one child to a product, 6-year-olds disapprove of free-riders, and 7-year-olds regard the amount of effort expended as a more important basis for allocating resources than the outcome of the effort (Yang, Choi, Misch, Yang, & Dunham, 2018; Noh, D'Esterie, & Killen, 2019).

A suspicion of unfairness hovers over the fact that the annual salaries of the women and men who collect rubbish, drive the trucks that supply supermarkets, put out fires, police streets, monitor the electric grid, test imported foods for contamination, decide on the safety of new medicines, and repair cars, toilets, and the many machines we have become dependent on are, in many cases, less than one-tenth of the salaries of the portfolio managers at investment firms. Although star actors and athletes also earn high salaries, Americans are more tolerant of this asymmetry because these men and women have a special talent, work hard, and entertain us.

The employees in one of the 31 departments of a large German firm who regarded the ambience of their department as unfair reported more somatic symptoms than those working in departments with a more just ambience (Herr et al., 2018). I suspect that the anger over the high level of income inequality in many nations rests on the more fundamental idea of proportionality. Children are exposed regularly to proportional relations between events. Large objects make more noise than small ones when they fall on a hard surface. Large wounds require more time to heal than small ones.

Serious violations of a moral standard are followed by more severe pun-ishments than minor violations. These and hundreds of other experiences establish a prototypic representation of proportional relations, especially a proportional relation between the amount of effort or talent applied to a task and the magnitude of reward.

Americans regard the monthly Social Security checks sent to 15 percent of Americans as fair because they assume the recipients deserved this money for their decades of work. However, many of the same citizens regard the welfare checks sent to only 1 percent of Americans as unfair because the money was not earned. The British share this belief (Biresi & Nunn, 2013). The government of Finland had to terminate a program that sent money to poor citizens in order to reduce inequality because the public objected to the unfairness of awarding resources to those who expended no effort. Continental Europeans, compared with the Americans and British, are less bothered by helping the less advantaged, because they value a more equal society and believe that luck plays a far more important role than effort in the failure or success in accumulating wealth. Hence, they are willing to have their taxes help the less fortunate (Alesina & Angeletos, 2005).

The European perspective on the disadvantaged is a partial product of a history marked by cruel monarchs, many wars, and Hitler's celebration of the superiority of the Aryan race. These memories motivate the wish for a society of more equal citizens. These memories are missing from the Ameri-can psyche. The lives of Benjamin Franklin, Abraham Lincoln, Henry Ford, Andrew Carnegie, and Thomas Edison, who rose from poverty to wealth and a position of power through hard work, are among the salient memo-ries held by many Americans.

Agency

Adults who occupy higher class positions possess greater access to those in power, material resources that allow more moments of pleasure, and a sense of personal agency that persuades them they can reject popular norms and alter their life itinerary. The diary of Friedrich Kellner, a German civil servant who privately opposed Hitler, described the absence of a sense of agency among the less well-educated Germans living in rural areas, who accepted Hitler's orders without questioning their arbitrariness, irrational-ity, or cruelty (Kellner, 2018).

This conception of personal agency is more popular in Europe and North America than in most regions of the world. I suggest that Christianity's emphasis on each person's ability to freely choose the behaviors that might lead to salvation was one of the sources of this idea. It is a short ideological leap from agency to Adam Smith's assertion, a millennium and a half later, that community harmony was guaranteed if every person made his or her welfare the sole criterion when making an economic decision.

This conception of agency was missing from the belief systems of most ancient cultures because gods, rulers, family members, community norms, and worry over community gossip imposed serious limits on a person's freedom of choice. The rebellion by American youth against the Vietnam war, sexism, and racism during the late 1960s was a watershed moment in the public's awareness of personal agency. High school and college students were unpunished after breaking long-standing institutional rules. Late adolescents found this a heady experience. One middle-class senior at a private high school in 1969 told me that she and her friends could not believe that school authorities imposed no punishment on the many students who left the school during a class and marched to Boston Common to join a rally against the war. Such experiences potentiate the conviction that each person ought to award their wishes precedence over the legitimate sources of restraint in the community. This idea is now spreading to many societies that traditionally awarded primacy to the family and larger community.

Some professional groups sense a threat to their sense of agency. Professions that have always enjoyed unfettered autonomy are encountering new restraints. American physicians, for example, have always had the freedom to choose the best treatment for their patients. The rise over the past 20 years in the number of doctors working in large bureaucratic clinics or hospitals has reduced this autonomy considerably. The larger structures limit the therapeutic procedures doctors can prescribe, and require them to fill out many forms and record all decisions on a computer. As a result, many doctors who picked this career expecting to enjoy a sense of agency have become frustrated and are leaving their profession.

A similar restraint on a scientist's agency has emerged over the past 50 years. The increased number of scientists has not been accompanied by a comparable rise in research funds. This asymmetry has led some investigators to publish results that have low power that are often not replicated.

Psychologists, in particular, have been embarrassed by the lack of replicability of many studies.

One response to this crisis was a requirement by funding agencies and journal editors to state, ahead of time, the results the investigator expected. This demand tempts investigators to perform safe research that is likely to be affirmed, unlikely to provoke criticism, but unlikely to lead to a significant discovery. Charles Darwin, David Hubel, Torsten Wiesel, Barbara McClintock, Rosalind Franklin, Vera Rubin, James Watson, Francis Crick, Eleanor Gibson, Jennifer Doudna, Arnold Penzias, Harry Harlow, Brenda Milner, James Olds, and many others whose observations led to major advances did not know what they would find when they began their work.

The Price of Mobility

A small number of adults who ascended from a working-class or poor family to a position of prominence live with gnawing doubts over their right to enjoy a privileged position. John Updike (2012) and Frank Kermode (1995) are classic examples. Both men confessed in memoirs to an uncomfortable feeling when they were in the presence of those born into an elite family. The acclaimed writer John Wideman, born poor and black in a Pittsburgh ghetto, wrote that on most mornings he could not suppress the thought that this was the day the world would discover that he was a fraud. Isiah Berlin, whose family emigrated from St. Petersburg to London in 1921 when he was 12, experienced harsh prejudice from his elite English peers for his modest class rank and Jewish ethnicity. Although his writings recruited fame and respect from British elites, he once wrote, "I know nothing . . . my bluff will be called."

These feelings of doubt among those who ascended in class share some features with the feeling of *huzun* experienced by the residents of Istanbul who are saddened by the city's loss of its past eminence and ashamed of its current backwardness (Pamuk, 2006). V. S. Naipaul, a Nobel Laureate in Literature who died in August 2018, once confessed, "My most difficult thing to overcome was being born in Trinidad. That crazy resort place" (*New York Times*, August 12, 2018).

Some of these adults worry about being disloyal to the values of their less advantaged parents or feel guilty over making more money than their siblings. The adults who have preserved a strong identification with a disadvantaged class of rearing are vulnerable to occasional shame over the minimal education of their parents (Lubrano, 2004).

On the other hand, some working-class Americans who perform a distinctive service, such as tow truck operators, fire fighters, and policemen, possess an identification with their occupational category that calls for a level of loyalty to other members that is rare among those in higher-status jobs requiring more education. For example, when a tow truck operator is killed while on duty, hundreds of other tow operators, many of whom did not know the victim, gather within a week to memorialize their colleague. Memorials for professionals are attended by those who knew the victim and rarely by strangers from the same profession.

Class and Trait Preservation

Investigators who find a predictive relation between a behavioral or biological measure in an infant or young child and an outcome in late childhood often attribute the outcome to preservation of the earlier trait. In many cases, however, the experiences linked to continued rearing in a more or less advantaged family provide a more valid explanation (Kagan, Lapidus, & Moore, 1978; Rose, Feldman, & Jankowski, 2015; Sylvester et al., 2017; Bailey, Duncan, Watts, Clements, & Sarama, 2018; Lewis, 2018; Rudolph et al., 2018). A correlation between frequent babbling at 7 months and size of vocabulary at 10 years does not necessarily mean that the processes that mediated the infant babbling were preserved and account for the larger vocabulary. It is more likely that the behaviors of well-educated parents contributed to both the more frequent babbling and the larger vocabulary.

A marble in a groove preserves its direction of motion without an inherent disposition to move in a straight line. A child's class of rearing is a groove that restricts or enlarges possible opportunities. This suggestion finds support in a study of French infants born to disadvantaged mothers and adopted before age three by parents from a range of class positions. The school performances of the adolescents who had been adopted by the most educated parents were clearly superior to the academic records of those adopted by less well-educated parents (Duyme, 1988). More than 50 years ago, scientists at a number of universities studied the development of thousands of American infants born in different cities. Parental education, the index of class, accounted for more variation in IQ scores at ages 4 and 7 than combinations of the pregnant mother's health and the biological integrity of the newborn (Broman, Nichols & Kennedy, 1975).

Magnitude of Income Inequality

As with gender, each person's comparison of their class position with respect to others is a critical determinant of the outcomes of class rank. The larger the difference in income and education, the more frequent the prevalence of poor health, mental illness, crime, and lack of intergenerational mobility among the less advantaged in every nation studied (Sapolsky, 2005; Clough-Gorr, Enger, & Spoerri, 2015; Conejero, Guerra, Abundis-Gutierrez, & Rueda, 2018; Kishiyawa, Boyce, Jimenez, Perry, & Knight, 2009; McLeod, Horwood, & Fergusson, 2016; Rentfrow, Jakela, & Lamb, 2015; Bjornsdottir & Rule, 2017; Prins, Bates, Keyes, & Muntaner, 2015; Manuck, Flory, Ferrell, & Muldoon, 2004; Tackett, Herzhoff, Smack, Reardon, & Adam, 2017; Du Paul, Morgan, Farkas, Hillemeier, & Maczuga, 2017; Figlio, Freese, Karbownik, & Roth, 2017; Fajnzylber, Lederman, & Loayza, 2002; Christensen, Osler, Avlund, & Lund, 2014).

A perception of improved opportunities and enhanced respect can quiet the resentments of the less privileged in unequal societies without a major improvement in their economic security. A small number of American cities suffered more than 200 race riots each year during the 1960s. But the number of riots declined after 1970. Some of the reasons for the decline include the fact that more blacks in the riot cities received a high school diploma, an African-American was twice elected president, blacks are hosts of or commentators on television programs, Hollywood films feature black actors and actresses, and many white youths reject any form of prejudice against blacks.

These gains appear to be an important reason for the reduced number of riots, even though the black unemployment rate and income gain relative to whites in the riot cities had not improved much over this interval (Gooden & Myers, 2018). A perception of increased respect by a previously hostile majority can mute some of the anger over income inequality. Eliza Doolittle made the same request to Henry Higgins in the film *My Fair Lady.*

When an adult in a seriously unequal society decides he or she is a victim of unjust conditions there is some danger that this view of self will become stronger than national identity or identity as an employee or member of a labor union. When this happens the individual becomes reluctant to contribute to the welfare of the larger group. In *Janus v. American Federation of State, County and Municipal Employees*, the Supreme Court in 2018 sided with Mark Janus, an employee of the state of Illinois, who refused to pay dues to the union that was bargaining for better working conditions for all state employees.

The inverse relation between magnitude of income inequality and intergenerational mobility is larger in Great Britain and the United States than in the Scandinavian nations (Perez-Arce, Amaral, Huang, & Price, 2006). Two-fifths of the world's adults whose wealth places them in the top 1 percent (a net worth of about $870,000) live in the United States (*The Economist*, October 27, 2018). The occupational mobility of America's sons and daughters has decreased steadily over the interval from 1994 to 2016, with coefficients as high as 0.50 between the father's occupation and the class rank of his adult children (Hout, 2018).

A combination of high inequality and low mobility can have unwanted consequences. The 12 states in 2013 with the highest Gini coefficients, the economist's index of inequality, had higher homicide rates than the dozen states with the lowest coefficients. The relation between the Gini coefficient and murder rates in 39 nations revealed that Latin America was high on both indices, while the Scandinavian nations were low (Fajnzylber, Lederman, & Loayza, 2002). The magnitude of inequality has to reach a tipping point before consequences occur. A tipping point was reached in the United States in the 1880s when anger at the high level of inequality provoked violent worker strikes.

England and the United States in 2010 had high Gini coefficients and a high proportion of mentally ill adults. Japan, Germany, and the Scandinavian nations had lower coefficients and a smaller burden of mental illness. (Domenech-Abella et al., 2018; Gilman et al., 2017; Steenkamp et al., 2017; Brendgen, Girard, Vitaro, Dionne, & Boivin, 2016; Bekhuis, Boschloo, Rosmalen, de Boer, & Schoevers, 2016; Bosma, Brandts, Simons, Groffen, & van den Akker, 2015; Betancourt et al., 2016; Garratt, Chandola, Purdom, & Wood, 2017; Karevold, Roysamb, Ystrom, & Mathiesen, 2009; Fleming et al., 2017.)

Some European nations try to reduce inequality by increasing taxes on the wealthy. The United States and England, unwilling to use this tactic, live with an underclass growing increasingly desperate. The health of this group is one sign of this unfortunate situation. The health of less well-educated citizens in 27 of 28 nations improved across the interval from 2002 to 2014. The United States was the lone exception (Mackenbach et al., 2018).

Frank Bruni, a writer for the *New York Times*, proposed that America's elite colleges admit equal proportions of advantaged and disadvantaged youths, even if this plan ignored the applicant's qualifications. This proposal rankles those who believe that the distribution of privileges should be correlated with effort and ability, rather than guided only by an egalitarian ideal.

Bruni did not acknowledge that the quality of the student body makes a critical contribution to the prestige of the institution. The City University of New York, during the 1930s and 1940s, enjoyed elite status because it admitted high school seniors with the highest grades and test scores. As a result, those who graduated extracted considerable pride from their accomplishment. The recent, reasonable demand to admit more students from less advantaged minority groups, some of whom were not ready for college because of inadequate preparation in high school, has led over the years to a less talented student body which, in turn, removed the City University of New York from the group of prestige colleges. Sonja Sotomayor would have been deprived of the pride of achievement and enhanced confidence following her graduation from Princeton University if she believed that her admission was based only on her minority status and had nothing to do with her excellent performance in high school.

Humans possess two powerful motives that appear inconsistent. On the one hand, no one wants to feel dominated by, subordinate to, or less respected by other members of their society. An egalitarian ethos satisfies this need. On the other hand, children and adults like the feeling of vitality that bubbles up when they develop a talent that recruits an enhanced respect from others. A meritocratic society satisfies this desire. The Scandinavian nations have, at the moment, achieved the best balance between these wishes.

Status in a Community

It is useful to distinguish between a person's class in a society, on the one hand, and the respect he or she enjoys in their community. Many adults belonging to less advantaged class ranks enjoy the respect of many in their community because of a reputation for moral integrity, generosity, and/ or a family member who is known for a distinguished accomplishment. Although class and status are correlated, and some social scientists treat them as synonyms, I use the term status to refer to those who enjoy the respect of others in a particular community or setting.

The person occupying a higher class or status often invites a deferential posture in those from a lower rank. The former often looks directly at the other, who may bow the head a little and look away (Toscano, Schubert, & Glessner, 2018). An interaction between adults differing in status can affect subtle features in the speech of the subordinate member. When the television host Larry King was interviewing a guest with higher status, say a sitting president, Nobel Laureate, or Pulitzer Prize winner, he unconsciously began to match the physical qualities of his voice to those of his guest (Gregory & Webster, 1996). A small proportion of adults automatically evoke a subservient role in others because of a blend of energy and confidence that exudes psychic power. An unknown, poor, twenty-one year-old Pablo Picasso was such a person (Unger, 2018).

Although many adults combine a higher- or lower-class rank with a corresponding status, some enjoy only one of these positions. Presidents of major universities, physicians, famous scientists, and some judges enjoy both a privileged class rank as well as high status in their community. The portfolio managers in investment banks with an MBA from an elite business school and a high income are members of a privileged class but might not enjoy equally high status at a party with liberal Democrats or historians of Mesopotamia. Bank clerks in small towns in rural America who graduated from a prestige university and, in addition, had a grandfather whom everyone knew was a famous hero in the first world war have high status in that community, while occupying a modest class position in the society. The opportunity for British working-class men and women to earn a high salary in financial institutions grew in a major way during the 1980s. British writers and comedians satirized the boorish behavior of these *nouveau riche* because proper behavior was an important basis of respect in many communities (Biresi & Nunn, 2013).

Those who knew a little about a lot of things, from ants to astrophysics, enjoyed an enhanced status before the internet. This sign of status lost most of its power when anyone with access to Google could acquire the same information. This historical change devalued what had been an important product of a college education. When this challenge to the mission of a college was combined with the increased matriculation of youth from working-class families who thought they needed to get a college degree to obtain a good job, the colleges and universities felt pressured to make the preparation of young adults for a well-paying job in their society's economy a major reason for their existence,

Nations are sensitive to their status among nations of comparable size or power. Had fifteenth-century Spanish nobility not decided that their country's status had sunk below that of France, Italy, and Germany, they might not have urged Spain's rulers to expel Jews and Muslims in order to announce to their neighbors that they were the purest Catholic nation in Europe. The leaders of Russia and Germany during most of the nineteenth-century envied the higher status of France and England, which were rational, liberal democracies that nurtured famous artists and scientists. The German response was to declare that their nation had a more highly developed *Geist*, translated as spirit (Kohn, 1960).

The current leaders of China and Russia, aware that many of their citizens envy the economic, media, and military power of the United States, are trying to engender a more intense national pride. Putin is persuading the Russian people that they belong to a distinct ethnic group of *russki*. Putin hopes that this idea will generate an enhanced pride that will compensate for the feeling of loss following the dissolution of the Soviet Union.

The dominant themes of a nation's films often reflect attempts to articulate the accomplishments, values, or traits that enhance national pride. The French make many films celebrating art, either the lives of their famous painters or the interest in art among its citizens. German producers, aware that their viewers want to be released from the collective guilt of the Nazi era, make films depicting Germans who opposed Hitler or helped Jews. British filmmakers emphasize the glories of the Victorian era, when the nation was arguably the richest and most powerful in the world. Hollywood celebrates the themes that Americans believe render their society unique, especially tolerance, the opportunity for social mobility among those raised in modest circumstances, and the unexpected successes of the underdog.

Animals from varied species are sensitive to the relation between their status, defined as the likelihood of dominating others, and the status of others in the group. Male chimpanzees who are about to assume a subordinate role with a dominant male emit vocalizations called pant grunts (Sherrow, 2012). The daughter of a high-ranking female in a baboon troop evokes a subordinate posture with other females. The presence of a male in a species of African cichlid fish suppresses displays of dominance among the females in his harem. However, should the male die or be removed, one or more females immediately display dominant actions (Renn, Fraser, Aubin-Horth, Trainor, & Hofmann, 2012).

The Changing Status of Professional Groups

Philanthropic organizations supporting science during most of the last century typically assumed a subordinate role by asking scientists which phenomena were ready for their support. After the increase in government funding by NIH and NSF during the 1970s, the scientific staff at these agencies, who had stopped or never did research, began to tell the active investigators what ideas their agency would support. The private philanthropies soon followed suit. In less than a quarter-century, the status of many scientists vis-à-vis the staff at funding agencies was altered. They were now supplicants who had lost the freedom to probe the phenomena they thought would reveal significant insights when the research required a great deal of money.

The attacks on scientists performing experiments on monkeys or chimps are additional signs of a loss of status over the past 50 years. As a result, a smaller proportion of American college seniors plan to pursue a career in science in 2018, compared with the proportions in the two previous generations. This loss of interest in science has been accompanied by an examination of the integrity of all fields by scientists in varied disciplines. Essays in *Science* and *Nature* bemoan the number of non-replicable results and the reasonable critiques of popular practices, such as meta-analysis.

The situation is more serious in the social sciences. A trio of investigators using pseudonyms and false affiliations submitted 20 papers containing fabricated results supporting a political position to journals that favored that perspective. Seven of the 20 have been published or were accepted for publication. One example was a paper accepted by the journal *Sex Roles* examining table dialogue, which found that heterosexual men preferred to eat at one of the *Hooters* restaurants (Schuessler, 2018). Teaching, journalism, and the arts have also lost an earlier status that rendered them attractive, despite their modest salaries. This leveling of the status awarded to occupations that once enjoyed unfreckled respect is part of a broader anti-elitist movement that has removed the taint that had been attached to those who pursued careers whose primary reward is a high salary.

Can There Be a Classless Society?

Few societies have been able to arrange a lasting system in which most citizens believe their opportunities to obtain the prizes symbolic of worthiness are not seriously different from the access possessed by the small proportion occupying an elite class rank. Mao Zedong's attempt to promote the status of those who had grown up in peasant families, at the expense of the few who enjoyed a privileged childhood, lasted for only two generations.

I recall an afternoon in the fall of 1973 when I was a member of a group of social scientists visiting Mao's China. A Chinese professor of psychology replied to our question of what he taught by repeating Marx. "A person's social class is the only important source of variation." One of my colleagues challenged the professor by noting that China was attempting to establish a classless society. When that goal was reached, Chinese psychologists would have nothing to teach. The faculty member was silent for several minutes as he searched for an answer. The cadre who traveled with us rescued the embarrassed professor by reminding the group, "A society only approaches classlessness, it never fully attains it."

A formidable obstacle to a classless society is the human resistance to relinquishing the notion that some exemplars of every category are better than others, whether dogwood trees, pizza, sunsets, rainbows, speeches, or physical attractiveness. Attractive adults are more likely to occupy positions of responsibility (Urbatsch, 2018). Every society needs some citizens who possess the moral authority needed to persuade a majority of an unpopular idea or action. Many of these adults have attained a class or status, based on education, bravery, moral integrity, wealth, or mastery of a technical skill, that is higher than most in their audience. The enhanced status of military officers over enlisted soldiers permits them to feel they have the right to order young men and women into battle. An important function of a degree from an elite institution is to persuade the graduates that they possess the talents needed to assume a position of responsibility. A society lacking these adults is less likely to produce an Archibald Cox or Sonia Sotomayor.

This discussion implies that the members of a particular class vary on many measures that range from quality of childhood diet to kinds of parental punishments. Investigators who use statistics to remove the contribution of class to a relation between a predictor and outcome cannot be certain of the meaning of their result, because the members of a particular class do not share all the properties of the members of that class. Not all adults who grew up in a disadvantaged family attended schools with poorly trained teachers, had a depressed parent, were physically abused, or suffered from poor health. Each condition makes a unique contribution to the probability of the outcomes that scientists measure. Therefore, the results of a statistical analysis that removes the effect of class do not allow an unambiguous inference.

Ethnicity and Ethnic Identity

The term ethnicity was introduced into the American vocabulary in 1913 to replace race. US immigration forms in 1898 listed more than 50 races, most of which referred to a person's nation of origin (Perlman, 2018). Some of these national groups possessed a small number of distinctive genes. This fact explains why a popular definition of ethnicity is based on the genes that are more frequent in adults whose ancestors occupied a specific region thousands of years ago (Tateno et al., 2014). However, the reproductively isolated populations that existed many thousands of years ago have become so rare it is more difficult to find populations within a society that possess distinctive DNA sequences. That is why social scientists prefer the concept of ethnic identity,

The Bases of an Ethnic Identity

An ethnic identity is a belief that one belongs to a group possessing distinctive properties, including invisible bodily tissues that have been transferred from generation to generation for thousands of years. The hope held by sociologists at the University of Chicago during the first decade of the last century that immigrants to the United States would lose their ethnic identity as they assimilated to the Anglo-American culture lies unfulfilled. About one-third of white Americans in 2018 resent the growing numbers of other ethnic groups. The broadly advertised fact that Caucasians will be a minority in the United States by 2050 has made the members of this group acutely aware of their ethnic identity.

Some sociologists and anthropologists believe that capitalism bred an individualism that was necessary for the development of class and ethnic identities with the potential to generate strong emotions. This view ignores the robust fact that all humans automatically classify objects, events, and people that possess salient physical or symbolic features into distinct categories.

Unfortunately, answers to a questionnaire are the most popular measure of ethnic identity. Because many of the inferences about ethnic identity are based only on self-report evidence, readers should reflect on their meaning and limited validity. The problem with a self-report measure of identity is that an unknown number of adults who deny their ethnic identity on a questionnaire experience a vicarious shame or pride when a member of their ethnic group commits an immoral or praiseworthy action. These feelings, which are automatic, imply that the person possesses an ethnic identity he or she denied on a questionnaire. Many American Jews who reported the lack of a Jewish identity said they were surprised by a feeling of vicarious joy when the Israelis won the Six-Day War in 1967. The Jews in fifteenth-century Spain who converted to Catholicism did not experience the vicarious pride of the majority of Spanish Catholics who acquired their ethnic identity as children.

A dissociation between self-reports of a trait and direct observations or biological measures is common. German college students who reported empathy for individuals pictured in a distressed situation failed to show any changes in heart rate, heart rate variability, and skin conductance that would imply a feeling of empathy (Deuter et al., 2018). If adults reporting a firm ethnic identity are more likely to experience vicarious pride while those who deny it feel vicarious shame, many statements in the published literature are misleading. The phenomenon of vicarious affect due to an identification a person did not know he or she possessed challenges Chater's (2018) claim that there are no ideas that escape awareness.

Social scientists do not understand why only some members of a group feel a vicarious pride when a member of their group wins a prize or vicarious shame when a member commits a moral error. German youth who were genetically related to a high-ranking Nazi official varied in their reaction to learning of the actions of their relative. The adolescent grand-son of Rudolph Hoess felt ashamed when he learned of the horrendous actions of his grandfather, who ran Auschwitz for many years. But Hein-rich Himmler's daughter, Gudrun, denied that her father was director of the concentration camps, and she remained loyal to his memory until her death in 2018.

Individuals with an ethnic identity believe they are the heirs of an ances-tral population that lived in a particular place, spoke a distinctive language, shared distinctive values, and possessed unique physical features. Americans whose ancestors came from either east, south, or southeast Asia have differ-ent ethnic identities. The Americans whose grandparents lived in China or Japan usually have more education, higher incomes, professional careers, and are less likely to be victims of prejudice than those from the other two Asian groups, partly because a majority of Americans regard the members of these groups as conscientious and law abiding (Hsin & Xie, 2014).

Distinctive names can contribute to an ethnic identity (Rahman, 2013). African-American parents are most likely to give their infants uncommon names, such as Dion or Jayla. The ethnic identity of many Italians born in the United States is based on last names as well as distinctive foods and lifestyles (Nardell, 2004). An unknown proportion of Italian-Americans experienced intense conflict when the United States declared war on Italy in December 1941 as well as later when American troops, including some Italian-Americans, invaded Sicily with orders to kill Italian soldiers. Groups that maintain their isolation from neighboring groups possess a strong eth-nic identity. The Inuit Eskimo of Baffin Island in Canada, surrounded by a larger white population, are proud of an identity based on form of work, values, and distinctive names that transfer to a newborn the temperamen-tal biases, personality traits, and skills of a dead ancestor with the same name (Searles, 2008).

Although a Jewish identity includes the idea of an ancestral group in a particular place, it also includes the less common features of no homeland until 1948, a minority religion, and a victim of prejudice in many societies for more than 2,000 years. This latter feature generates doubt about one's acceptability to strangers. The American polymath Norbert Wiener, who contributed significant ideas to several domains, wrote that his Jewish iden-tity "forced on me a sense of inferiority which contributed greatly to my insecurity" (Wiener, 1956).

A Polish journalist told me in 2002 that, until she was 20, she assumed she was born to Polish Catholic parents whose ancestors were also Polish Catholics. The day her mother confessed to being Jewish, her ethnic identity was altered. Presumably, she imagined her body containing some Jewish cells. This idea precipitated a depression because she was aware of the virulent anti-Semitic views held by her Polish friends and supposed they would somehow detect her tainted pedigree. A non-Jew who was a victim of frequent rejections might entertain the notion that they possessed a psychological property that was salient to the Jewish identity. A psychiatrist told me of a 7-year-old Catholic daughter of Catholic parents who was a target of peer rejection. This girl surprised her mother one evening by saying, "I feel I'm Jewish."

The ethnic identity of the Hazaras, who are scattered across several Middle Eastern nations, are a persecuted minority without a homeland, partly because they practice the Shia religion in the majority-Sunni nations of Afghanistan, Syria, and Iraq in which they reside. Although the Kurds occupy parts of Turkey, Iran, Syria, and Iraq, they are a majority in northern Iraq, where they experience more pride in their ethnic identity than the Hazaras.

The distinct ethnic identities of the Yoruba, Ibo, and Hausa-Fulani of Nigeria have a greater influence on their behaviors than their wealth and education. Class divisions in Nigeria are often based on variation within each of these three ethnic groups (Ifidon, 1999). This practice makes it difficult to generate a national identity. The ruling dynasty of China at the end of the seventeenth century recognized this truth and tried to persuade the Han and non-Han populations to adopt a Chinese identity (Zhao, 2006). Contemporary Chinese enjoy an enhanced ethnic pride because of the nation's extraordinary gains over the past 40 years in GDP, income, and status in the world of nations (Chen, 2018).

Individuals can have more than one ethnic identity depending on the setting. A person can possess the identity of a Caribbean black in her visits to Ghana, and an African-American identity in her home community of Boise, Idaho. Older children born to parents who, years earlier, had migrated to a society with a different religion or values are susceptible to a conflicted ethnic identity. Youths born to parents who left Tibet in 1959 to settle in Kashmir are not sure whether they are Tibetans or Kashmiris. Edward Said, a former professor of literature at Columbia University, was born in Palestine in 1935 but educated in British and American schools. He confessed to a confused ethnic identity because of a British first name and a Palestinian surname.

Ethnicity and the Primacy of the Person or the Community

Scholars do not agree on the reasons why medieval Europeans began to replace the welfare of the family or the community as the primary beneficiary of decisions with the welfare of each individual. Some historians emphasize the many wars that required individual valor. Other scholars suggest that Christianity may have contributed to the ascendance of the individual because the God in the New Testament loved individuals, not groups. Each person was responsible for his or her salvation. This premise made it easy for Europeans to celebrate the entrepreneurial merchant and the premises of capitalism.

The concern with the welfare of each person and faith in a technological fix for any problem render Americans and the British distinctive among the world's nations. The focus on the properties of the individual, instead of the individual in a setting, is one reason why many Western commentators writing on the poverty in select nations in Africa, Latin America, and Asia place the blame on the traits of the residents and their leaders.

The anthropologist Jason Hickel (2017) argues that the problems these nations face are the product of earlier actions by Europeans and Americans that kept them impotent. These acts include exploitation of their material wealth, assassinations of leaders trying to institute policies inimical to both European and American interests, and, after 1980, loans that burdened them with an annual debt service in 2017 that approached a trillion dollars. The white rhinoceros is close to extinction because humans kill them, not because they possess defective genes, physiologies, or behavioral traits.

The historical contexts of the past 500 years have made a major contribution to the currently large gap between the economic and political development of these nations and levels in Europe, North America, Japan, and a few other nations. Europeans and Americans typically credit their position of dominance to the possession of greater talent and an ethos that values hard work. This explanation fails to acknowledge the good luck that gave their regions a relatively benign climate, rich supplies of fuel, and a Middle

Eastern monotheism that allowed an illusion of superiority because they honored a moral imperative to improve the self through accomplishments.

The conditions in asociety are rarely due only to the actions of its members. The eastern half of the United States contributed more carbon dioxide to the atmosphere during the last 100 years than the western half because of more factories and cars. But the western half is currently suffering the consequences of a warmer atmosphere in the form of droughts and large fires. The seventeenth-century poet John Donne could not have anticipated the relevance for this century of his famous lines, "Do not ask for whom the bell tolls; it tolls for thee."

The Changing American Premises

The individualistic, self-reliant ethic that dominated America for more than two centuries began to change a little during the depression of the 1930s, when Franklin Roosevelt used government resources to help the millions of unemployed. Today, a majority of Americans believe their government has a responsibility to come to the aid of any person that is a victim of circumstances they cannot control, whether a flood, hurricane, drought, or unemployment (Fender, 2012).

Young scientists in 2018 are extending the idea of government responsibility to their professional group. The oversupply of young scientists—there were about 3,000 desirable jobs for the 40,000 new PhDs in science in 2017—has generated a fierce competition for tenure-track appointments and grants that is precipitating bouts of anxiety and depression, as well as demands that universities and the government do something to relieve their distress. No prior generation of adults who chose science as a career assumed that their institution or government was obligated to support them in times of need.

A concern with the welfare of the group is spreading to the scientific laboratory, because a large number of labs run by senior scientists employ many junior scientists and assistants. An essay in the May 17, 2018, issue of *Nature* advised these senior scientists to be concerned with the harmony of the group they lead. The assistants who helped Tycho Brahe, I. P. Pavlov, and other investigators who profited from a large number of aspiring scientists regarded their roles as a privilege, and their mentors did not assume that they had a responsibility to ensure the happiness of their helpers.

The Premises of the Ancient Chinese

The histories of China and England reveal the sharp contrast between promoting the harmony of the group or protecting the freedom of the individual. The English, who enjoyed a benign climate, celebrated the individual artisan, businessman, and professional. The agricultural Chinese were often victims of catastrophic floods or droughts that required collective action. The ancient Chinese had no gods, no origin of the world, no slaves, no word for truth, little interest in metaphysical ideas, a concern with wholes rather than parts, a denigration of artisans, and an acceptance of the need to yield to nature. They also preferred a calm over an aroused mood, silence over speaking, written texts over natural phenomena, cycles over a linear metric for history, and complementary forces instead of things as the foundation of events that are always dependent on the setting (Bodde, 1981).

The Chinese insisted that no object, event, or person could be the strongest, biggest, or most beautiful in all settings. This idea is the basis of a famous set of comparisons. Wood, in the form of a spade, conquers earth by turning it over, metal conquers wood, fire conquers metal, water conquers fire, and earth, in the form of a dam, conquers water.

East Asians have been willing to inhibit desired actions if their expression dishonored the family. American children born to Asian parents usually perform well in school because of an imperative requiring obedience to parents and protecting the family from embarrassment over a poor grade (Kingdon & Cassen, 2010). I once had a bright female graduate student born in America to South Korean parents, who had arranged her marriage to an older man she did not want to marry. Instead of simply telling her parents of her refusal to comply with their wish, she felt obligated to take a leave of absence for a year. She said it was necessary to return to her Washington, D.C., home in order to gradually persuade her parents of the reasons for her decision.

A flowing river is the most popular symbol of the Chinese civilization because it implies continuous change owing to the balance among forces. Confucius wrote, "When the sun stands at midday, it begins to set. When the moon is full, it begins to wane." East Asians are far more sensitive than Europeans or Americans to the setting in which an event occurs (Masuda, Gonzalez, Kwan, & Nisbett, 2008). A solitary eagle high on a mountain cliff, a popular symbol of the United States, implies that the eagle's dominance is preserved in all settings.

Mandarin contains 20 verbs that describe the varying ways an object can be held or carried; English has only two. Chinese speakers also prefer to use concrete rather than abstract words to describe a person's traits. In settings in which an English speaker might say, "Mary is an affectionate person," a speaker of Mandarin is likely to say, "Fei hugs her friends at parties."

The Japanese share the Chinese preference for the whole over the parts. Three-year-old Japanese children have already acquired this bias (Kuwabata & Smith, 2016). The patterns of maternal play with infants may facilitate this perceptual style. Japanese mothers typically use a toy as a basis for an interactive event, rather than an occasion to label an object and its parts, as Americans do. For example, a Japanese mother who picked up a toy dog might say, "Woof, woof, it's a dog, give it a love, now give it to me, thank you" (Fernald & Morikawa, 1993).

The Japanese concern with the setting is revealed in the important distinction between *uchi,* meaning inside, and *soto* meaning outside. This distinction dictates how one behaves. When preschool children arrive at school they remove their shoes and replace them with shoes appropriate for the inside. Their mothers, too, respect the boundary separating the street from the school. This is the place where the parent gives control of the child to the teachers (Walsh 2002). These experiences teach the child to be continually aware of the setting before they act. Few American children or adults honor this imperative with the regularity found in Japan.

Is This the Best of Times?

The Chinese belief in historical cycles governed by the changing balance of forces rubs against the view that humans in 2018 are luckier than all prior generations because of many material advances. The emphasis on the material gains ignores the undesirable outcomes, material as well as psychological, that are direct consequences of the benevolent advances. Nicholas Kristof (*New York Times,* January 5, 2019) and Steven Pinker (2018), who support this sunny perspective, cherry-pick the desirable material outcomes while failing to devote equal time to their costs.

No one questions the fact that medical advances, antibiotics, chlorination of water, and indoor plumbing have, over the past millennium, extended the average life span of hundreds of millions of humans by 40 to 50 years. The longer life spans, however, are accompanied by an increasing number of mutations that increase the risk for a serious disease. As a result, the world has a large number of aging, infirm adults whose health care costs comprise a large proportion of a nation's GDP. Although Americans older than 65 represent 15 percent of the population, 80 percent of whom are not working, their illnesses eat up about one-third of the federal dollars spent on health. When the expenditures for social security are added to the health costs the total comes to about $1.6 trillion, which was about 40 percent of all government spending in 2017.

These expenditures limit the resources that would benefit the younger working population whose taxes contributed to the support of the elderly. Because the proportion of older Americans will be much larger in 2060, it is not clear that the United States and other nations can sustain this burden unless it raises taxes, as many European nations have done, American women decide to bear more than two children, or the government accepts more immigrants. These facts invite a less celebratory assessment of the medical advances that prolong the lives of many citizens who make little or no contribution to the larger community while consuming products that add to the non-biodegradable mass.

The products of reason, science, and technology gave us electricity, more reliable and faster means of transportation, improved crop yields, plastics, machines that perform many unpleasant tasks, smart phones, and the internet. But these same advances are also responsible for increased pollution of air, rivers, and oceans, the killing of large numbers of animals, nuclear and non-biodegradable waste, climate change, an electronic interconnectedness that is vulnerable to cyber attacks that can cripple a nation's functions, online scams, theft of bank account numbers, vulnerabilities to infectious agents that have developed resistance to antibiotics, and, among Americans, increases in loneliness, deaths due to opioid overdoses, and the highest suicide rate in over 70 years. The history of life on this planet is marked by quiet intervals that are suddenly punctuated by an unpredictable catastrophe. The 100-mile-wide asteroid that struck northern Mexico about 70 million years ago, the bubonic plague, and the two world wars are four familiar examples. War or unrest in Syria, Ukraine, Latvia, and Lesotho in this century interrupted the linear increase in longevity characteristic of most nations.

The current and possible future problems that no one wants led Todd May, a philosopher at Clemson University, to suggest that reducing the size of the species that destroys more life than any other animal would not be a tragedy (*New York Times,* December 17, 2018). If flora, fauna, sky, streams, and seas could speak they would protest the idea that reason and science have been gifts for them. No wedding of reason and the facts of evolution leads to the conclusion that the welfare of Homo sapiens *assumes* a privileged priority over the welfare of other claimants. "The present historical time invites . . . a new vision of humanity no longer obstructed by . . . human supremacy" (Crist, 2018, p. 1243).

A greater awareness of the less desirable outcomes of the material advances has led to a decline in reports of well-being over the past 25 years. An annual Gallup poll that asks adults in many countries about the occurrence of episodes of worry reached their highest value in 2017 when 40 percent of respondents said they experienced serious worry the previous day. This rise in unhappiness occurred during the same interval that medical discoveries led to cures for what had been incurable illnesses, the ability to communicate with others improved, and anyone with access to the internet could learn about any topic that tickled their curiosity. Close to three-quarters of Americans polled in 2018 said they favor euthanasia. The public pressure on state legislatures to legalize euthanasia implies that the medical advances that allow bed-ridden older patients to remain alive are not a gift to those who extract few moments of joy during each day's interminable hours.

Robert Wuthnow (2018) documented the current unhappiness among the mainly white populations living in small towns in rural America. Prior to 1970 these Americans had enjoyed a sense of community based on town rituals, familiarity with many residents who shared the same values, and the belief that neighbors and the local church would help them if necessary. These adults in 2018 are troubled by their town's shrinking populations as youths leave for jobs in urban areas, the loss of local PTA organizations, youth sports leagues, hospitals, and physicians, and the increased use of drugs by adolescents. The loss of community vitality is the main cause of their melancholy.

Equally important, scientific discoveries have confirmed Macbeth's melancholic lament, "Life's but a tale written by an idiot, full of sound and fury, signifying nothing." Those who agree with this view are provoked to question the existence of a metaphysical force that created a universe with meaning and purpose. A large proportion of the youths and adults who have accepted this conclusion, but had not yet found a life mission, become depressed, confused, and unable to commit to a life goal because they cannot commit to an idea that they have to invent.

Amy Binder, co-author of *Becoming Right* (Binder & Wood, 2012), interviewed Harvard and Stanford seniors who, as freshmen, were considering careers that might help others or the society. Four years later these same students were considering a job in consulting or finance When asked why, they replied that the starting salaries were high ($70 to 100,000) and obtaining a position at one of the best firms brought the satisfaction of winning a competition with rivals.

Their culture has taught them that the primary purpose of life is to be a winner. The prize won need not be useful or have benevolent consequences. The sad aspect of this state of affairs is that these 21-year-olds had been selected earlier by the admissions committees of these and other prestige universities because they were among America's most talented youth. The ambience of their culture, replete with material advances, robbed them of their earlier wish to give back to a society that had been so generous to them.

More than half of the Harvard seniors who graduated in 2017 or 2018 (a similar proportion applies to other high prestige universities) were seeking a job in finance or consulting, even though many acknowledged that these jobs were boring and devoid of any praiseworthy moral standard. But their reasoning skills, applied to the facts as they saw them, invited this conclusion. Far fewer considered a career in a field that could contribute to the society, whether finding less polluting sources of energy, discovering the causes of and cures for an illness, or becoming a public defender. Sentiment, not reason, was needed to pick one of these domains and this generation's experiences taught them to be suspicious of sentiment.

An emphasis on the measurable consequences of the products of reason has led some social scientists to arrive at the obvious conclusion that the decision to have children results in a decline of family wealth. Children do cost money (Maroto, 2018). Although these authors never explicitly say that couples should not have children, they rarely acknowledge that adults want children because they believe that the experiences involved in raising a child will bring satisfactions that are difficult to measure and missing from any consumable.

The diverse electronic gadgets that eliminate the need to exert effort for many simple tasks, such as making coffee, deprive each person of the tiny surge of satisfaction that follows a goal attained after the expenditure of effort. I do not want an app that makes my coffee and toasts my bread before I get to the kitchen. Many wise commentators have recognized that the joy is in the effort. If the scientists acclaimed for a discovery that required years of work had made the same discovery in less than one day the intensity of their pride would be diluted. The videos of the Nobel Prize winners describing the sequence of events that led to their insight reveal the joy that accompanied resolving each frustration in the journey to victory.

Many years ago, in a meeting with a dozen graduate students studying for a degree in clinical psychology, I asked them why they wanted to become psychotherapists. The group agreed that their primary motive was to help those with mental problems. My reply evoked some guilt a day later because it seemed a bit cruel. I said, "If I gave each of you a magic wand that immediately healed every person it touched, you would become bored in less than a month. What you want is to use your knowledge, wisdom, and empathy, over a period of time, to help patients." A long interval of silence followed.

Most commentators assume that the material advances only deserve celebration if they increase human happiness. If not, why celebrate them? Advances in technology made it possible to manufacture inexpensive cigarettes that brought pleasure to many millions. But a large number of happy smokers stopped when they learned of the health risks. The generation of patients with chronic pain that was gladdened by the availability of synthetic opioids was replaced with patients who worried about acquiring an addiction.

Each person's judgment of their happiness requires a comparison, usually between the past and the present or the present and the future. Those who report a high level of happiness usually believe their life is improving or is likely to improve. The average level of happiness in a society cannot be inferred from the number of material advances. A 2017 poll of adults from 28 countries enjoying material advances found that over half of the respondents expected their living conditions to stagnate or worsen (*The Economist*, December 22, 2018). Although Americans enjoy a plethora of advances, their average level of happiness in 2018 ranked 18 among the world's major nations. The largest decline in the answer, "Very happy" to a question about well-being asked of a representative sample of Americans each year from 1972 to 2014 occurred among whites living in the northeast (Iceland & Ludwig-Dehm, 2019).

This result seems odd since, during this 42-year interval, more members of this population obtained a college degree and had access to some of the nation's outstanding medical facilities and research universities. On the other hand, this group of Americans became less religious, were less likely to be married, and witnessed a large increase in income inequality—three conditions that reduce happiness, but are often correlates of material progress.

The happiest adults live in one of the Scandinavian countries, which are smaller, agree on values, trust their governments, and enjoy a low level of income inequality, crime, and homelessness. None of these six features is a material advance and these conditions may have been present in select societies that existed before the industrial revolution.

The themes of the most popular films, books, and essays reflect the dark mood of many Americans in 2018. It is not unreasonable to suggest that a larger proportion of Americans alive in 1803, following independence from Britain and the Louisiana Purchase, would have reported feeling very happy than the proportion of contemporary Americans, despite the fact that Americans in 1803 had an average life span of 37 years. I suspect that more Americans experienced a larger jolt of happiness in 1964 when Congress passed the Civil Rights Bill than when they learned, the same year, that a vaccine for measles was available and the first heart transplant occurred.

A full refrigerator, improved transportation, smart phones, watching movies at home, online shopping, personalized cures for select diseases, and a longer life span cannot silence the melancholy that emerges from feelings of loneliness, moral confusion, distrust of authority, and worry about the future. Isaac Newton was right. For every action there is an equal and opposite reaction. I am not suggesting that the material advances have not brought happiness to many individuals. But free lunches are rare. I am willing to speculate that the proportion of humans older than 13 years who believed they were very happy or very unhappy has remained relatively stable for the last 100,000 years.

Biology and Ethnicity

Despite the profound significance of a person's ethnic identity, contemporary ethnic groups differ in genes that affect the risk for select diseases, reproductive functions, brain states, physiological profiles, anatomy, olfactory receptors, pain sensitivities, and behaviors (Zhu, Manichaikul, Hu, Chen, Liang, Steffen et al., 2016; Nisbett, Peng, Choi, & Norenzyan, 2001; Kredlow, Pineles, Inslicht, Marin, Milad, Otto, & Orr, 2017; Lu, Zeltzer, & Tsao, 2013; Majid & Kruspe, 2018; Manuck, 2017; Galanter et al., 2017; Glatt, Tampilic, Christie, De Young, & Freimer, 2004).

The first component of a principal components analysis of the variation in 130 short sequences of DNA (about 300 base pairs) containing two or more SNPs on populations scattered around the world revealed differences among the populations in sub-Saharan Africa, southwest Asia, south central Asia, east Asia, Europe, the Americas, and the Pacific islands (Bulbul et al., 2017). To the surprise of many obstetricians, this genetic variation is associated with variation in the shape of the pelvis. Some shapes make it easier and some make it harder for the fetus to pass through the birth canal (*New York Times*, October 27, 2018).

East Asians and Africans possess the largest number of differences in DNA sequences (Kidd et al., 2017). One difference has implications for the response to medicines. The cytochrome family of genes, CYP2D6, which is the origin of an enzyme that metabolizes drugs, has more than 40 alleles. Asians are most likely to be born with an allele that is minimally functional (Bradford, 2002). This observation implies that Asians are more likely than other ethnic groups to develop unwanted side effects to drugs prescribed for an illness.

The two major alleles of the gene for the progesterone receptor vary among East Asians, Africans, and Europeans. More Asians possess the allele that allows a woman to carry her fetus to term (Li et al., 2018). Native Americans, like their East Asian ancestors, possess alleles of the alcohol dehydrogenase gene whose products interfere with the metabolism of alcohol (Peng, Gizer, Wilhelmsen, & Ehlers, 2017). Indigenous populations living in the high altitudes of the Andes and Tibet possess alleles that aid adaptation to these uncommon ecologies, but also increase the risk for a cancer at older ages (Voskarides, 2018).

Some alleles found in African-Americans contribute to a higher risk of hypertension (Hatzfeld, La Veist, & Gaston-Johansson, 2012). One allele of the APOL1 gene renders pregnant women with an African pedigree vulnerable to very high blood pressure prior to the birth of the fetus (called preeclampsia). In some cases, this state is followed by a more dangerous syndrome that places the fetus at risk (called eclampsia). Instances of preeclampsia in 10 percent of African-American mothers were due to the fact that the fetus, not the mother, possessed the risk allele and transferred it to the mother (Reidy et al, 2018).

On some occasions an allele has different consequences in different ethnic groups. A variant of the gene for acetylcholine is correlated with a lower heart rate and greater heart rate variability in black infants, but with a higher heart rate and less variability in white infants (Jones, Gray, Theall, & Drury, 2018; Qu & Leerkes, 2018). Alleles whose frequencies vary in different ethnic groups can increase the risk for macular degeneration among whites (Klein et al. 2013), lower the incidence of alcoholism among Asians (Wall, Luczak, & Hiller-Sturmhofel, 2016), increase the risk for breast cancer, Crohn's disease, and ulcerative colitis in Ashkenazi Jews (Jackson et al., 2014) or affect the size of the follicular reserve in older African women (Bleil et al., 2014).

Chinese and Chinese-American 4-month-old infants are less aroused by unexpected events and more easily soothed when distressed, compared with European-American infants (Kagan et al., 1994; Freedman & Freedman, 1969). This ethnic difference might be due, in part, to a variant of the gene for the serotonin transporter. East Asians are most likely to have inherited a shorter DNA sequence in the promoter region of this gene. This allele is associated with reduced expression of the gene for the transporter and, therefore, slower re-uptake of serotonin (Liu et al., 2015).

An infrequent allele of the gene for the dopamine receptor, called DRD4, renders the receptor less responsive to dopamine. Individuals with this allele ought to feel a more persistent urge to seek new experiences because novel events are accompanied by a phasic increase in dopamine. Caucasian populations with this allele are more likely than others to have a diagnosis of ADHD (Nikolaidis & Gray, 2010). Furthermore, the 16 percent of the free ranging juvenile rhesus macaques on the island of Cayo Santiago who possess this allele are more restless than the other animals (Coyne, Lindell, Clemente, Barr, Parker, & Maestripieri, 2015).

In light of these facts it is intriguing to learn that Europeans, South Americans, and Africans are more likely than the Chinese to inherit the DRD4 allele. The frequency of this allele in a population happens to correlate with the probability that the population will undertake long distance migrations. The human groups who migrated more than 9,000 miles thousands of years ago had the highest proportion with this allele. The ancient Chinese, who were less likely to possess this allele, were less likely to migrate long distances (Chen, Burton, Greenberger, & Dmitrieva, 1999).

The gene for catechol-o-methyltransferase, or COMT, has two major alleles. One contains the amino acid valine at a particular location in the exon, while the other contains methionine. The latter metabolizes dopamine in the synapses of the frontal lobe less effectively than the former. Hence, dopamine remains in the synapse for a slightly longer time. Theory implies that those homozygous for the methionine allele should have a better working memory and more effective control of impulsive responding. Northern Europeans were more likely than 29 other ethnic groups to possess methionine rather than valine in the COMT gene (Palmatier, Kang, & Kidd, 1999).

Many Africans inherit a small number of repeats of CAG trinucleotides in exon 1 of the gene for the androgen receptor. This variant results in high levels of androgen receptor activity in sites that affect muscle mass. Most East Asians, on the other hand, have the largest number of repeats and the lowest levels of receptor activity. Caucasians and Hispanics fall in between (Ackerman et al., 2012). Despite these facts, investigators who find a small correlation between a gene or genes and a psychological outcome in an ethnically diverse sample often fail to check the evidence to see whether the relation holds for only one ethnic group.

Skin Color

The many genes that are the origins of variation in skin color may make a small contribution to physiological states that, under certain conditions, could affect behavior. The pro-opiomelanocortin gene is the source of a large peptide that is cleaved into a number of molecules, one of which is a variant of melanin-stimulating hormone (Slominski, Wortsman, Luger, Paus, & Solomon, 2000). When this hormone binds to one of the five melanocortin receptors (MCR1) on the surface of a melanocyte, eumelanin is produced and transported to the keratinocytes in the upper layer of the skin to give it a darker color. If, however, agouti signaling peptide binds to the MCR1 receptor on the melanocyte, instead of the variant of melanin-stimulating hormone, the resulting pigment is reddish-brown, called pheomelanin. The balance between eumelanin and pheomelanin determines the color of the skin, hair, and iris. Fair-skinned, blonde, blue-eyed humans possess a balance favoring the agouti protein. Those with darker skin, hair, and iris were born with a balance favoring the binding of melanin-stimulating hormone to the receptor (D'Alba & Shawkey, 2019).

The variation in pigmentation in skin, hair, or fur is correlated with a variety of outcomes in fish, reptiles, birds, mice, lions, sheep, cattle, deer, foxes, dogs, and apes. The darker members of a species are usually larger in size, display higher levels of motor activity, are better protected from inflammatory states, and, in some species, are tamer and less resistant to human handling (Ducrest, Keller, & Roulin, 2008; Kim et al., 2010). These correlates are not surprising given the fact that all five melanocortin receptors are found in the brain (Slominski, Wortsman, Luger, Paus & Solomon, 2000).

Most darker-skinned humans have a higher vagal than sympathetic tone on the heart and, a lower and more variable heart rate compared with Asians and Caucasians (Tagliaferri et al., 2017). These results match the author's unpublished observations on 4-month-old African-American, European-American, and Chinese-American infants living in Boston. The African-American infants had the largest heart rate variabilities, implying high levels of vagal control of the heart. The Chinese-American infants had the smallest variabilities and least vagal influence.

The balance between sympathetic and vagal tone on the heart is reasonable given the latitudes these populations occupied originally. An autonomic nervous system that favored parasympathetic over sympathetic activity is adaptive in the warm climate of sub-Saharan Africa, where dilation of skin capillaries allows body heat to escape. A brisker sympathetic arm, accompanied by constriction of the skin's capillaries in order to conserve body heat, is more advantageous in the colder regions of Europe and Asia that are above the fortieth latitude. The ethnic variation in vasodilation and constriction of skin capillaries to cold temperatures is in accord with this hypothesis (Maley, Eglin, House, & Tipton, 2014).

An ethnic group's settings can, of course, mute or enhance traits associated with its genes. The starkly dissimilar contexts in contemporary Japan and Nigeria invite behaviors that are independent of genes. Infants in the foraging economy of the Aka peoples of Central Africa are held by their primary caretaker for many hours of the day. As a result, they sleep more and cry less often than the infants born to Ngandu mothers, who belong to a sedentary farming community in a similar part of Africa (Hewlett, Lamb, Shannon, Leyendecker, & Scholnerich, 1998). Contexts usually exert a stronger influence on behavior than genes. Gangs of youth armed with knives are rare in communities with fewer than 10,000 residents.

The Problem with Statistical Control of Ethnicity

As noted in the discussion of class, investigators who use a statistical procedure to remove the contribution of ethnicity to a predictor-outcome relation are removing dissimilar contributions from participants with the same ethnicity. A measure of subjective well-being gathered on Americans who are white, black, Asian, or Hispanic is affected by each person's beliefs, identification with their group, genes, and minority status.

New England, the Deep South, Southwest, Upper Plains states, and West Coast have dissimilar proportions of the major ethnic groups. There are more blacks than Asians in the south, more Asians than blacks on the West Coast, more Hispanics than Asians in the Southwest, and whites are the majority in New England and the Upper Plains states. Moreover, these ethnic groups vary in years of education, income, and frequency of discrimination in the varied regions. Blacks in the South, for example, have less education, a lower income, and experience more prejudice than blacks in New England. These facts imply that investigators who controlled for ethnicity in a multi-ethnic, national sample removed different psychological contributions to well-being from residents of southern states compared with those living in Maine, Vermont, North and South Dakota, and Montana.

Scientists who employ Mechanical Turk adults as subjects in psychological studies are insufficiently concerned with the fact that more than a third reside in India on a modest income (Paolacci, & Chandler, 2014; Litman, Robinson, & Rosenzweig, 2015). Equally important, the MTurk employees who learned English after age 13 lack the associations between words, images, and feeling states that are present in those for whom English is the native language (Hayakawa & Keysar, 2018). As a result, the answers of these MTurk subjects to questions involving emotions may have a different meaning.

Henrich, Heine, & Norenzayan (2010) have criticized the fact that many inferences in social psychology, personality, and cognitive psychology are based on data that Americans provided. Nielsen, Haun, Kartner, and Legare (2017) made the same point for studies of children. More than 90 percent of 1,582 papers in which children were the participants relied on American or European samples. Welcome signs of progress appear in issues of *Child Development* (1998, 2017), *Developmental Psychology* (2017), and *Perspectives on Psychological Science* (2017). The authors of the papers in these issues document the importance of class and ethnicity on values, cognitive styles, and behaviors.

Perhaps the next generation of investigators will acknowledge that many functional relations discovered with middle-class white adults do not apply to all combinations of class and ethnicity. Until then, social scientists ought to reflect before assuming that the influence of class or ethnicity on a relation between a predictor and outcome can be removed with statistics without altering the relation and, therefore, the validity of the conclusions.

Coda

This slim book has tried to make three points. First, investigators studying human populations should consider the possibility that developmental stage, gender, class, and/or ethnic identity affect the relations they find. Because these four conditions are associated with exposures to different contexts, Mischel's (2004) insistence that the setting has to be acknowledged in all statements about a person's probable reactions is satisfied.

I hope that future investigators will discover some of the combinations of genes and experiences that render a person susceptible to particular psychological responses. When this knowledge is added to the person's circumstances at the time, a large number of possible outcomes will be pruned to a more reasonable number. But this happy state of affairs requires investigators to gather evidence in more than one setting, because each context selects a small envelope of likely responses from the large collection of alternatives. Many phenomena are more likely to be understood if scientists accept the possibility that, on some occasions, combinations of age, gender, class, and/or ethnicity make a significant contribution to the evidence.

Second, the popular practice of using statistics to remove the contribution of age, gender, class, or ethnicity so that the investigator can confirm a favored predictor-outcome relation, independent of these categories, is flawed. This inferential error occurs when one or more of the above conditions is correlated with the predictor or dependent variable, or the relations among the measures are nonlinear (Wheelan, 2017). The use of statistics to control for gender, class, and ethnicity in a study of the relation between reading ability in the fourth grade and adult incarceration for a crime does not capture the fact that black males from disadvantaged homes and white females from affluent families represent two distinct psychological categories that make unique contributions to the outcome.

Finally, the biological properties that are more common in one gender, class, or ethnic group are not a defensible basis for restricting access to an educational program, vocation, or position of authority. What is true in nature need not dictate the practices societies favor.

A society can ignore biological differences between or among groups in order to honor an ethical imperative for equality without incurring serious costs. American men commit far more murders, rapes, acts of arson, and counterfeiting than women. But our judicial system, with the support of the public, treats men and women who commit one of these crimes equally. Ethnic groups vary in their susceptibility to different diseases. But our laws prevent insurance companies from charging higher premiums for those with disabilities that are more frequent in one ethnic group. Investigators who discover or acknowledge a biological property that is more common in one gender or ethnic group should not be accused of prejudice or criticized for violating the current demand for politically correct language. A society's ethics need not accommodate the biological properties that distinguish between the genders or among ethnic groups. Each time a hospital's staff saves a 3-pound infant or keeps a 90-year-old comatose patient alive for months it defies nature's plan. A long sequence of natural processes happened to produce the only animal who invented and occasionally applied a community's concept of fairness as a balance to nature's biases.

References

Abeles, H. (2009). Are musical instrument gender associations changing? *Journal of Research in Music Education,* 57, 127–139.

Abelionsky, A. L., & Strulik, H. (2018). How we fall apart. *Demography,* 55, 341–359.

Abu-Akel, A., Bousman, C., Kafidas, E. F., & Pantelis, C. (2018). Mind the prevalence rate. *Psychological Medicine,* 48, 1225–1227.

Achen, C. H. (2005). Achen, C. H. (2005). Let's put garbage-can regressions and garbage-can probits where they belong. *Conflict Management and Peace Science,* 4, 22–36.

Ackerman, C. M., Lowe, L. P., Lee, H., Hayes, M. G., Dyer, A. R., Metzger, B. E., . . . Hapo Study Cooperative Research Group. (2012). Ethnic variation in allele distribution of the androgen receptor (AR) (CAG)n repeat. *Journal of Andrology,* 33, 210–215.

Aczel, B., Palfi, B., & Szasazi, B. (2017). Estimating the evidential value of significant results in psychological science. *PLoS One,* 12(8), e0182651. doi:10.1371/journal.pone.0182651.

Aftanas, M. S., & Solomon, J. (2018). Historical traces of a general measurement theory in psychology. *Review of General Psychology,* 22, 278–289.

Ahl, R. E., & Keil, F. C. (2017). Diverse effects, complex causes. *Child Development,* 88, 828–845.

Ahmed, W. (2018). Developmental trajectories of math anxiety during adolescence. *Journal of Adolescence,* 67, 458–466.

Aikhenvald, A. Y. (2012). Round women and long men. *Anthropological Linguistics,* 54, 33–86.

Ainsworth, M. D. S., Blehar, M. C., Waters, E., & Wall, S. (1978). *Patterns of Attachment.* Hillsdale, NJ: Erlbaum.

Albanesi, A. P. (2009). Eschewing sexual agency. *Race, Gender & Class,* 16, 102–132.

Albert, K., Pruessner, J., & Newhouse, P. (2015). Estradiol levels modulate brain activity and negative responses to psychosocial stress across the menstrual cycle. *Psychoneuroendocrinology, 59*, 14–24.

Alesina, A., & Angeletos, B. (2005). Fairness and redistribution. *The American Economic Review, 95*, 960–980.

Alexander, G. M., & Hines, M. (2002). Sex differences in response to children's toys in nonhuman primates (Ceropithecus aethiops sabgeus). *Evolution and Human Behavior, 23*, 467–479.

Allen, C. S., & Gorski, R. A. (1990). Sex differences in the bed nucleus of the stria terminalis of the human brain. *Journal of Comparative Neurology, 302*, 697–706.

Allport, F. (1937). *Personality: A Psychological Integration*. New York: Holt, Rinehart & Winston.

Almeida, D. M., & Kessler, R. C. (1998). Almeida, D. M., & Kessler, R. C. (1998). Everyday stressors and gender differences in daily distress. *Journal of Personality and Social Psychology, 75*, 670–680.

Aloisi, A. M., & Bonifazi, M. (2006). Sex hormones, central nervous system and pain. *Hormones and Behavior, 50*, 1–7.

Alrajih, S., & Ward, J. (2014). Increased facial width-to-height ratio and perceived dominance in the faces of the UK's leading business leaders. *British Journal of Psychology, 105*, 153–161.

Amunts, K., Armstrong, E., Malikovic, A., Homke, L., Mohlberg, H., Schleicher, A., & Zilles, K. (2007). Gender-specific left-right asymmetries in human visual cortex. *Journal of Neuroscience, 27*, 1356–1364.

Andersen, E. M., Hespos, S. J., & Rips, L. J. (2018). Five-month-old infants have expectations for the accumulation of nonsolid substances. *Cognition, 175*, 1–10.

Andersen, L. M., & Lundqvist, D. (2019). Somatosensory responses to nothing. *Neuroimage, 184*, 78–89.

Anobile, G., Arrighi, R., & Burr, D. C. (2019). Simultaneous and sequential subitizing on separate systems and neither predicts math ability. *Journal of Experimental Child Psychology, 178*, 86–103.

Ardekani, B. A., Figarsky, K., & Sidtis, J. J. (2013). Sexual dimorphisms in the human corpus callosum. *Cerebral Cortex, 23*, 2514–2520.

Arnold, M. R., Thallon, C. L. Pitkofsky, J. A., & Meerts, S. H. (2019). Sexual experience confers resilience to restraint stress in female rats. *Hormones and Behavior, 167*, 61–66.

Arnulf, J. K., Larsen, K. R., Martinsen, O. L., & Egeland, T. (2018). The failing measurement of attitudes. *Behavior Research Methods,* 50(6), 2345-2365. doi:10.3758/s13428-017-0999-y.

Aslin, R. N. (2007). What's in a look? *Developmental Science,* 10, 48–53.

Baek, S., Daitch, A. L., Pinheiro-Chagas, P., &., & Parvizi, J. (2018). Neuronal population responses in the human ventral temporal and lateral parietal cortex during arithmetic processing. *Journal of Cognitive Neuroscience,* 30, 1315–1322.

Bailey, D. H., Duncan, G. J., Watts, T., Clements, D. H., & Sarama, J. (2018). Risky business: Correlation and causation in longitudinal studies of skill development. *American Psychologist,* 73, 81–94.

Baillargeon, R. H., Zoccolillo, M., Keenan, K., Cote, S., Peruse, D., Wu, H. X., . . . Tremblay, R. E. (2007). Gender differences in physical aggression. *Developmental Psychology,* 43, 13–26.

Baker, A., Kalmbach, B., Morishima, M., Kim, J., Ajuavinett, A., Li, L., & Dembrow, N. (2018). Specialized subpopulations of deep-layer pyramidal neurons in the neocortex. *Journal of Neuroscience,* 38, 5441–5445.

Baker, N., & Kellman, P. J. (2018). Abstract shape representation in human visual perception. *Journal of Experimental Psychology: General,* 147, 1295–1308.

Bandelow, B., Sagebei, A., Belz, M., Gorlich, Y., Michelis, S., & Wedekind, D. (2018). Evaluating effects of psychological treatments for anxiety disorders. *British Journal of Psychiatry,* 212, 333–338.

Banks, R. R. (2018). An end to the class vs. race debate. *The New York Times,* March 21.

Bar-Anan, Y., & Nosek, B. A. (2014). A comparative investigation of seven indirect attitude measures. *Behavior Research Methods,* 46, 668–688.

Barker, T. V., Reeb-Sutherland, B., Degnan, K. A., Walker, O. L., Chronis-Tuscano, A., Henderson, H. A., . . . & Fox, N. A. (2015). Contextual startle responses moderate the relation between behavioral inhibition and anxiety in middle childhood. *Psychophysiology,* 52, 1544–1549.

Barnes, J. N. (2017). Sex-specific factors regulating pressure and flow. *Experimental Physiology,* 102, 1385–1392.

Barry-Anwar, R., Hadley, H., Comte, S., Keil, A., & Scott, L. S. (2017). The developmental time course and topographic distribution of individual-level monkey face discrimination in the infant brain. *Neuropsychologia,* 108, 25–31.

Bayer, J., Schultz, H., Gamer, M., & Sommer, T. (2014). Menstrual-cycle dependent fluctuations in ovarian hormones affect emotional memory *Neurobiology of Learning and Memory,* 110, 55–63.

Beard, M. (2017). *Women & Power*. New York: Liveright Publishing.

Beaty, R. E., Chen, Q., Christnesen, A. B., Qiu, J., Silva, P. J., & Schacter, D. L. (2018). Brain networks of the imaginative mind. *Human Brain Mapping*, 39, 811–821.

Becker, J. B. (1999). Gender differences in dopaminergic function in striatum and nucleus accumbens. *Pharmacology Biochemistry and Behavior*, 64, 803–812.

Bekhuis, E., Boschloo, L., Rosmalen, J. G. M., de Boer, M. M., & Schoevers, R. A. (2016). The impact of somatic symptoms on the course of major depressive disorder. *Journal of Affective Disorders*, 25, 122–118.

Beking, T., Geuze, R. H., van Faassen, M., Kema, I. P., Kreukels, B. P. C., & Groothius, T. G. G. (2017). Prenatal and pubertal testosterone affect brain lateralization. *Psychoneuroendocrinology*, 88, 78–91.

Benbow, C. P., Lubinski, D., Shea, D. L., & Effekhari-Sanjani, H. (2000). Sex differences in mathematical reasoning ability at age 13: Their status 20 years later. *Psychological Science*, 11, 474–480.

Benenson, J. F., Carder, H. P., & Geib-Cole, S. J. (2008). The development of boys' preferential pleasure in physical aggression. *Aggressive Behavior*, 34, 154–166.

Benenson, J. F., Tennyson, R., & Wrangham, R. W. (2011). Male more than female infants imitate propulsive motion. *Cognition*, 121, 262–267.

Berenbaum, S. A., Beltz, A. M., Bryk, K., & McHale, S. (2018). Gendered peer involvement in girls with congenital adrenal hyperplasia. *Archives of Sexual Behavior*, 47(4), 915–929. doi:10.1007/s10508-017-1112-4.

Bergman, L. R. (1998). A pattern-oriented approach to studying individual development. In R. B. Cairns, L. R. Bergman, & J. Kagan (Eds.), *Methods and Models for Studying the Individual* (pp. 83–121). Thousand Oaks, CA: Sage.

Bergman, L. R., & Andersson, H. (2017). The person or the variables in developmental psychology. Unpublished manuscript.

Bergold, S., Wendt, H., Kasper, D., & Steinmayr, R. (2017). Academic competencies. *Journal of Educational Psychology*, 109, 430–445.

Berman, A. S., Jobes, D. A., & Silverman, M. M. (2006). *Adolescent Suicide*. Washington, D. C., American Psychological Association.

Betancourt, L. M., Avants, B., Farah, M. J., Brodsky, N. L., Wu, J., Ashtari, M., & Hurt, H. (2016). Effect of socioeconomic status (SES) disparity on neural development in female African-American infants at age 1 month. *Developmental Science*, 19, 947–956.

Bian, L., Leslie, S. J., & Cimpian, A. (2017). Gender stereotypes about intellectual ability emerge early and influence children's interests. *Science*, 355, 389–391.

Biresi, A., & Nunn, H. (2013). *Class and Contemporary British Culture*. London: Palgrave Macmillan.

Bjornsdottir, R. T., & Rule, N. O. (2017). The visibility of social class from facial cues. *Journal of Personality and Social Psychology, 113*, 530–546.

Bixo, M., Johansson, M., Timby, E., Michalski, L., & Backstrom, T. (2018). Effects of GABA active steroids in the female brain with a focus on the premenstrual dysphoric disorder. *Journal of Endocrinology, 30*, doi: 10.1111/jne.12553.

Blakemore, S. J. (2012). Imaging brain development. *Neuroimage, 61*, 397–406.

Blanca, M. J., Alarcan, R., Arnau, J., Bono, R., & Bandayan, R. (2018). Effect of variance ratio on ANOVA robustness. *Behavior Research Methods, 50*, 937–962.

Blazhenkova, O., & Kumar, M. M. (2018). Angular versus curved shapes. *Perception, 47*, 67–89.

Bleakley, A., Ellithorpe, M. E., Hennessy, M., Jamieson, P. E., Khurana, A., & Weitz, I. (2017). Risky movies, risky behaviors, and ethnic identity among black adolescents. *Social Science and Medicine, 195*, 131–137.

Block, K., Gonzalez, A. M., Schmader, T., & Baron, A. S. (2018). Early gender differences in core values predict anticipated family versus career orientation. *Psychological Science, 29*, 1540–1547.

Blume, S. R., Freedberg, M., Vantrease, J. E., Chan, R., Padival, M., Record, M. J., . . . Rosenkranz, J. A. (2017). Sex-and estrus-dependent differences in rat basolateral amygdala. *Journal of Neuroscience, 37*(44), 10567–10586. doi:10.1523/JNEUROSCI.0758-17.2017.

Bodde, D. (1981). *Essays on Chinese Civilization*. Princeton, NJ: Princeton University Press.

Boelen, P. A., & Lenferink, L. L. M. (2018). Latent class analysis of indicators of intolerance of uncertainty. *Scandinavian Journal of Psychology, 29*(4), 435–445. doi:10.1037/pas0000357.

Bogartz, R. S., Shinskey, J. L., & Speaker, C. J. (1997). Interpreting infant looking. *Developmental Psychology, 33*, 408–422.

Bohr, Y., Potnick, D. L., Lee, Y., & Bornstein, M. H. (2018). Evaluating caregiver sensitivity to infants. *Infancy, 23*, 730–747.

Boo, J., Matsubayashi, T., & Ueda, M. (2019). Diurnal variation in suicide by gender. *Journal of Affective Disorders, 243*, 366–374.

Boorsboom, D., Cramer, A., & Kalis, A. (2018). Brain disorders? Not really. . . . Why network structures block reductionism in psychopathology research. *Behavioral and Brain Sciences*, 1–54. doi:10.1017/SO140525K17002266.

Borgi, M., & Majolo, B. (2016). Facial width-to-height ratio relates to dominance style in the genus Macaca. *Peer J*, 4, e1775. doi:10.7717/peerj.1775.

Borkenau, P., Hrebickova, M., Kuppens, P., Realo, A., & Allik, J. (2013). Sex differences in variability in personality. *Journal of Personality*, 81, 49–60.

Bosma, H., Brandts, L., Simons, A., Groffen, D., & van den Akker, M. (2015). Low socioeconomic status and perceptions of social inadequacy and shame. *European Journal of Public Health*, 25, 311–313.

Boudreau, A. M., Dempsey, E. E., Smith, I. M., & Garon, N. (2017). A novel working memory task or preschoolers. *Child Neuropsychology*, 24(6), 799-822. https://doi.org/10.1080/09297049.2017.1333592.

Boyer, C. B. (1944). The symbol, the concept, the number. *National Mathematics Magazine*, 18, 323–332.

Bradford, L. D. (2002). CYP2D6 allele frequency in European Caucasians, Asians, Africans, and their descendants. *Pharmacogenomics*, 3, 229–243.

Braga, R. M., & Buckner, R. L. (2017). Parallel interdigitated distributed networks within the individual estimated by intrinsic functional connectivity. *Neuron*, 95, 457–471.

Breckler, S. J. (1990). Applications of covariance structure modeling in psychology. *Psychological Bulletin*, 107, 260–273.

Brendgen, M., Girard, A., Vitaro, F., Dionne, G., & Boivin, M. (2016). Personal and familial predictors of peer victimization trajectories from primary to secondary school. *Developmental Psychology*, 52, 1103=1114.

Brick, R., Thibault-Sennett, S., Smagulova, F., Lam, K. G., Pu, Y., Pratto, T., . . . Petukhova, G. V. (2018). Extensive sex differences at the initiation of genetic recombination. *Nature*, 561, 338–342.

Broman, S. H., Nichols, P. L., & Kennedy, W. (1975). *Preschool IQ*. New York: Wiley.

Brooker, R. J., Canen, M. J., Davidson, R. J., & Goldsmith, H. H. (2017). Short-and long-term stability of alpha asymmetry in infants. *Psychophysiology*, 54, 1100–1109.

Brown, A. W., Kaiser, K. A., & Allison, D. B. (2018). Issues with data and analyses. *Proceedings of the National Academy of Sciences*, 115, 2563–2570.

Brown, I. (1992). A cross-cultural comparison of children's drawing development. *Visual Arts Research*, 18, 15–20.

Bruder, G. E., Tenke, C. E., Warner, V., & Weissman, M. M. (2007). Grandchildren at high and low risk for depression differ in EEG measures of regional brain asymmetry. *Biological Psychiatry*, 62, 1317–1323.

Bruno, J. L., Romano, D., Mazaika, P., Lightbody, A. A., Hazlett, J. C., Piven, J., & Reiss, A. L. (2017). Longitudinal identification of clinically distinct neurophenotypes in young children with fragile X syndrome. *Proceedings of the National Academy of Sciences,* 114, 10767–10772.

Brusini, I., Carneiro, M., Wang, C., Rubin, C. J., Ring, H., Alfonso, S., . . . & Andersson, K. (2018). Changes in brain architecture are consistent with altered fear processing in domesticated rabbits. *Proceedings of the National Academy* of Sciences, 115, 7380–7385.

Bulbul, O., Pakstis, A. J., Soundararajan, U., Gurkan, C., Brissenden, J. E., Roscoe, J. M., . . . Kidd, K. K. (2017). Ancestry inference of 96 population samples using microhaplotypes. *International Journal of Legal Medicine,* 132(3), 702–711. doi:1007/s00414.017-1748-6.

Burke, C. M., Manzouri, A. H., Dhejne, C., Bergstrom, K., Arvers, S., Feusner, J. D., & Savic-Berglund, I. (2018). Testosterone effects on the brain in transgender men. *Cerebral Cortex,* 28, 1582–1596.

Busby, C. (1997). Permeable and partible persons. *The Journal of the Royal Anthropological Institute,* 3, 265–278.

Buss, A. T., Ross-Sheehy, S., & Reynolds, G. D. (2018). Visual working memory in early development. *Journal of Neurophysiology,* 120, 1472–1483.

Buss, K. A., Jaffee, S., Wordsworth, M. E., & Kliewer, W. (2018). Impact of psychophysiological stress-response systems on psychological development. *Developmental Psychology,* 54, 1601–1605.

Butterworth, B., Gallistel, C. R., & Vallortigara, C. (Eds.). (2018). The origins of numerical abilities. *Philosophical Transactions of the Royal Society Biological Sciences B,* 373(1740). doi:10.1098/rstb.2016.0507.

Buzsaki, G. (2018). Q & A. *Neuron,* 91, 216–217.

Buzsaki, G., & Llinas, R. (2017). Space and time in the brain. *Science,* 358, 482–485.

Cacioppo, S., Bianchi-Demicheli, F., Bischof, P., Deziegler, D., Michel, C. M., & Landis, T. (2013). Hemispheric specialization varies with EEG brain resting states and phase of menstrual cycle. *PLoS One,* e63196.

Campbell, I. G., Grimm, K. J., de Bie, E., & Feinberg, I. (2012). Sex, puberty, and the timing of sleep EEG measures adolescent brain maturation. *Proceedings of the National Academy of Sciences,* 109, 5740–5743.

Campbell, J. M., Marcinowski, E. C., & Michel, G. F. (2018). The development of neuromotor skills and hand preference during infancy. *Developmental Psychobiology,* 60, 165–175.

Campbell, M. J., Toth, A. J., & Brady, N. (2018). Illuminating sex differences in mental rotation using pupillometry. *Biological Psychology,* 138, 19–26.

Carl, N. (2016). IQ and socioeconomic development across regions of the UK. *Journal of Biosocial Science,* 48, 406–417.

Carnevali, L., Thayer, J. F., Brosschot, J. F., & Ottaviani, C. (2017). Heart rate variability mediates the link between rumination and depressive symptoms. *International Journal of Psychophysiology,* pii: S0167–8760(17)30421-X.

Carpenter, J. S., Abelmann, A. C., Hattan, S. N., Robillard, R., Hermens, D. F., Bennett, M. R., . . . & Hickle, J. B. (2017). Pineal volume and evening melatonin in young people with affective disorder. *Brain Imaging and Behavior,* 11, 1741–1750.

Carrel, L., & Brown, C. J. (2017). When the Lyon(ized chromosome) roars. *Philosophical Transactions of The Royal Society B: Biological Sciences,* 372, pii:.20160365.

Caspi, A., & Moffitt, T. E. (2018). All for one and one for all. *American Journal of Psychiatry,* 175, 831–844.

Cassia, V. M., Valenza, E., Simion, F., & Leo, I. (2008). Congruency as a non-specific perceptual principle contributing to newborns' face preferences. *Child Development,* 79, 807–820.

Castillejos, M. C., Martin-Perez, C., & Moreno-Kustner, B. (2018). A systematic review and meta-analysis of psychotic disorders. *Psychological Medicine,* 48, 2101–2115.

Cavanagh, J., Krishnadas, R., Batty, G. D., Burns, H., Deans, K. A., Ford, I., . . . McLean, J. (2013). Socioeconomic status and the cerebellar gray matter volume. *Cerebellum,* 12, 882–891.

Caves, E. M., Green, P. A., Zipple, M. N., Peters, S., Johnsen, S., & Nowicki, S. (2018). Categorical perception of colour signals in a songbird. *Nature,* 560, 365–367.

Chai, X. J., & Jacobs, L. F. (2012). Digit ratio predicts sense of direction in women. *PLoS One,* 7, e32816.

Chan, N. Y., Na, J., Agres, D. F., Savalia, N. K., Park, D. C., & Wig, G. S. (2018). Socioeconomic status mediates age-related differences in the brain's functional network organization and anatomy across the adult lifespan. *Proceedings of the National Academy of Sciences,* 115, E5144-E5153.

Chase, E., & Walker, R. (2012). The co-construction of shame in the context of poverty. *Sociology,* 47, 739–754.

Chater, N. (2018). *The Mind is Flat.* New Haven, CT: Yale University Press.

Chauhan, P., Schuck, A. M., & Widom, C. S. (2017). Child maltreatment, problem behaviors, and neighborhood attainment. *American Journal of Community Psychology,* 60, 555–567.

Chen, C., Burton, M., Greenberger, E., & Dmitrieva, J. (1999). Population migration and the variation of the dopamine D4 receptor (DRD4)allele frequencies around the globe. *Evolution and Human Behavior, 20*, 309–324.

Chen, J., Snow, J. C., Culham, J. C., & Goodale, M. A. (2018). What role does "elongation" play in "tool-specific" activation and connectivity in the dorsal and ventral streams? *Cerebral Cortex, 28*, 1117–1131.

Chen, M., Li, B., Guang, J., Wei, L., Wu, S., Liu, Y., & Zhang, M. (2016). Two subdivisions of macaque LIP process visual-oculomotor information differently. *Proceedings if the National Academy of Sciences, 113*, E6263-E6266.

Chernow, R. (2010). *Washington.* New York: Penguin Books.

Chi, C. W., & Baldwin, C. (2004). Gender and class stereotypes. *Race, Gender & Class, 11*, 156–175.

Choe, M. S., Ortiz-Mantilla, S., Makris, N., Gregas, M., Bacic, J., Haehn, D., . . . Grant, P. E. (2013). Regional infant brain development. *Cerebral Cortex, 23*, 2100–2117.

Choleris, E., Galea, L. A. M., Sohrabji, F., & Frick, K. M. (2018). Sex differences in the brain. *Neuroscience and Biobehavioral Reviews, 85*, 126–145.

Chomsky, N. (1957). *Syntactic Structures.* The Hague, Netherlands: Mouton & Co.

Christensen, D., Taylor, C. L., & Zubrick, S. R. (2017). Patterns of multiple risk exposures for low receptive vocabulary growth 4–8 years in the longitudinal study of Australian children. *PLoS One*, e0168804.

Christodoulou, J., Lac, A., & Moore, D. S. (2017). Babies and math. *Developmental Psychology, 53*, 1405–1417.

Chugani, H. T. (1991). Imaging human brain development with PET. *Journal of Nuclear Medicine, 32*, 23–26.

Chugani, H. T. (1994). Development of regional brain glucose metabolism. In G. Dawson & K. Fischer (Eds.), *Human Behavior and the Developing Brain* (pp.53–175). New York: Guilford.

Chugani, H. T. (1998). A critical period of brain development. *Preventive Medicine, 27*, 184–188.

Chung, W. C., & Auger, A. P. (2013). Gender differences in neurodevelopment and epigenetics. *Pflugers Archives, 465*, 573–584.

Clauss, J. A., Avery, S. N., van DerKlok, R. M., Rogers, B. P., Cowan, R. L., Benningfield, M. M., & Blackford, J. U. (2014). Neurocircuitry underlying risk and resilience to social anxiety. *Depression and Anxiety, 31*, 822–833.

Clough-Gorr, K. M., Enger, M., & Spoerri, A. (2015). A Swiss paradox? *European Journal of Epidemiology, 30*, 627–630.

Coelho, B. M., Santana, G. L., Duarte-Guerra, L. S., Viana, M. C., Neto, F. L., Andrade, L. H., & Wang, Y. D. (2018). The role of gender in the structure of the network of childhood adversity. *Psychiatry Research, 270*, 348–356.

Cohen, E. D. (2018). Gendered styles of student-faculty interaction. *Social Science Research, 75*, 117–129.

Cohen, L. B., & Marks, K. S. (2002). How infants process addition and subtraction events. *Developmental Science, 5*, 186–201.

Cohen, L. B., & Oakes, L. M. (1993). How infants perceive a single causal event. *Developmental Psychology, 29*, 421–433.

Cole, P. M., Zahn-Waxler, C., Fox, N. A., Usher, B. A., & Welsh, J. D. (1996). Individual differences in emotion regulation and behavior problems in preschool children. *Journal of Abnormal Psychology, 105*, 518–529.

Conant, J. (2017). *Man of the Hour*. New York: Simon & Schuster.

Conejero, A., Guerra, S., Abundis-Gutierrez, A., & Rueda, M. R. (2018). Frontal theta activation *associated* with error detection in toddlers. *Developmental Science, 21*(1), 1–10. doi:10.1111/desc.12494.

Conley, D., & Zhang, S. (2018). The promise of genes for understanding cause and effect. *Proceedings of the National Academy of Sciences, 115*, 5626–5628.

Constantinescu, M., Moore, D. S., Johnson, S. P., & Hines, M. (2018). Early contributions to infants' mental rotation abilities. *Developmental Science, 21*(4), e12613. doi:10.1111/desc.12613.

Conway, C. (2000). Gender and musical instrument choice. *Bulletin of the Council for Research in Music Education, 146*, 1–17.

Conway, J. K. (1999). *When Memory Speaks*. New York: Vintage.

Courage, M. L., Reynolds, G. D., & Richards, J. E. (2006). Infants' attention to patterned stimuli. *Child Development, 77*, 680–695.

Cowan, R. L., Frederick, B. B., Rainey, M., Levin, J. M., Maas, L. C., Bang. J., . . . Renshaw, P. F. (2000). Sex differences in response to red and blue light in human primary visual cortex. *Psychiatry Research: Neuroimaging, 100*, 129–138.

Cox, D. R. (2017). Statistical science. *European Journal of Epidemiology, 32*, 465–471.

Coyne, S. P., Lindell, S. G., Clemente, J., Barr, C. S., Parker, K. J., & Maestripieri, D. (2015). Dopamine D4 receptor genotype variation in free-ranging rhesus macaques and its association with juvenile behavior. *Behavioral Brain Research, 292*, 50–55.

Crocq, M. A. (2017). The history of generalized anxiety disorder as a diagnostic category. *Dialogues in Clinical Neuroscience, 19*, 107–115.

Csibra, G., Hernik, M., Mascaro, O., Tatone, D., & Lengyel, M. (2016). Statistical treatment of looking-time data. *Developmental Psychology, 52*, 521–536.

Cuevas, K., Bell, M. A., Marcovitch, S., & Calkins, S. D. (2012). Electroencephalogram and heart rate measures of working memory at 5 and 10 months of age. *Developmental Psychology, 48*, 907–917.

Culbert, K. M., Sinclair, E. B., Hildebrandt, B. A., Klump, K. L., & Sisk, C. L. (2018). Perinatal testosterone contributes to mid-to-post pubertal sex differences in risk for binge eating in male and female rats. *Journal of Abnormal Psychology, 127*, 239–250.

Cundiff, J. M., & Matthews, K. A. (2017). Is subjective social status a unique correlate of physical health? *Health Psychology, 36*, 1109–1125.

Curtis, H. D. (2007). *Faith in the Great Physician.* Baltimore, MD: The Johns Hopkins University Press.

Cvencek, D., Meltzoff, A. N., & Greenwald, A. G. (2011). Math-gender stereotypes in elementary school children. *Child Development, 82*, 766–779.

D'Alba, L. & Shawkey, M. D. (2019). Melanosomes. *Physiological Reviews, 99*, 1–19.

D'Hooge, L., Achterberg, P., & Reeskens, T. (2018). Imagining class. *Social Science Research, 70*, 71–89.

Dalton, M. A., Zeidman, P., Mc Cormick, K. C., & Macguire, E. A. (2018). Differentiable processing of objects, associations, and scenes within the hippocampus. *Journal of Neuroscience, 38*, 8146–8159

Damaraju, E., Caprihan, A., Lowe, J. R., Allen, E. A., Calhoun, V. D., & Phillips, J. P. (2014). Functional connectivity in the developing brain. *Neuroimage, 84*, 169–180.

Davis, E., & Buss, K. A. (2012). Moderators of the relation between shyness and behavior with peers. *Social Development, 21*, 801–820.

De Boisferon, A. H., Dupierrix, E., Quinn, P. C., Loevenbruck, H., Lewkowicz, D. J., Lee, K., & Pascalis, O. (2015). Perception of multisensory gender coherence in 6- and 9-month-old infants. *Infancy, 20*, 661–674.

De Zambotti, M., Javitz, H., Franzen, P. L., Brumback, T., Clark, D. B., Colrain, I. M., & Baker, F. C. (2018). Sex-and age-dependent differences in autonomic nervous system functioning in adolescents. *Journal of Adolescent Health, 62*, 184–190.

Degnan, K. A., Almas, A. N., Henderson, H. A., Hane, A. A., Walker, O. L., & Fox, N. A. (2014). Longitudinal trajectories od social reticence with unfamiliar peers across early childhood. *Developmental Psychology, 50*, 2311–2323.

Degnan, K. A., Hane, A. A., Henderson, H. A., Moas, O. L., Reeb-Sutherland, B. C., & Fox, N. A. (2011). Longitudinal stability of temperamental exuberance and social-emotional outcomes in early childhood. *Developmental Psychology, 47,* 765–780.

Delacroix, R. (2017). Exploring the experiences of nurse practitioners who have committed medical errors. *Journal of the American Association of Nurse Practitioners, 29,* 413–429.

DeLoache, J. S., Simcock, G., & Macari, S. (2007). Planes, trains, automobiles—and tea sets. *Developmental Psychology, 43,* 1579–1586.

Deuter, C. E., Nowacki, J., Wingenfeld, K., Kuehl, L. K., Finke, J. B., Dziobek, J., & Otte, C. (2018). The role of physiological arousal for self-reported emotional empathy. *Autonomic Neuroscience, 214,* 9–14.

Diamond, A. (1988). Abilities and neural mechanisms underlying AB phenomena. *Child Development, 59,* 523–527.

Diamond, A. (1990). Rate of maturation of the hippocampus and the developmental progression of children's performance on the delayed non-match to sample and visual paired comparison tasks. In A. Diamond (Ed.), *Development and Neural Bases of Higher Cognitive Functions* (pp. 394–426). New York: New York Academy of Sciences Press.

Diamond, A., Lee, E. Y., & Hayden, M. (2003). Early success in using the relation between stimuli and rewards to deduce an abstract rule. *Developmental Psychology, 39,* 825–847.

Diehl, M. N., Lampert, K. M., Parr, A. C., Ballard, I., Steele, V. R., & Smith, D. V. (2018). Toward an integrative perspective on the neural mechanisms underlying persistent maladaptive behaviors. *European Journal of Neuroscience, 48*(3), 1870–1883. doi:10.1111/ejn.14083.

DiPietro, J. A., Costigan, K. A., & Voegtline, K. M. (2015). Studies in fetal behavior. *Monographs of the Society for Research in Child Development, 80,* 1–94.

Dluzen, D. E. (2005). Unconventional effects of estrogen uncovered. *Trends in Pharmacological Sciences, 26,* 485–487.

Domenech-Abella, J., Mundo, J., Leonardi, M., Chatterji, S., Tobasz-Adamczyk, B., Koskinen, S., . . . Haro, J. M. (2018). The association between socioeconomic status and depression among older adults in Finland, Poland and Spain. *Journal of Affective Disorders, 241,* 311–318.

Dorn, L. D., Gayles, J. G., Engeland, C. G., Houts, R., Cizza, G., & Denson, L. A. (2016). Cytokine patterns in healthy adolescent girls. *Psychosomatic Medicine, 78,* 646–656.

Du Paul, G. J., Morgan, P. L., Farkas, G., Hillemeier, M. M., & Maczuga, S. (2017). Eight-year latent class trajectories of academic and social functioning in children with Attention-Deficit/Hyperactivity disorder. *Journal of Abnormal Child Psychology, 46*(5), 979–992. http://dx.doi.org/10.1007/s10802-017-0344-z.

Ducrest, A. L., Keller, L., & Roulin, A. (2008). Pleiotropy in the melanocortin system, coloration and behavioural syndromes. *Trends in Ecology and Evolution, 23*, 502–510.

Duerden, E. G., Arsalidou, M., Lee, M., & Taylor, M. J. (2013). Lateralization of affective processing in the insula. *Neuroimage, 78*, 159–175.

Duyme, M. (1988). School success and social class. *Developmental Psychology, 24*, 203–209.

Ecuyer-Dab, I., & Robert, M. (2004). Spatial ability and hone-range size. *Journal of Comparative Psychology, 118*, 217–231.

Ehrlich, S. B., Levine, S. C., & Goldin-Meadow, S. (2006). The importance of gesture in children's spatial reasoning. *Developmental Psychology, 42*, 1259–1268.

Eliot, T. S. (1949). *Notes Towards the Definition of Culture*. New York; Harcourt Brace.

Ellemers, N. (2018). Gender stereotypes. *Annual Review of Psychology, 69*, 275–298.

Elliott, C. A., & Yoder-White, M. (1997). Masculine/feminine associations for instrumental timbre among children seven, eight, and nine years of age. *Contributions to Music Education, 24*, 30–39.

Ellis, L. (2006). Gender differences in smiling. *Physiology and Behavior, 88*, 303–305.

Erikson, E. H. (1959). *Identity and the Life Cycle*. Oxford, UK: International Universities Press.

Fagan, J. F. (1977). Infant recognition memory. *Child Development, 48*, 68–78.

Fajnzylber, P., Lederman, D., & Loayza, N. (2002). Inequality and violent crime. *The Journal of Law and Economics, 45*, 1–39.

Fales, E. (1937). A comparison of the vigorousness of play activities of preschool boys and girls. *Child Development, 8*, 144–159.

Falk, A., & Hermle, J. (2018). Relationship of gender differences in preferences to economic development and gender equality. *Science, 362*, 307.

Fan, C. C. (1996). Gender and Chinese culture. *International Journal of Politics, Culture, and Society* 10, 95–114.

Fanselow, M. S., & Pennington, Z. T. (2018). A return to the psychiatric dark ages with a two-system framework for fear. *Behaviour Research and Therapy, 100*, 24–29.

Farah, M. J. (2017). The neuroscience of socioeconomic status. *Neuron, 96*, 56–71.

Federman, D. D. (2006). The biology of human sex differences. *The New England Journal of Medicine*, 354, 1507–1514.

Fender, S. (2012). *Nature, Class, and New Deal Literature*. New York: Routledge.

Feng, X., Shaw, D. S., & Silk, J. S. (2008). Developmental trajectories of anxiety symptoms among boys across early and middle childhood. *Journal of Abnormal Psychology*, 117, 32–47.

Fenson, L., Kagan, J., Kearsley, R. B., & Zelazo, P. R. (1976). The developmental progressions of manipulative play in the first two years. *Child Development*, 47, 232–236.

Ferguson, B., & Waxman, S. (2017). Linking language and categorization in infancy. *Journal of Child Language*, 44, 527–552.

Fernald, A. & Morikawa, H. (1993). Common themes and cultural variations in Japanese and American mothers' speech to infants. *Child Development*, 64, 637–656.

Figlio, D. N., Freese, J., Karbownik, K., & Roth, J. (2017). Socioeconomic status and genetic influences on cognitive development. *Proceedings of the National Academy of Sciences*, 114, 13441–13446.

Fischer, K., & Bidell, T. R. (2006). Dynamic development of action, thought, and emotion. In R. M. Lerner (Ed.), *Handbook of Child Psychology*, 6th ed., vol. 1. (pp. 313–399). New York: Wiley.

Fischer, U., Hess, C. W., & Rosler, K. M. (2005). Uncrossed cortico-muscular projections in humans are abundant to facial muscles of the upper and lower face, but may differ between sexes. *Journal of Neurology*, 252, 1–6.

Fish, A. M., Cachia, A., Fischer, C., Mankiw, C., Reardon, P. K., Clasen, L. S., . . . Reznahan, A. (2017). Influences of brain size, sex, and sex chromosome complement on the architecture of human sulcal folding in cerebral cortex. *Cerebral Cortex*, 27, 5557–5567.

Fisher, A. J., Medaglia, J. D., & Jeronimus, B. F. (2018). Lack of group-to-individual generalizability is a threat to human subjects research. *Proceedings of the National Academy of Sciences*, 115, E6106-E6115.

Fisher, A. J., Reeves, J. W., Lawyer, G., Medaglia, J. D., & Rubel, J. A. (2017). Exploring the ideographic dynamics of mood and anxiety via network analysis. *Journal of Abnormal Psychology*, 126, 1044–1056.

Fiske, P. (2018). Why scientists need to market themselves. *Nature*, 555, 275–276.

Fiske, S. T. (2017). Prejudices in cultural contexts. *Perspectives on Psychological Science*, 12, 791–799.

Fiske, S. T. (2018). Stereotype content. *Current Directions in Psychological Science*, 27, 67–75.

Fleming, M., Fitton, C. A., Steiner, M. F. C., McLay, J. S., Clark, D., King, A., . . . Pell, J. P. (2017). Educational and health outcomes of children treated for Attention-Deficit/Hyperactivity Disorder. *JAMA Pediatrics, 171*(7), e170691. doi:10.1001/jamapediatrics.2017.0691.

Flensborg-Madsen, T., & Mortensen, E. L. (2018). Developmental milestones during the first three years as precursors of adult intelligence. *Developmental Psychology, 54,* 1434–1444.

Flesch, T., Balaguer, J., Dekker, R., Nili, H., & Summerfield, C. (2018). Comparing continual task learning in minds and machines. *Proceedings of the National Academy of Sciences, 115,* E10313-E10322.

Flory, C. D. (1935). Sex differences in skeletal development. *Child Development, 6,* 205–211.

Foley, W. A. (2000). The languages of New Guinea. *Annual Review of Anthropology, 29,* 357–404.

Foster, D. G. (2017). Dramatic decrease in US abortion rates. *American Journal of Public Health, 107,* 1860–1862.

Foulkes, L., & Blakemore, S. J. (2018). Studying individual differences in human adolescent brain development. *Nature Neuroscience, 21,* 315–323.

Fox, N. A., Henderson, H. A., Rubin, K. H., Calkins, S. D., & Schmidt, L. A. (2001). Continuity and discontinuity of behavioral inhibition and exuberance. *Child Development, 72,* 1–21.

Fox, N. A., Kagan, J., & Weiskopf, S. (1979). The growth of memory during infancy. *Genetic Psychology Monographs, 99,* 91–130.

Francken, J. C., & Slors, M. (2018). Neuroscience and everyday life. *Brain and Cognition, 120,* 67–74.

Freedman, D.G., & F reedman, N. C. (1969). Behavioural differences between Chinese-American and European-American newborns. *Nature, 224,* 1227.

Furichi, T. (2011). Female contributions to the peaceful nature of bonobo society. *Evolutionary Anthropology, 20,* 131–142.

Gagliano, H., Nadal, R., & Armario, A. (2014). Sex differences in the long-lasting effects of a single exposure to immobilization stress in rats. *Hormones and Behavior, 66,* 793–801.

Gagnon, K. T., Cashdan, E. A., Stefanucci, J. K., & Creem-Regehr, S. H. (2016). Sex differences in exploration behavior and the relationship to harm avoidance. *Human Nature, 27,* 1182–1197.

Gagnon, K. T., Thomas, B. J., Munion, A., Creem-Regehr, S. H., Cashdan, E. A., & Stefanucci, J. K. (2018). Not all those who wander are lost. *Cognition*, 180, 105–117.

Galanter, J. M., Gignoux, C. R., Oh, S. S., Torgerson, D., Pino-Yanes, M., Thakur, N., . . . Zaitlen, N. (2017). Differential methylation between ethnic sub-groups reflects the effect of genetic ancestry and environmental exposures. *Elife*, 6: e20532. doi:10.7554/eLife.20532.

Gao, J., Su, Y., Tomonaga, M., & Matsuzawa, T. (2018). Learning the rules of the rock-paper-scissors game. *Primates*, 59, 7–17.

Garratt, E. A., Chandola, T., Purdam, K., & Wood, A. M. (2017). Income and social rank influence UK children's behavioral problems. *Child Development*, 88, 1302–1320.

Gartstein, M. A., Prokasky, A., Bell, M. A., Calkins, S., Bridgett, D. J., Braumgart-Rieker, . . . Seamon, E. (2017). Latent profile and cluster analysis of infant temperament. *Developmental Psychology*, 53, 1811–1825.

Gaucher, D., Friesen, J., & Kay, A. C. (2011). Evidence that gendered wording in job advertisements exists and sustains gender inequality. *Journal of Personality and Social Psychology*, 101, 109–128.

Geangu, E., Ichikawa, H., Lao, J., Kanazawa, S., Yamaguchi, M. K., Caldara, R., & Turati, C. (2016). Culture shapes 7-month-olds' perceptual strategies in discriminating facial expressions of emotion. *Current Biology*, 26, R663–4. doi:10.1016/j,cub.2016.05.072.

Geangu, E., Senna, I., Croci, E., & Turati, C. (2015). The effect of biomechanical properties of motion on infants' perception of goal-directed grasping actions. *Journal of Experimental Child Psychology*, 129, 55–67.

Geary, D. C. (2016). Evolution of sex differences in trait-and age-specific vulnerabilities. *Perspectives on Psychological Science*, 11, 855–876.

Geary, D, C. (2017). Evolution of human sex-specific cognitive vulnerabilities. *Quarterly Review of Biology*, 92, 361–410.

Gelman, A., & Hill, J. (2007). *Data Analysis Using Regression and Multilevel/Hierarchical Models*. Cambridge, UK: Cambridge University Press.

Genc, S., Malpes, C. B., Ball, G., Silk, T. J., & Seal, M. C. (2018). Age, sex, and puberty related development of the corpus callosum. *Brain Structure and Function*, 223(6), 2753–2765. doi:10.1007/s00429-018-1658-5.

German, A., Shmoish, M., & Hochberg, Z. (2015). Predicting pubertal development by infantile and childhood height, BMI, and adiposity rebound. *Pediatric Research*, 78, 445–450.

Gianaros, P. J., Marsland, A. L., Sheu, L. K., Erickson, K. I., & Verstynen, T. D. (2013). Inflammatory pathways link socioeconomic inequalities to white matter architecture. *Cerebral Cortex, 23,* 2058–2071.

Giannini, M., Alexander, D. M., Nikolaev, A. R., & van Leeuwen, C. (2018). Large-scale traveling waves in EEG activity following eye movement. *Brain Topography,* 31(4), 608–622. doi:1007/s10548-018-0622-2.

Giedd, J. N., Snell, J. W., Lange, N., Rajapakse, J. C., Casey, B. J., & Kozuch, P. (1996). Quantitative magnetic resonance imaging of human brain development. *Cerebral Cortex, 6,* 551–560.

Gilbert, O. M. (2018). Altruism or association? *Proceedings of the National Academy of Sciences,* 115, E3069–E3070.

Giles, J. W., & Heyman, G. D. (2005). Young children's beliefs about the relationship between gender and aggressive behavior. *Child Development, 76,* 107–121.

Gillies, G. E., Virdee, K., Pienaar, I., Al-Zaid, F., & Dalley, J. V. V. (2016). Enduring sexually dimorphic impact of in utero exposure to elevated levels of glucocorticoids on midbrain dopaminergic populations. *Brain Science, 7*(1), 5. doi:10.3390/brainsci7010005.

Gilman, S. E., Hornig, M., Ghassabian, A., Hahn, J., Cherkerzian, S., Albert, P. S., & Buka, S. L. (2017). Socioeconomic disadvantage, gestational immune activity, and neurodevelopment in early childhood. *Proceedings of the National Academy of Sciences,* 114, 6728–6733.

Gilmore, D. G. (1990). *Mankind in the Making.* New Haven, CT: Yale University Press.

Giroux, H. A. (1998). Nymphet fantasies. *Social Text,* 87, 31–53.

Glatt, C. E., Tampilic, M., Christie, C., DeYoung, J., & Freimer, N. B. (2004). Re-screening serotonin receptors for genetic variants identifies population and molecular genetic complexity. *American Journal of Medical Genetics B Neuropsychiatric Genetics,* 124, 92–100.

Goldberg, S. K., & Halpern, C. T. (2017). Sexual initiation patterns of U. S. sexual minority youth. *Perspectives on Sexual Reproduction and Health,* 49, 55–67.

Goller, J., Leder, H., Cursiter, H., & Jenkins, R., (2018). Anchoring effects in facial attractiveness. *Perception,* 47, 1043–1053.

Gomes, N., Soares, S. C., Silva, S., & Silva, C. F. (2018). Mind the snake. *Emotion,* 18, 886–895.

Gooden, S. T., & Myers, S. L. (2018). The Kerner commission report fifty years later. *The Russell Sage Foundation Journal of the Social Sciences,* 4, 1–17.

Goodyer, I. M., Ban, M., Croudace, T., & Herbert, J. (2009). Serotonin transporter genotype, morning cortisol, and subsequent depression in adolescents. *British Journal of Psychiatry*, 195, 33–45.

Gould, R. V. (2003). *Collision of Wills*. Chicago, IL: University of Chicago Press.

Graham, C., Laffan, K., & Pinto, S. (2018). Well-being in metrics and policy. *Science*, 362, 287–288.

Grant, P. R., & Grant, B. R. (2008). *How and Why Species Multiply*. Princeton, NJ: Princeton University Press.

Gratch, G. (1982). Responses to hidden persons and things by 5-, 9-, and 16-month-old infants in a visual tracking situation. *Developmental Psychology*, 18, 232–237.

Greenberg, G. D., & Trainor, B. C. (2016). Sex differences in the social behavior network and mesolimbic dopamine system. In R. M,. Shansky (Ed.), *Sex Differences in the Central Nervous System*, (pp. 77–106), New York Academic Press.

Greenberg, M. T., Lengua, L. L., Coie, J. D., & Pinderhughes, E. E. (1999). Predicting developmental outcomes at school entry using a multiple-risk model. *Developmental Psychology*, 35, 403–417.

Gregory, S. W., & Webster, S. (1996). A nonverbal signal in voices of interview partners effectively predicts communication accommodation and social status perceptions. *Journal of Personality and Social Psychology*, 70, 1731–1740.

Griffin, D. R., & Speck, G. B. (2004). New evidence of animal consciousness. *Animal Cognition*, 7, 5–18.

Griffin, R., Richardson, J. B., Kerby, J. D., & McGwin, G. (2017). A decompositional analysis of firearm-related mortality in the United States, 2001–2012. *Preventive Medicine*, 106, 194–199. doi:10.1016/j.ypmed.2017.10.031.

Grootswagers, T., Cicby, R. M., & Carlson, T. A. (2018). Finding decodable information that can be read out in behavior. *Neuroimage*, 179, 252–262.

Guiso, L., Monte, F., Sapienza, P., & Zingales, L. (2008). Culture, gender, and math. *Science*, 320, 1164–1165.

Guloksuz, S., Pries, L. K., & van Os, J. (2017). Application of network methods for understanding mental disorders. *Psychological Medicine*, 47, 2743–2752.

Haith, M. M. (1998). Who put the cog in infant cognition? *Developmental Psychology*, 21, 167–179.

Hamama-Raz, Y., Palgi, Y., Shrira, A., Goodwin, R., Kaniasty, K., & Ben-Ezra, M. (2015). *Psychiatry Quarterly*, 86, 285–296.

Hampson, E., Levy-Cooperman, N., & Kalman, J. M. (2014). Estradiol and mental rotations. *Hormones and Behavior*, 65, 238–248.

Handa, R. J., & McGivern, R. F. (2015). Steroid hormones, receptors, an114d perceptual and cognitive sex differences in the visual system. *Current Eye Research*, 40, 110–127.

Harden, K. P., Mann, F. D., Grotzinger, A. D., Patterson, M. W., Stenberg, L., Takett, J. L., & Tuvker-Drob, E. M. (2018). Developmental differences in reward sensitivity and sensation seeking in adolescence. *Journal of Personality and Social Psychology*, 115, 161–178.

Hare, B., & Yamamoto, S. (Eds.). (2017). *Bonobos: Unique in Mind, Brain, and Behavior*. New York: Oxford University Press.

Harro, M., Eensoo, D., Kiive, E., Merenakk, L., Alep, J., Oreland, L., & Harro, J. (2001). Platelet monoamine oxidase in healthy 9- and 15-year-old children. *Progress in Neuropsychopharmacology and Biological Psychiatry*, 25, 1497–1511.

Harter, S. (1996). Developmental changes in self transitions. In A. G. Sameroff & M, M. Haith (Eds.), *The Five to Seven Year Shift* (pp. 207–236), Chicago, IL: University of Chicago Press.

Haslam, N. (2018). Unicorns, snarks, and personality types. *Australian Journal of Psychology*. doi:10.1111/ajpy.12228.

Hassett, J. M., Siebert, E. R., & Wallen, K. (2008). Sex differences in rhesus monkey toy preferences parallel those of children. *Hormones and Behavior*, 54, 359–364.

Hattwick, L. A. (1937). Sex differences in behavior of nursery school children. *Child Development*, 8, 343–356.

Hatzfeld, J. J., LaVeist, T. A., & Gaston-Johansson, F. G. (2012). Racial/ethnic disparities in the prevalence of selected chronic diseases among US Air Force members, 2008. *Prevention and Chronic Disease*, 9, E112. doi:10.5888.pcd9/110136.

Hausmann, M., Schoofs, D., Rosenthal, H. E. S., & Jordan, K. (2009). Interactive effects of sex hormones and gender stereotypes on cognitive sex differences. *Psychoneuroendocrinology*, 34, 389–401.

Hawkley, L. C., Lavelle, L. A., Bernston, G. G., & Cacioppo, J. T. (2011). Mediators of the relationship between socioeconomic status and allostatic load in the Chicago Health, Aging, and Social Relations Study (CHASRS). *Psychophysiology*, 48, 1134–1145.

Hayakawa, S., & Keysar, B. (2018). Using a foreign language reduces mental imagery. *Cognition*, 173, 8–15.

Heil, M., & Jansen-Osmann, P. (2008). Sex differences in mental rotation with polygons of different complexity. *Quarterly Journal of Experimental Psychology*, 61, 683–689.

Helo, A., Rama, P., Pannasch, S., & Meary, D. (2016). Eye movement patterns and visual attention during scene viewing in 3- to 12-month-olds. *Visual Neuroscience*, 33, E014.

Henrich, J., Heine, S. J., & Norenzayan, A. (2010). The weirdest people in the world? *Behavioral and Brain Sciences*, 33, 61–83.

Herr, R. M., Bosch, J. A., Loerbroks, A., Genser, B., Almer, C., van Vianen, A. E. M., & Fischer, J. E. (2018). Organizational justice, justice climate, and somatic complaints. *Journal of Psychosomatic Research*, 111, 15–21.

Hertig, M. M., Maxwell, E. C., Irvine, C., & Nagel, B. J. (2012). The impact of sex, puberty, and hormone status on white matter microstructure in adolescents. *Cerebral Cortex*, 22, 1979–1992.

Herzog, M., Sucec, J., Van Diest, I., Van den Bergh, O, & Von Leupoldt, A. (2019). The presence of others reduces dyspnea and cortical processing of respiratory sensations. *Biological Psychology*, 140, 48–54.

Hewlett, B. S., Lamb, M. E., Shannon, D., Leyendecker, B., & Scholnerich, A. (1998). Culture and early infancy among Central African foragers and farmers. *Developmental Psychology*, 34, 653–661.

Hickel, J. (2017). *The Divide*. New York: W. W. Norton & Company.

Hildebrandt, B. A., Racine, S. E., Keel, P. K., Burt, S. A., Neale, M., Boker, S., . . . Klump, K. L. (2015). The effects of ovarian hormones and emotional eating on changes in weight preoccupation across the menstrual cycle. *International Journal of Eating Disorders*, 48, 477–486.

Hinde, R. A. (1998). Through categories toward individuals. In R. B. Cairns, L. R. Bergman, & J. Kagan (Eds.), *Methods and Models for Studying the Individual* (pp. 11–29). Thousand Oaks, CA: Sage.

Hochmann, J. R., Benavides-Varela, S., Flo, A., Nespar, M., & Mehler, J. (2018). Bias for vocalic over consonantal information in 6-month olds. *Infancy*, 23. 136–151.

Holmquist, J. C. (1991). Semantic features and gender dynamics in Cantabrian speech. *Anthropological Linguistics*, 33, 57–80.

Honjo, K., Iso, H., Inoue, M., Sawada, N., & Tsugane, S. (2014). Socioeconomic status inconsistency and risk of stroke among Japanese middle-aged women. *Stroke*, 45, 2592–2598.

Hood, B., Cole-Davies, V., & Dias, M. (2003). Looking and search measures of object knowledge in preschool children. *Developmental Psychology, 39*, 61–70.

Hooks, K. B., Koosman, J. P., & O'Malley, M. A.(2018). Microbiota-gut-brain research. *Behavioral and Brain Sciences, 12*:1–40. doi:10.1017/S0140525X18002133.

Hossenfelder, S. (2018). *Lost in Math.* New York: Basic Books.

Hout, M. (2018). Americans' occupational status reflects the status of both of their parents. *Proceedings of the National Academy of Sciences, 115*, 9527–9532.

Howard, S. A., Avargues-Weber, A., Garcia, J. E., Greentree, A. D., & Dyer, A. D. (2018). Numeral ordering of zero in honey bees. *Science, 360*, 1124–1126.

Hsin, A., & Xie, Y. (2014). Explaining Asian Americans' academic advantage over whites. *Proceedings of the National Academy of Sciences, 111*, 8416–8421.

Hubner, N., Wille, E., Cambria, J., Osschatz, K., Nagengast, B., & Trautwein, V. (2017). Maximizing gender equality by minimizing course options? *Journal of Educational Psychology, 109*, 993–1009.

Hurely, R. S., Mesulam, M. M., Sridhar, J., Rogalski, E. J., & Thompson, C. K. (2018). A nonverbal route to conceptual knowledge involving the right anterior temporal lobe. *Neuropsychologia, 117*, 92–101.

Huynh, H. K., Willemsen, A. T., & Holstege, G. (2013). Female orgasm but not male ejaculation activates the pituitary. *Neuroimage, 76*, 178–182.

Hyde, J. S. (2005). The gender similarities. *American Psychologist, 60*, 581–592.

Hyde, J. S., & Mertz, J. E. (2009). Gender, culture, and mathematics performance. *Proceedings of the National Academy of Sciences, 106*, 8801–8807.

Ifidon, E. A. (1999). Social rationality and class analysis of national conflict in Nigeria. *African Development, 24*, 145–164.

Imperato-McGinley, J., Petersen, R., Gautier, T., & Sturla, E. (1979). Androgens and the evolution of male gender identity among male pseudohermaphrodites with 5-alpha-reductase deficiency. *New England Journal of Medicine, 300*, 1233–1237.

Inhelder, B., & Piaget, J. (1958). *The Growth of Logical Thinking from Childhood to Adolescence.* New York: Basic Books.

Inman, C. S., Manns, J. R., Bijanki, K. R., Bass, D. I., Hamann, S., Drane, D. L., . . . Willie, J. T. (2018). Direct electrical stimulation of the amygdala enhances declarative memory in humans. *Proceedings of the National Academy of Sciences, 115*, 98–103.

Ivancovsky, T., Kleinmetz, O., Lee, J., Kurman, J., & Shamay-Tsoory, S. G. (2018). The neural underpinnings of cross-cultural differences in creativity. *Human Brain Mapping, 39*, 4493–4508.

Jackson, S. A., Davis, A. A., Li, J., Yi, N., McCormick, S. R., Grant, C., . . . Northwestern Cancer Genetics Group. (2014). Characteristics of individuals with breast cancer rearrangements in BRACA1 and BRCA2. *Cancer*, 120, 1557–1564.

Jacobs, E. G., Holsen, L. M., Lancaster, K., Makris, N., Whitfield-Gabrielli, S., Remington, A., . . . Goldstein, J. M. (2015). 17beta-estradiol differentially regulates stress circuitry activity in healthy and depressed women. *Neuropsychopharmacology*, 40, 566–576.

Jacobsohn, L., Rodrigues, P., Vasemelos, O., Corbetta, D., & Barreiros, J. (2014). Lateral manual asymmetries. *Developmental Psychobiology*, 56, 58–72.

Jasanoff, S. (2018). Science, common sense and judicial power un U. S. courts. *Daedalus*, 147, 15–27.

Jeffery, N. D., Bate, S. T., Safayi, S., Howard, M. A., Moon, L., & Jeffery, U. (2018). When neuroscience met clinical pathology. *European Journal of Neuroscience*, 47, 371–379.

Jimenez, J. C., Su, K., Goldberg, A. R., Luna, V. M., Biane, J. S., Ordek, G., . . . Kheirbek, A. (2018). Anxiety cells in hippocampal-hypothalamic circuit. *Neuron*, 97, 670–683.

Johnson, S. B., Riis, J. L., & Noble, K. G. (2016). State of the art review: Poverty and the developing brain. *Pediatrics*, 137(4), pii: e20153075. doi:10.1542/peds.2015–3076.

Jones, C. W., Gray, S. A. O., Theall, K P., & S. S. Drury (2018). Polymorphic variation in the SLCSA7 gene influences infant autonomic reactivity and self-regulation. *Psychoneuroendocrinology*, 97, 28–36.

Jones, L. K., Jennings, B. M., Higgins, M. K., & de Waal, F. B. M. (2018). Ethological observations of social behavior in the operating room. *Proceedings of the National Academy of Sciences*, 115, 7575–7580.

Judah, M. R., Shurkova, E. Y., Hager, N. M., White, E. J., Taylor, D. L., & Grant, D. M. (2018). The relationship between social anxiety and heartbeat evoked potential amplitude. *Biological Psychology*, 139, 1–7.

Judd, C. M., McClelland, G. H., & Culhane, S. E. (1995). Data analysis. *Annual Review of Psychology*, 46, 433–465.

Kagan, J. (1971). *Change and Continuity in Infancy*. New York: John Wiley.

Kagan, J. (1981). *The Second Year*. Cambridge, MA: Harvard University Press.

Kagan, J. (2012). *Psychology's Ghosts*. New Haven, CT: Yale University Press.

Kagan, J. (2013). *The Human Spark*. New York: Basic Books.

Kagan, J. (2017). *Five Constraints on Predicting Behavior.* Cambridge, MA: The MIT Press.

Kagan, J. (2018). Three unresolved issues in human morality. *Perspectives on Psychological Science,* 13, 346–358.

Kagan, J., Arcus, D., Snidman, N., Feng, W. Y., Hendler, J., & Greene, S. (1994). Reactivity in infants. *Developmental Psychology,* 30, 342–345.

Kagan, J., Snidman, N., & Arcus, D. (1998). Childhood derivatives of high-and low-reactivity in infancy. *Child Development,* 69, 1483–1495.

Kagan, J., & Herschkowitz, N. (2005). *A Young Mind in a Growing Brain.* Mahwah, NJ: Lawrence Erlbaum.

Kagan, J., Kearsley, R. B., & Zelazo, P. R. (1978). *Infancy.* Cambridge, MA: Harvard University Press.

Kagan, J., Klein, R. E., Finley, C. E., Rogoff, B., & Nolan, E. (1979). A cross-cultural study of cognitive development. *Monographs of the Society for Research in Child Development,* 44, 1–66.

Kagan, J., Lapidus, D. R., & Moore, M. (1978). Infant antecedents of cognitive functioning. *Child Development,* 49, 1005–1023.

Kagan, J., Snidman, N., McManis, M., Woodward, S., & Hardway, C. (2002). One measure, one meaning: Multiple measures, clearer meaning. *Development and Psychopathology,* 14, 463–475.

Kagan, J., & Snidman, N. (2004). *The Long Shadow of Temperament.* Cambridge, MA: Harvard University Press.

Kaiser, J., Crespo-Llado, M. M., Turati, C., & Geangu, E. (2017). The development of spontaneous facial responses to others' emotions in infancy. *Science Reports,* 7, 17500. doi:10.1038.s4i598.

Kaldy, Z., & Leslie, A. M. (2005). A memory span of one? *Cognition,* 97, 153–177.

Kann, S., Zhang, S., Manza, P., Leung, H. C., & Li, C. R. (2016). Hemispheric lateralization of resting-state functional connectivity of the anterior insula. *Brain Connectivity,* 6, 724–734.

Karalunas, S. L., Gustafsson, H. C., Dieckmann, N. F., Tipsord, J., Mitchell, S. M., & Nigg, J. T. (2017). Heterogeneity in development of aspects of working memory predicts longitudinal attention deficit hyperactivity disorder symptom change. *Journal of Abnormal Psychology,* 126, 774–792.

Karevold, E., Roysamb, E., Ystrom, E., & Mathiesen, K. S. (2009). Predictors and pathways from infancy to symptoms of anxiety and depression in early adolescence. *Developmental Psychology,* 45, 1051–1060.

Kato, K., Sullivan, P. F., & Pedersen, N. L. (2010). Latent class analysis of functional somatic Symptoms in a population-based sample of twins. *Journal of Psychosomatic Research*, 68. 447–453.

Katz, B., Shah, P., & Meyer, D. E. (2018). How to play 20 questions with nature and lose. *Proceedings of the National Academy of Sciences*, 115, 9897–9904.

Kay, K., & Frank, L. M. (2018). Three brain states in the hippocampus and cortex. *Hippocampus*. doi:10.1002/hipo.22956.

Keller, K., & Menon, V. (2009). Gender differences in the functional and structural neuroanatomy of mathematical cognition. *Neuroimage*, 47, 342–352.

Kellner, R. S. (Ed.). (2018). *My Opposition*. New York: Cambridge University Press.

Kelly, A. M., & Goodson, J. L. (2015). Functional interactions of dopamine cell groups reflect personality, sex, and social context in highly social finches. *Behavioural Brain Research*, 280, 101–112.

Kendler, K. S., & Halberstadt, L. J. (2013). The road not taken. *Molecular Psychiatry*, 18, 975–984.

Kermode, F. (1995). *Not Entitled*. New York: Farrar Straus & Giroux.

Kersey, A. J., & Cantlon, J. F. (2017). Neural tuning to numerosity relates to perceptual tuning in 3–6-year old children. *Journal of Neuroscience*, 37, 512–522.

Keyes, K. M., & Galea, S. (2017). Commentary: The limits of risk factors revisited. *Epidemiology*, 28, 1–5.

Kidd, C., Piantadosi, S. T., & Aslin, R. N. (2014). The Goldilocks effect in infant auditory attention. *Child Development*, 85, 1795–1804.

Kidd, K. K., Speed, W. C., Pakstis, A. J., Podini, D. S., Lagace, R., Chang, J., . . . Sound-ararajan, U. (2017). Evaluating 130 microhaplotypes across a global set of 83 populations. *Forensic Science International: Genetics*, 29, 29–37.

Kiesner, J. (2011). One woman's low is another woman's high. *Psychchoneuroendocrinology*, 36, 68–76.

Kim, A. G., Moon, NJ, Han, J. J., & Choi, J. W. (2017). Quantification of myelin in children using multiparametric quantitative MRI. *Neuroradiology*, 59, 1043–1051.

Kim, D. J., Davis, E. P., Sandman, C. A., Sporns, O., O'Donnell, B. F., Buss, C., & Hetrick, W. P. (2017). Prenatal maternal cortisol has sex-specific associations with child brain network properties. *Cerebral Cortex*, 27, 5230–5241.

Kim, Y. K., Lee, S. S., Oh, S. I., Kim, J. S., Suh, E. H., Houpt, K. A., . . . Yeon, S. C. (2010). Behavioural reactivity of the Korean native Jindo dog varies with coat color. *Behavioural Processes*, 84(2), 568-72. doi:10.1016/j.beproc.2010.02.012.

Kimmel, M. (2012). *Manhood in America*. New York: Oxford University Press.

Kimura, D., & Hampson, E. (1994). Cognitive pattern in men and women is influenced by fluctuations in sex hormone. *Current Directions in Psychological Science*, 3, 57–61.

Kingdon, G., & Cassen, R. (2010). Ethnicity and low achievement in England's schools *British Educational Research Journal*, 36, 403–431.

Kivlighan, K. T., Granger, D. A., & Booth, A. (2005). Gender differences in testosterone and cortisol *response to competition*. *Psychoneuroendocrinology*, 30, 58–71.

Klein, R., Li, X., Kuo, J. Z., Klein, B. E., Cotch, M. F., Wong, T. Y., . . . Rotter, J. L. (2013). Associations of candidate genes to age-related macular degeneration among racial/ethnic groups in the multi-ethnic study of atherosclerosis. *American Journal of Ophthalmology*, 156, 1010–1020.

Kling, J., Gattario, K. H., & Frisen, A. (2017). Swedish women's perceptions of and conformity to feminine norms. *Scandinavian Journal of Psychology*, in press.

Knutson, J. F. (1995). Psychological characteristics of maltreated children. *Annual Review of Psychology*, 46, 401–431.

Kobayashi, M., Macchi-Cassia, V., Kanazawa, S., Yamagichi, M. K., & Kakigi, R. (2016). Perceptual narrowing towards adult faces is a cross-cultural phenomenon in infancy. *Developmental Science*, 21(1). doi:10.1111/desc.12498.

Kohn, H. (1960). *The Mind of Germany*. New York: Charles Scribner's and Sons.

Koscik, T., O'Leary, D., Moser, D. J., Andreasen, N. C., & Nopoulos, P. (2008). Sex differences in parietal lobe morphology. *Brain and Cognition*, 69, 451–459.

Kosinski, M. (2017). Facial width-to-height ratio does not predict self-reported behavioral tendencies. *Psychological Science*. doi:10.1177/095679761771699.

Kraemer, H. C. (2015). A source of false findings in published research studies. *JAMA Psychiatry*, 72, 961–962.

Kredlow, M. A., Orr, S. P., & Otto, M. W. (2018). Who is studied in de novo fear conditioning paradigms? *International Journal of Psychophysiology*, 130, 21–28.

Kredlow, M. A., Pineles, S. L., Inslicht, S. S., Marin, M. F., Milad, M. R., Otto, M. W., & Orr, S. P. (2017). Assessment of skin conductance in African American and non-African American participants in studies of conditioned fear. *Psychophysiology*, 54, 1741–1754.

Kuhl, P. K., Ramirez, R. R., Bosseler, A., Lin, J. F., & Imada, T. (2014). Infants' brain responses to speech suggest analysis by synthesis. *Proceedings of the National Academy of Sciences*, 31, 11238–11245.

Kuhl, P., & Rivera-Gaxiola, M. (2008). Neural substrates of language acquisition. *Annual Review of Neuroscience, 31*, 511–534.

Kuhlman, K. R., Robles, T. F., Dickensen, L., Reynolds, B., & Repetti, R. L. (2018). Stability of diurnal cortisol measures across days, weeks, and years during middle childhood and early adolescence. *Psychoneuroendocrinology, 100*, 67–74.

Kung, T. T. F., Li, G., Golding, J., & Hines, M. (2018). Preschool gender-typed play behavior at age 3.5 years predicts physical aggression at age 13 years. *Archives of Sexual Behavior, 47*, 905–914.

Kurdi, B., & Banaji, M. (2017). Repeated evaluative pairings and evaluative statements. *Journal of Experimental Psychology: General, 146*,194–213.

Kutter, E. F., Bostroem, J., Elger, C. E., Mormann, F., & Nieder, A., (2018). Single neurons in the human brain encode number. *Neuron, 100*, 753–761.

Kwon, M. K., Setoodehnia, M., Baek, J., Luck, S. J., & Oakes, L. M. (2016). The development of visual search in infancy. *Developmental Psychology, 52*, 537–555.

Ladd, G. W., Ettekal, I., & Kochenderfer-Ladd, B. (2017). Peer victimization trajectories from kindergarten through high school. *Journal of Educational Psychology, 09*, 826–841.

Lahti, M., Raikkonen, K., Lemola, S., Lahti, J., Heinonen, K., Kajantie, E., Pesonen, A. K., . . . , Eriksson, J. G. (2013). Trajectories of physical growth and personality dimensions of the Five-Factor model. *Journal of Personality and Social Psychology, 105*, 154–169.

Lambeck, R., Sonuga-Barken, E., Tannock, R., Sorendon, A. V., Damm, D., & Thomsen, P. H. (2018). Are there distinct cognitive and motivational sub-groups of children with ADHD? *Psychological Medicine, 48*, 1722–1730.

Lamp, G., Alexander, B., Laycock, R., Crewther, D. P., & Crewther, S. G. (2016). Mapping of the underlying neural mechanisms of maintenance and manipulation in visuo-spatial working memory using an n-back mental rotations task. *Frontiers in Behavioral Neuroscience, 10*, 87. doi:10.3389/fnbeh.2016.00087.

Langlois, J. H., Roggman, L. A., Casey, R. J., Ritter, J. M., Rieser-Danner, L. A., & Jenkins, V. Y. (1987). Infant preferences for attractive faces. *Developmental Psychology, 23*, 363–369.

Langsdorf, P., Izard, C. E., Rayias, M., & Hembree, E. A. (1983). Interest expression, visual fixation, and heart rate changes in 2- to 8-month-old infants. *Developmental Psychology, 19*, 375–386.

Lapiedra, O., Schoener, T. W., Leal, M., Losos, J. B., & Kolbe, J. J. (2018). Predator-driven natural selection on risk-taking in anole lizards. *Science, 360*, 1017–1020.

Larsen, B. & Luna, B. (2018). Adolescence as a neurobiological critical period for the development of higher order cognition, *Neuroscience and Biobehavioral Reviews, 94,* 179–195.

Lauer, J. E., Udelson, H. B., Jeon, S. O., & Lourenco, S. F. (2015). An early sex difference in the relation between mental rotation and object preference. *Frontiers in Psychology,* 6, 558. doi:m10.3389/fpsyg.2015.00558.

Lazzaro, S. C., Rutledge, R. B., Burghart, D. R., & Glimcher, P. W. (2016). The impact of menstrual cycle phase in economic choice and rationality. *PLoS One,* e0144080.

Lee, A. G., Capanzana, R., Brockhurst, J., Cheng, M. Y., Buckmaster, C. L., Absher, D., . . . Lyons, D. M. (2016). Learning to cope with stress modulates anterior cingulate cortex stargazing expression in monkeys and mice. *Neurobiology of Learning and Memory,* 131, 95–100.

Lee, S., & Schwarz, N. (2014). Question context and priming meaning of health. *American Journal of Public Health,* 104, 179–185.

Leeming, J. (2018). How researchers ensure that their work has an impact. *Nature,* 556, 139–141.

Legewie, J. (2018). Living on the edge. *Demography,* 55, 1957–1977.

Leibovich, T., & Henik, A. (2014). Comparing performance in discrete and continuous comparison tasks. *Quarterly Journal of Experimental Psychology,* 67,1–19.

Leibovich, T., Katzin, N., Harel, M., & Henik, A. (2017). From "sense of number" to "sense of magnitude." *Behavioral and Brain Sciences,* 40, 1–62.

Leslie, A. M. (1982). The perception of causality in infants. *Perception,* 11, 173–186.

Leslie, S. J., Cimpian, A., Meyer, M., & Freeland, E. (2015). Expectations of brilliance underlie gender distributions across academic disciplines. *Science, 347, 262–265.*

Levine, S. C., Huttenlocher, J., Taylor, A., & Langrock, A. (1999). Early sex differences in spatial skill. *Developmental Psychology,* 35, 940–949.

Levman, J., MacDonald, P., Lim, A. R., Forgeron, C., & Takahashi, E. (2017). A pediatric structural MRI analysis of healthy brain development from newborn to young adult. *Human Brain Mapping,* 381, 5931–5942.

Lewin, A., Brandeer, R., Benmarhnia, T., Frederique, T., & Basile, C. (2018). Attrition bias related to missing outcome data. *Epidemiology,* 29, 87–95.

Lewis, M. (2014). *The Rise of Consciousness and the Development of the Emotional Life.* New York: Guilford Press.

Lewis, G. J. (2018). Early-childhood conduct problems predict economic and political discontent in adulthood. *Psychological Science,* 29, 711–722.

Li, J., Hong, X., Mesiano, S., Muglia, L. J., Wang, X., Snyder, M., . . . Shaw, G. M. (2018). Natural selection has differentiated the progesterone receptor among human populations. *American Journal of Human Genetics, 103*, 45–57.

Liben, L. S., & Downs, R. M. (1993). Understanding person-space-map relations. *Developmental Psychology, 29*, 739–752.

Lin, C., Adolphs, R. & Alvarez, R. M. (2018). Inferring whether officials are corruptible from looking at their faces. *Psychological Science, 29*, 1807–1823.

Litman, L., Robinson, J., & Rosenzweig, C. (2015). The relationship between motivation, money compensation and data quality among US- and India-based workers on Mechanical Turk. *Behavior Research Methods, 47*, 515–528.

Liu, C., Snidman, N., & Kagan, J. (2016). Ethnic differences in infant reactivity. Unpublished manuscript.

Liu, J., Mo, Y., Ge, T., Wang, Y., Luo, X. J., Feng, J., Li, M., & Su, B. (2015). Allelic variation at 5-HTTLPR is associated with brain morphology in a Chinese population. *Psychiatry Research, 226*, 399–402.

Liu, X. C., Chen, H., Liu, Z. Z., Wang, J. Y., & Jia, C. X. (2017). Prevalence of suicidal behavior and associated factors in a large sample of Chinese adolescents. *Epidemiology and Psychiatric Science.* doi:10.1017/S2045796017000488.

Liu, Y., Su, Y., Xu, G., & Pei, M. (2018). When do you know what you know? *Journal of Experimental Child Psychology, 166*, 34–48.

Livesay, D. J., & Intili, P. (1996). A gender difference in visual-spatial ability in 4-year-old children. *Journal of Experimental Child Psychology, 63*, 436–444.

Loken, E. (2004). Using latent class analysis to model temperamental types. *Multivariate Behavioral Research, 39*, 625–650.

Loken, E., Leichtman, M. D., & Kagan, J. (2002). Integration of past and present. Unpublished manuscript.

Lombardo, M. P., & Deaner, R. (2018). On the evolution of the sex differences in throwing. *Quarterly Review of Biology, 93*, 91–119.

Lombardo, M. V., Ashwin, E., Auyeung, B., Chakrabarti, B., Taylor, K., Hackett, G., . . . Baron-Cohen, S. (2012). Fetal testosterone influences sexually dimorphic gray matter in the human brain. *Journal of Neuroscience, 32*, 674–680.

Long, C. C., Sadler, K. E., & Kolber, B. J. (2016). Hormonal and molecular effects of restraint stress on formalin-induced pain-like behavior in male and female mice. *Physiology and Behavior, 165*, 278–285.

Long, X., Benischek, A., Dewey, D., & Lebel, C. (2017). Age-related functional brain changes in young children. *Neuroimage, 155*, 322–330.

Lonigan, C. J., Phillips, B. M., Clancy, J. L., Landry, S. H., Swank, P. R., Assel, M., . . . Barnes, M. (2015). Impacts of a comprehensive school readiness curriculum for preschool children at risk for educational difficulties. *Child Development, 86,* 1773–1793.

Lonsdorf, E. V. (2017). Sex differences in nonhuman primate behavioral development. *Journal of Neuroscience Research, 95,* 213–221.

Lonsdorf, E. V., Markham, A. C., Heintz, M. R., Anderson, K. E., Ciuk, D. J., Goodall, J., . . . Wheatley, T. (2010). The tipping point of animacy. *Psychological Science, 21,* 1854–1862.

Lopez-Perez, B., & Wilson, E. L. (2015). Parent-child discrepancies in the *assessment* of children's and adolescents' happiness. *Journal of Experimental Child Psychology, 139,* 249–255.

Lovden, M., Karalija, N., Andersson, M., Wahlin, A., & Axelsson, J. (2018). Latent profile analysis reveals behavioral and brain correlates of dopamine-cognition associations. *Cerebral Cortex, 28,* 3894–3907.

Lu, Q., Zeltzer, L., & Tsao, J. (2013). Multiethnic differences in responses to laboratory pain stimuli among children. *Health Psychology, 32,* 905–914.

Lubrano, A. (2004). *Limbo.* New York: John Wiley.

Lundh, L. G., Wangby-Lundh, M., & Bjarehed, J. (2008). Self-reported emotional and behavioral problems in Swedish 14- to 15-year-old adolescents. *Scandinavian Journal of Psychology, 49,* 523–532.

MacCallum, R. C., & Austin, J. T. (2000). Applications of structural equation modeling in psychological research. *Annual Review of Psychology, 51,* 201–226.

Machin, S., & Pekkarinen, T. (2008). Global sex differences on test score variability. *Science, 322,* 1331–1332.

Mackenbach, J. P., Valverde, J. R., Artnik, B., Bopp, M., Brannum-Hansen, H., Deboosere, P., . . . Nusselder, W. J. (2018). Trends in health inequalities in 27 European countries. *Proceedings of the National Academy of Sciences, 115,* 6440–6445.

MacNeill, L. A., Ram, N., Bell, M. A., Fox, N. A., & Perez-Edgar, K. (2018). Trajectories of infants' biobehavioral development. *Child Development, 89,* 711–724.

MacTurk, R. H., McCarthy, M. E., Vietze, P. M., & Yarrow, L. J. (1987). Sequential analyses of mastery behavior in 6- and 12-month-old infants. *Developmental Psychology, 23,* 199–203.

Madgwick, P. G., Stewart, B., Belcher, L. J., Thompson, C. R. L., & Wolf, J. B. (2018). Strategic investment explains patterns of cooperation and cheating in a microbe. *Proceedings of the National Academy of Sciences, 115,* E4823-E4832.

Magnusson, D. (1998). The logic and implications of a person-oriented approach. In R. B. Cairns, L. R. Bergman, & J. Kagan (Eds.), *Methods and Models for Studying the Individual* (pp. 33–62). Thousand Oaks, CA: Sage.

Magnusson, D., & Torestad, B. (1993). A holistic view of personality. *Annual Review of Psychology*, 44, 427–452.

Majid, A., & Kruspe, N. (2018). Hunter-gatherer olfaction is special. *Current Biology*, 28(3), 409–413.e2. doi:10.1016/j.cub2017.12. 014.

Majid, A., Roberts, S. G., Cilssen, L., Emmorey, K., Nicodemus, B., O'Grady, L., ... Levinson, S. C. (2018). Differential coding of perception in the world's languages. *Proceedings of the National Academy of Sciences*, 115, 11369–11376.

Malaty, H. M., & Graham, D. Y. (1994). Importance of childhood socioeconomic class on the current prevalence of Helicobacter pylori infections. *Gut*, 35,742–745.

Maley, M. J., Eglin, C. M., House, J. R., & Tipton, M. J. (2014). The effect of ethnicity on the vascular responses to cold exposure of the extremities. *European Journal of Applied Physiology*, 114, 2369–2379.

Mandel, H. (2018). A second look at the process of occupational feminization and pay reduction in occupations. *Demography*, 55, 669–690.

Manuck, S. B., Flory, J. D., Ferrell, R. E., & Muldoon, M. F. (2004). Socio-economic status covaries with central nervous system serotonergic responsivity as a function of allelic variation in the serotonin transporter gene-linked polymorphic region. *Psychoneuroendocrinology*, 29, 651–668.

Manuck, S. B., Phillips, J. E., Gianaros, P. J., Flory, J. D., & Muldoon, M. F. (2010). Subjective socioeconomic status and presence of the metabolic syndrome in midlife community volunteers. *Psychosomatic Medicine, 72*, 35–45.

Manuck, T. A. (2017). Racial and ethnic differences in preterm birth. *Seminars in Perinatology*, pii:. S0146–0005(17)30098–8.

Marzi, S. J., Sugden, K., Arsenault, L., Belsky, D. W., Burrage, J., Corcoran, D. L., Danese, A., . . . Caspi, A. (2018). Analysis of DNA methylation in young people. *American Journal of Psychiatry*, 175, 517–525.

Masuda, T., Gonzalez, R., Kwan, L., & Nisbett, R. E. (2008). Culture and aesthetic preference. *Personality and Social Psychology Bulletin*, 14, 1260–1275.

McCarthy, M. M. (2008). Estradiol and the developing brain. *Physiological Reviews*, 88, 91–134.

McCarthy, M. M., de Vries, G. J., & Forge, N. G. (2017). Sexual differentiation of the brain. In D. W. Pfaff & M. Joels (Eds.), *Hormones, Brain and Behavior*, 3d ed., (pp. 3–32), Amsterdam: Elsevier/Academic Press.

McCarthy, M. M., Woolley, C. S., & Arnold, A. P. (2017). Incorporating sex as a variable in neuroscience. *Nature Reviews Neuroscience, 18*, 1–2.

McDonald, N. M., & Perdue, K. L. (2018). The infant brain in the social world. *Neuroscience and Biobehavioral Reviews, 87*, 38–49.

McElroy, E., Shevlin, M., & Murphy, J. (2017). Internalizing and externalizing disorders in childhood and adolescence. *Comprehensive Psychiatry, 75*, 75–84.

McEwen, B. S., & Milner, T. A. (2017). Understanding the broad influence of sex hormones and sex differences in the brain. *Journal of Neuroscience Research, 95*, 24–39.

McIntyre, M. H., Cohn, B. A., & Ellison, P. T. (2005). Sex dimorphism in digital formulae of children. *American Journal of Physical Anthropology, 129*, 143–150.

McKenzie, K., Murray, A., & Booth, T. (2013). Do urban environments increase the risk of anxiety, depression, and psychosis? *Journal of Affective Disorders, 150*, 1019–1024.

McLaughlin, K. A., Rith-Najarian, L., Dirks, M. A., & Sheridan, M. A. (2015). Low vagal tone Magnifies the association between psychosocial stress exposure and internalizing psychopathology in adolescents. *Journal of Clinical Child and Adolescent Psychology, 44*, 314–328.

McLeod, G. F. H., Horwood, L. J., & Fergusson, D. M. (2016). Adolescent depression, adult mental health and psychosocial outcomes at 30 and 35 years. *Psychological Medicine, 46*, 1401–1412.

McRae, R. R. (2002). NEO-PI-R-data for 36 countries. In R. R. Mc Rae & J. Allik (Eds.), *The Five Factor Model of Personality Across Cultures* (pp. 105–125). New York: Kluwer/Plenum.

Mehnert, J., Akhrif, A., Telkemeyer, S., Rossi, R., Schmitz, C. H., Steinbrink, J., . . . Neufang, S. (2013). Developmental changes in brain activation and functional connectivity during response inhibition in the early childhood brain. *Brain Development, 35*, 94–904.

Mehrabian, A. (2001). Characteristics attributed to individuals on the basis of their first names. *Genetic, Social, and General Psychology Monographs, 127*, 59–88.

Melynyte, S., Wang, G. Y., & Griskova-Bulanova, I. (2018). Gender differences on auditory P300. *International Journal of Psychophysiology, 133*, 55–65.

Menegas, W., Akiti, K., Amo, R., Uchida, N., & Watabe-Uchida, M. (2018). Dopamine neurons projecting to the posterior striatum reinforce avoidance of threatening stimuli. *Nature Neuroscience, 21*, 1421–1430.

Menikoff, D. E., & Bargh, J. A. (2018). The mythical number two. *Trends in Cognitive Sciences, 22*, 280–293.

Meyer-Bahlburg, H. F. L., Khuri, J., Reyes-Portillo, J., Ehrhardt, A. E., & New, M. I. (2018). Stigma associated with classical adrenal hyperplasia in women's sexual lives. *Archives of Sexual Behavior, 47*, 943–951.

Miller, G. E., Chen, E., & Parker, K. J. (2011). Psychological stress in childhood and susceptibility to the chronic diseases of aging. *Psychological Bulletin, 137*, 959–997.

Miller, P. M., Dancher, D. L., & Forbes, D. (1986). Sex-related strategies for coping with interpersonal conflict. *Developmental Psychology, 22*, 543–548.

Mireault, G. G., Crockenberg, S. C., Heilman, K., Soarrow, J. S., Cousineau, K., & Rainville, B. (2018). Social, cognitive, and physiological aspects of humour perception from 4 to 8 months. *British Journal of Developmental Psychology, 36*, 98–109.

Mirkovic, J. & Altmann, G. T. M. (2019). Unfolding meaning in context. *Cognition, 83*, 19–43.

Mischel, W. (2004). Toward an integrative science of the person. *Annual Review of Psychology, 55*, 1–22.

Mix, K. S., Levine, S. C., & Newcombe, N. S. (2016). Development of quantitative thinking across correlated dimensions. In A. Henik (Ed.), *Continuous Issues in Numerical Cognition, (pp.3–35)*. New York: Elsevier.

Miller, G. E., Lachman, M. E., Chen, E., Gruenewald, T. L., Karlamangla, A. S., & Seeman, T. E. (2011). Pathways to resilience. *Psychological Science, 22*,1591–1599.

Moding, K. J., & Stifter, C. A. (2016). Stability of food neophobia from infancy through early childhood. *Appetite, 97*, 72–78.

Moes, P. E., Brown, W. S., & Minnema, M. T. (2007). Individual differences in interhemispheric transfer time (IHTT) as measured by event related potentials. *Neuropsychologia, 45*, 2626–2630.

Moffett, L., Moll, H., & FitzGibbon, L. (2018). Future planning in preschool children, *Developmental Psychology, 54*, 866–874.

Monto, M. A., McRee, N., & Dercyk, F. S. (2018). Nonsuicidal self-injury among a representative sample of US adolescents, (2015).*American Journal of Public Health, 108*, 1042–1048.

Moore, D. S., & Cocas, L. A. (2006). Perception precedes computation. *Developmental Psychology, 42*, 666–678.

Moran, K. R., & Del Valle, S. Y. (2016). A meta-analysis of the association between gender and *Protective* behaviors in response to respiratory epidemics and pandemics. *PLoS One*, e0164541.

Moreau, D., & Corballis, M. C. (2018). When averaging goes wrong. *Journal of Experimental Psychology: General*, doi: 10.1037/xge.0000504.

Morris, M. L. (2016). Vocational interests in the United States. *Journal of Counseling Psychology*, 63, 604–615.

Morrison, R., & Reiss, D. (2018). Precocious development of self-awareness in dolphins. *PLoS One*, Jan 10, 13, e0189813.

Mrzljak, L., Uylings, H. B., van Eden, C. J., & Judas, M. (1990). Neuronal development in human prefrontal cortex in prenatal and postnatal stages. *Progress in Brain Research*, 85, 185–222.

Muller, L., Chavane, F., Reynolds, J., & Sejnowski, T. J. (2018). Cortical travelling waves, *Nature Reviews Neuroscience*, 19, 255–268.

Muller, N., Campbell, S., Nonaka, M., Rost, T. M., Pipa, G., Konrad, G. N., . . . Genzel, L. (2018). 2D:4D and spatial abilities. *Neurobiology of Learning and Memory*, 151, 85–87.

Nardell, M. (2004). My Italian-American identity. *Italian Americana*, 22, 208–213.

Nazareth, A., Weisberg, S. M., & Newcomb, S. (2018). Charting the development of cognitive maps. *Journal of Experimental Child Psychology*, 170, 86–106.

Needham, B. L., Adler, N., Gregorich, S., Rehkopf, S., Lin, J., Blackbum, E. H., & Epel, E. S. (2013). Socioeconomic status, health behavior, and leukocyte telomere length in the National Health and Nutrition Examination Survey, 1999–2002. *Social Science and Medicine*, 85, 1–8.

Needham, L., Diez, B., Roux, A. V., Bird, C. E., Bradley, R., Fitzpatrick, A. L., . . . Wang, S. (2014). A test of biological and behavioral explanations for gender differences in telomere length. *Biodemography and Social Biology*, 60, 156–173.

Neigh, G. N., Nemeth, C. L., & Rowson, S. A. (2016). Sex differences in immunity and inflammation. In R. M. Shansky (Ed.), *Sex Differences in the Central Nervous System*, (pp. 1–26), New York: Academic Press.

Nesselroade, J. R., & Molenaar, P. C. (2016). Some behavioral science measurement concerns and proposals. *Multivariate Behavioral Research*, 51, 396–412.

Nguyen, T. V. (2018). Developmental effects of androgens in the human brain. *Journal of Endocrinology*, 30(2). doi:10.1111/jne.12486.

Nielsen, M., Haun, D., Kartner, J., & Legare, C. H. (2017). The persistent sampling bias in developmental psychology. *Journal of Experimental Child Psychology*, 162, 31–38.

Nieuwenhuys, R. (2012). The insula cortex. *Progress in Brain Research*, 195, 123–163.

Nikolaidis, A., & Gray, J. R. (2010). ADHD and the DRD4 exon III 7-repeat polymorphism. *Social Cognitive and Affective Neuroscience*, 5, 188–193.

Nisbett, R. E., Peng, K., Choi, I., & Norenzayan, A. (2001). Culture and systems of thought. *Psychological Review, 108,* 291–310.

Nitsch, R., & Stabnisch, F. W. (2018). Neural mechanisms recording the stream of consciousness—A reappraisal of Wilder Penfield's (1891–1976) concept of experiential phenomena elicited by electrical stimulation of the human cortex. *Cerebral Cortex, 28,* 3347–3355.

Noble, K. G., Houston, S. M., Brito, N. H., Bartsch, H., Kan, E., Kuperman, J. M., . . . Sowell, E. R. (2015). Family income, parental education, and brain structure in children and adolescents. *Nature Neuroscience, 16,* 773–778.

Noh, J. Y., D'Esterie, A., & Killen, M. (2019). Effort or outcome? *Journal of Experimental Child Psychology, 178,* 1–14.

Nordenstrom, A., Servin, A., Bohlin, G., Larsson, A., & Wedell, A. (2002). Sex-typed toy play behavior correlates with the degree of prenatal androgen exposure assessed by CYP21 genotype in girls with congenital adrenal hyperplasia. *Journal of Clinical Endocrinology and Metabolism, 87,* 5119–5124.

Nowell, A., & Hedges, L. V. (1998). Trends in gender differences in academic achievement from 1960 to 1994. *Sex Roles, 39,* 21–43.

Nummenmaa, L., Hari, R., Hetanen, J. K., & Glerean, E. (2018). Maps of subjective feelings. *Proceedings of the National Academy of Sciences, 115,* 9198–9203.

Nunez, R. E. (2017). Is there really an evolved capacity for number? *Trends in Cognitive Sciences, 21,* 409–422.

Nystrom, B., & Bengtsson, H. (2017). A psychometric evaluation of the Temperament in Middle Childhood Questionnaire (TMCQ) in a Swedish sample. *Scandinavian Journal of Psychology, 58,* 477–484.

Oakes, L. M. (1994). Development of infants' use of continuity cues in their perception of causality. *Developmental Psychology, 30,* 869–879.

Oakes, L. M., Ross-Sheehy, S., & Luck, S. J. (2006). Rapid development of feature binding in visual short term memory. *Psychological Science, 17,* 781–787.

Odone, A., Landsiscini, T., Amerio, A., & Costa, G. (2018). The impact of the current economic crisis on mental health in Italy. *European Journal of Public Health, 28,* 490–495.

Oetjens, M. T., Shen, F., Emery, S. B., Zou, Z., & Kidd, J. M. (2016). Y-chromosome structural diversity in the bonobo and chimpanzee lineages. *Genomes and Biological Evolution, 8,* 2231–2240.

Ortiz-Mantilla, S., Hamalainen, J. A., Realpe-Bonilla, T., & Benasich, A. A. (2016). Oscillatory dynamics underlying perceptual narrowing of native phoneme mapping from 6 to 12 months of age. *Journal of Neuroscience, 36*, 12095–12105.

Osgood, C. E., May, W. H., & Miron, M. S. (1975). *Cross-Cultural Universals of Affective Meaning.* Urbana, IL: University of Illinois Press.

Osler, M., McGue, M., Lund, R., & Christensen, K. (2008). Marital state and twins' health and behavior. *Psychosomatic Medicine, 70*, 482–487.

Oswald, A. J., & Wu, S. (2010). Objective confirmation of subjective measures of human well-being. *Science, 327*, 576–577.

Otsuka, Y., Ichikawa, H., Kanazawa, S., Yamaguchi, M. K., & Spehar, B. (2014). Temporal dynamics of spatial processing in infants. *Journal of Experimental Psychology: Human Perception and Performance, 40*, 995–1008.

Paletta, P., Sheppard, P. A. S., Matta, R., Ervin, K. S. J., & Choleris, E. (2018). Rapid effects of estrogens on short-term memory. *Hormones and Behavior,* pii:S0018–506X(18)30062-X

Palmatier, M. A., Kang, A. M., & Kidd, K. K. (1999). Global variation in the frequencies of functionally different catechol-0-methyltransferase alleles. *Biological Psychiatry, 46*, 557–567.

Pamuk, O. (2006). *Istanbul.* New York: Alfred A. Knopf.

Panno, A., Donati, A. M., Millioni, M., Chiesi, F., & Primi, C. (2018). Why women take fewer risks than men do. *Sex Roles, 78*, 286–297.

Paolacci, G., & Chandler, J. (2014). Inside the Turk. *Current Directions in Psychological Science, 23*, 184–188.

Papadopoulos, A., Sforazzini, F., Egan, G., & Jamadar, S. (2018). Functional subdivisions within the human intraparietal sulcus are involved in visuospatial transformations in a non-context-dependent manner. *Human Brain Mapping, 39*, 354–368.

Pappa, I., Mileva-Seitz, V. R., Szekely, E., Verhulst, F. C., Bakermans-Kranenburg, M. J., Jaddoe, V. W., . . . van IJzendoorn, M. H. (2014). DRD4 VNTRs, observed stranger fear in preschoolers and later ADHD symptoms. *Psychiatry Research, 30*, 982–986.

Paris, L. D., Howell, J. P., Dorfman, P. W., & Hanges, P. J. (2009). Preferred leadership prototypes of male and female leaders in 27 countries. *Journal of International Business Studies, 40*, 1396–1405.

Park, G., Yaden, D. B., Schwartz, H. A., Kern, M. L., Eichstaedt, J. C., Kosinski, M., . . . Seligman, M. E. (2016). Women are warmer but no less assertive than men: Gender and language on Facebook. *PLoS One,* e0155885.

Park, H. D., Bernasconi, F., Salomon, P., Tallon-Baudry, C., Spinell, L., Seeck, M., ... Blanke, O. (2018). Neural sources and underlying mechanisms of neural response to heartbeats, and their relation to bodily self-consciousness. *Cerebral Cortex*, 28, 2351–2364.

Paul, J. M., Reeve, R. A., & Forte, J. D. (2017). Taking a(c)count of eye movements. *Journal of Vision*, 17(3), 16. doi:10.1167/17.3.16.

Pavlova, M. A., Sokolov, A. N., & Bidet-Ildei, C. (2015). Sex differences in the neuromagnetic cortical response to biological motion. *Cerebral Cortex*, 25, 3468–3474.

Pearl, J., & Mackenzie, D. (2018). *The Book of Why*. New York: Basic Books.

Pedersen, F. A., & Bell, R. Q. (1970). Sex differences in preschool children without histories of complications of pregnancy and delivery. *Developmental Psychology*, 3, 10–15.

Pelphrey, K. A., Reznick, J. S., Goldman, B. D., Sasson, N., Morrow, J., Donahue, A., & Hodgson, K. (2004). Development of visuospatial short-term memory in the second half of the 1st year. *Developmental Psychology*, 40, 836–851.

Peng, Q., Gizer, I. R., Wilhelmsen, K. C., & Ehlers, C. L. (2017). Associations between genomic variants in alcohol dehydrogenase genes and alcohol symptomology in American Indians and European Americans. *Alcohol and Clinical Experimental Research*, 41, 1695–1704.

Perez-Arce, F., Amaral, E. F. C., Huang, H., & Price, C. C. (2016). *Inequality and Opportunity*. Santa Monica, CA: Rand Corporation.

Perlman, J. (2018). *America Classifies the Immigrants*. Cambridge, MA: Harvard University Press.

Perry, A., Wen, W., Kochan, N. A., Thalamuthu, A., Sachdev, P. S., & Breakspear, M. (2017). The independent influences of age and education on functional brain networks and cognition in healthy older adults. *Human Brain Mapping*, 38, 5094–5114.

Pervin, L. A. (1978). Theoretical approaches to the analysis of individual-environment interaction. In L. A. Pervin & M. Lewis (Eds.), *Perspectives in Interactional Psychology*. (pp. 67–85), New York: Plenum.

Phares, E. J., & Lamiell, J. T. (1977). Personality. *Annual Review of Psychology*, 28, 113–140.

Piaget, J. (1950). *Psychology of Intelligence*. London: Routledge & Kegan Paul.

Piantadosi, S. T., Kidd, C., & Aslin, R. (2014). Rich analysis and rational models. *Developmental Science*, 17, 321–337.

Piantadosi, S. T., Palmeri, H., & Aslin, R. (2018). Limits on composition of conceptual operations in 9-month-olds. *Infancy*, 23, 310–324.

Piazza, M., de Feo, V., Panzeri, S., & Dehaene, S. (2018). Learning to focus on number. *Cognition, 181,* 35–45.

Pnevmatikos, D. (2018). When do children start to take mitigating circumstances into account when judging the act of killing? *Cognitive Development, 48,* 94–104.

Podcasy, J. C., & Epperson, C. N. (2016). Considering sex and gender in Alzheimer disorder and other dementias. *Dialogues in Clinical Neuroscience, 18,* 437–446.

Polevoy, C., Muckle, G., Seguin, J. R., Ouellet, E., & Saint Amour, D. (2017). Similarities and differences between behavioral and electrophysiological visual acuity thresholds in healthy infants during the second half of the first year of life. *Documenta Ophthalmologia, 134,* 99–110.

Ponce, C. R., Hartmann, T. S., & Livingstone, M. S. (2017). End-stopping predicts curvature tuning along the ventral stream. *Journal of Neuroscience, 37,* 648-659.

Ponsot, E., Burred, J. J., Belin, P., & Aucouturier, J. J. (2018). Cracking the social code of speech prosody using reverse correlation. *Proceedings of the National Academy of Sciences, 115,* 3972–3977.

Powell, L. J., & Spelke, E. S. (2017). Human infants' understanding of social imitation cognition. *Cognition, 170,* 31–48.

Prins, S. J., Bates, L. M., Keyes, K. M., & Muntaner, C. (2015). Anxious? Depressed? You might be suffering from capitalism. *Social Health and Illness, 37,* 1352–1372.

Prioreschi, A., Brage, S., Hesketh, K. D., Hnatiuk, J., Westgate, K., & Micklesfield, L. K. (2017). Describing objectively measured physical activity levels, patterns, and correlates in a cross sectional sample of infants and toddlers from South Africa. *International Journal of Behavioral Nutrition and Physical Activity, 14,* 176. doi:10.1186/s12966-017-0633-5.

Pruden, S. M., & Levine, S. C. (2017). Parents' spatial language mediates a sex difference in preschoolers' spatial language use. *Psychological Science, 28,* 1583–1596.

Pruett, J. R., Kandala, Hoertel, S., Snyder, A. Z., Elison, J. T. Nishino, T., . . . Piven, J. (2015). Accurate age classification of 6 and 12 month-old infants based on resting-state functional connectivity magnetic resonance imaging data. *Developmental Cognitive Neuroscience, 12,* 123–133.

Prum, R. O. (2017). *The Evolution of Beauty.* New York: Doubleday.

Purves-Tyson, T. D., Owens, S. J., Double, K. L., Desai, R., Handelsman, D. J., & Weickert, C. S. (2014). Testosterone induces molecular changes in dopamine signaling pathway molecules in the adolescent male rat nigrostriatal pathway. *PloS One,* e91151. doi:10.1371/jpurnal.pone0091151.

Pyle, R. E., & Davidson, J. D. (2003). The origins of religious stratification in Colonial America. *Journal for the Scientific Study of Religion, 42*, 57–76.

Qu, J., & Leerkes, E. M. (2018). Patterns of RSA and observed distress during the still-face paradigm predict later attachment, compliance and behavior problems. *Developmental Psychobiology, 60*, 707–721.

Quinn, P. C., Cummins, M., Kase, J., Martin, E., & Weissman, S. (1996). Development of categorical representations for above and below spatial relations in 3- to 7-month old infants. *Developmental Psychology, 32*, 942–956.

Racine, S. E., Culbert, K. M., Keel, P. K., Sisk, C. L., Burt, S. A., & Klump, K. L. (2012). Differential associations between ovarian hormones and disordered eating symptoms across the menstrual cycle in women. *International Journal of Eating Disorders, 45*, 333–344.

Rahman, T. (2013). Personal names add to Islamic identity in Pakistan. *Islamic Studies, 52*, 239–296.

Rai, D., Zitko, P., Jones, K., Lynch, J., & Araya, R. (2013). Country-and individual-level socioeconomic determinants of depression. *The British Journal of Psychiatry, 202*, 195–203.

Rajalingham, R., Issa, E. B., Bashiran, P., Kar, K., Schmidt, K., & Di Carlo, J. J. (2018). Large-scale, high resolution comparison of the core visual object recognition behavior of humans, monkeys, and state-of–the-art deep artificial neural networks. *Journal of Neuroscience, 38*, 7355–7369.

Rakison, D. H., & Butterworth, G. E. (1998). Infants' use of object parts in early categorization. *Developmental Psychology, 34*, 49–62.

Rankin, A. (2013). *Panaceia's Daughters*. Chicago, IL: University of Chicago Press.

Ranson, R., Stratton, G., & Taylor, S. R. (2015). Digit ratio (2D:4D) and physical fitness in school children. Early *Human Development, 91*, 327–331.

Raymond, C. L., & Benbow, C. P. (1986). Gender differences in mathematics. *Developmental Psychology, 22*, 808–819.

Razavi, S. M. K., Martin, R., Pantazis, D., & Oliva, A. (2018). Spatiotemporal neural dynamics of real-world object size and animacy in the human brain. *Journal of Cognitive Neuroscience, 30*, 1559–1576.

Reardon, C., Murray, K., & Lomax, A. E. (2018). Neuroimmune communication in health and disease. *Physiological Reviews, 95*, 2287–2316.

Redmond, S. M., & Ash, A. C. (2017). Associations between the 2D:4D proxy biomarker for prenatal hormone exposures and symptoms of developmental language disorder. *Journal of Speech, Language, and Hearing Research, 30*, 1–11.

Rees, M. (2018). *On the Future.* Princeton, NJ: Princeton University Press.

Reidy, K. J., Hjorten, R. C., Simpson, C. L., Rosenberg, A. Z., Rosenblum, S. D., Kovesdy, C. P., . . . Davis, R. L. (2018). Fetal-not maternal-APOL1 genotype associated with risk for preeclampsia in those with African ancestry. *American Journal of Human Genetics,* 103, 367–376.

Reiss, F. (2013). Socioeconomic inequalities and mental health problems in children and adolescents. *Social Science & Medicine,* 90, 24–31.

Reizel, Y., Spiro, A., Sabaq, O., Skversky, Y., Hecht, M., Keshet, I., . . . Cedar, H. (2015). Gender-specific postnatal demethylation and establishment of epigenetic memory. *Genes and Development,* 29, 923–933.

Renn, S. C., Fraser, E. J., Aubin-Horth, N., Trainor, B. C., & Hofmann, H. A. (2012). Females of an African cichlid fish display male-typical social dominance behavior and elevated androgens in the absence of males. *Hormones and Behavior,* 61, 496–503.

Rentfrow, P. J., Jakela, M., & Lamb, M. E. (2015). Regional personality differences in Great Britain. *PLoS One,* 10, e122245.

Reynolds, G. D. (2015). Infant visual attention and object recognition. *Behavioral Brain Research,* 285, 34–43.

Reynolds, G. D., & Richards, J. E. (2017). Infant visual attention and stimulus repetition effects on object recognition. *Child Development.* doi:10.1111/cdev.12982.

Reynolds, G. D., & Romano, A. C. (2016). The development of attention systems and working memory in infancy. *Frontiers in Systems Neuroscience.* https://doi.org/10.3389/fnsys.2016.00015.

Reynolds, G. D., Guy, M. W., & Zhang, D. (2010). Neural correlates of individual differences in infant visual attention and recognition memory. *Infancy,* 16, 368–391.

Rhodes, A. (1937). A comparative study of motor ability of Negroes and Whites. *Child Development,* 8, 369–374.

Richards, J. E., & Rader, N. (1981). Crawlig-onset age predicts the age of first visual cliff avoidance in infants. *Journal of Experimental Psychology: Human Perception and Performance,* 7, 382–387.

Rieger, G., Linsenmeier, J. A. W., Gygax, L., & Bailey, J. M. (2008). Sexual orientation and childhood gender nonconformity. *Developmental Psychology,* 44, 46–58.

Roberts, S. O., Ho, A. K., Rhodes, M., & Gelman, S. A. (2017). Making boundaries great again. *Personality and Social Psychology Bulletin,* 43(12), 1643–1658. doi:10.1177/0146167217724801.

Robinson, J. L., Kagan, J., Reznick, J. S., & Corley, R. (1992). The heritability of inhibited and uninhibited behavior. *Developmental Psychology,* 28, 1030–1037.

Rodrigues, M. A., & Boeving, E. R. (2018). Comparative social grooming networks in captive chimpanzees and bonobos. *Primates.* doi:10.1007/s10329-018-0670-y.

Rogers, M., Franklin, A., & Knoblauch, K. (2018). A novel method to investigate how dimensions interact to inform perceptual salience in infancy. *Infancy, 23,* 833–856.

Rohrer, J. M. (2018). Thinking clearly about correlations and causation. *Advances in Methods and Practices in Psychological Science, 1,* 27–42.

Rose, S. A., Feldman, J. F., & Jankowski, J. J. (2001). Visual short-term memory in the first year of life. *Developmental Psychology, 37,* 539–549.

Rose, S. A., Feldman, J. F., & Jankowski, J. J. (2015). Pathways from toddler information processing to adolescent lexical proficiency. *Child Development, 86,* 1935–1947.

Roy, P., & Benenson, L. (2002). Sex and contextual effects on children's use of interference competition. *Developmental Psychology, 38,* 306–312.

Rudd, R. A., Seth, P., David, F., & Scholl, L. (2016). Increases in drug and opioid-involved overdose deaths, United States, 2010–2015. *Centers for Disease Control and Prevention: Morbidity and Mortality Weekly Report, 65,* 1445–1452.

Rudolph, M. D., Graham, A. M., Feczki, E., Miranda-Dominguez, O., Rasmussen, J. M., Nardos, R., . . . Fair, D. A. (2018). Maternal IL-6 during pregnancy can be estimated from newborn brain connectivity and predicts future working memory in offspring. *Nature Neuroscience, 21,* 765–772.

Sabbagh, K. (2009). *Remembering Our Childhood.* New York: Oxford University Press.

Sabuncu, M. R., Ge, T., Holmes, A. J., Smoller, J. W., Buckner, R. L., & Fischl, B. (2016). Morphometricity as a measure of the neuroanatomical signature of a trait. *Proceedings of the National Academy of Sciences, 113,* E5749-E5756.

Saffran, J. R., & Kirkham, N. Z. (2018). Infant statistical learning. *Annual Review of Psychology, 69,* 181–203.

Safranski, R. (2016). *Goethe.* (trans. D. Dollenmayer), New York: Liveright.

Salinas, J., Mills, E. D., Conrad, A. L., Koscik, T., Andreasen, N. C., & Nopoulos, P. (2012). Sex Differences in parietal lobe structure and development. *Gender Medicine, 9,* 44–55.

Salvatore, M., Wiersielis, K. R., Luz, S., Waxler, D. E., Bhatnagar, S., & Bangasser, D. A. (2018). Sex differences in circuits activated by corticotropin releasing factor in rats. *Hormones and Behavior, 97,* 145–153.

Sameroff, A. J., & Haith, M. M. (Eds.). (1996). *The Five to Seven Year Shift.* Chicago, IL: University of Chicago Press.

Sand, M., Hessam, S., Sand, D., Bechara, F. G., Vorstius, C., Bromba, M., . . . Shiue, I. (2016). Stress-coping styles of 459 emergency care physicians in Germany. *Anaesthesist*, 65, 841–846.

Sano, K., Nakata, M., Morishita, M., Sakamoto, T., Tsukahara, S., & Ogawa, S. (2016). Pubertal activation of estrogen receptor alpha in the medial amygdala is essential for the full expression of male social behavior in mice. *Proceedings of the National Academy of Sciences*, 113, 7632–7637.

Sapienza, P., Zingales, L., & Maestripieri, D. (2009). Gender differences in financial risk aversion and career choices are affected by testosterone. *Proceedings of the National Academy of Sciences*, 106, 16268–16273.

Sapolsky, R. (2005). Sick of poverty. *Scientific American*, 293, 93–99.

Sarkisian, N., Gerena, M., & Gerstel, N. (2007). Extended family integration among Euro and Mexican Americans. *Journal of Marriage and Family*, 69, 40–54.

Sasser, T. R., Bierman, K. L., Heinrichs, B., & Nix, R. L. (2017). Preschool intervention can promote sustained growth of children exhibiting early deficit. *Psychological Science*, 28, 1719–1730.

Satterthwaite, T. D., Shinohara, R. T., Wolf, D. H., Hopson, R. D., Elliott, M. A., Vandekar, S. N. . . . Gur, R. E. (2014). Impact of puberty on the evolution of cerebral perfusion during adolescence. *Proceedings of the National Academy of Sciences*, 111, 8643–8648.

Satterthwaite, T. D., Wolf, D. H., Roalf, D. R., Ruparel, K., Erus, G., Vandekar, S., . . . Gur, R. C. (2015). Linked sex differences in cognition and functional connectivity in youth. *Cerebral Cortex*, 25, 2383–2394.

Sawyer, R. P., Sekar, P., Osborne, J., Kittner, S. J., Moomaw, C. J., Flaherty, M. L., . . . Woo, D. (2018). Racial/ethnic variation of APOE alleles for lobar intracerebral hemorrhage. *Neurology*, 91(5), e410–e420. doi:10.1212/WNL.000000000000590.

Scherer, K. R., Zentner, M. R., & Stern, D. (2004). Beyond surprise. *Emotion*, 4, 38

Schmidt, L. A., Trainor, L. J., & Santesso, D. L. (2003). Development of frontal electroencephalogram (EEG) and heart rate (ECG) responses to affective musical stimuli during the first 12 months of post-natal life. *Brain and Cognition*, 52, 27–32.

Schmitt, J. E., Giedd, J. N., Raznahan, A., & Neale, M. C. (2018). The genetic contributions to maturational coupling In the human cerebrum. *Cerebral Cortex*, 28, 3184–3191.

Schuessler, J. (2018). Hoaxers slip restaurants and dog-park sex into journals. *New York Times*, October 7, 2018.

Schumann, K., & Ross, M. (2010). Why women apologize more than men. *Psychological Science, 21*, 1649–1655.

Schwartz, H. A., Eichstaedt, J. C., Kern, M. L., Dziurzynski, L., Ramones, S. M., Agrawal, M., . . . Ungar, L. H. (2013). Personality, gender, and age in the language of social media. *PLoS One*, e73791.

Schwarz, J. M., & McCarthy, M. M. (2008). The role of neonatal NMDA receptor activation in defeminization and masculinization of sex behavior in the rat. *Hormones and Behavior, 54*, 662–668.

Schweren, L., Hoekstra, P., von Lieshait, M., Oosterlaan, J., Lambregts-Rommelse, N., Buitelaar, J., Franke, B., & Hartman, C. (2019). Long-term effects of stimulant treatment on ADHD symptoms, social- emotional functioning and cognition. *Psychological Medicine, 49*, 217–223.

Scott, L. S. (2006). Featural and configural face processing in adults and infants. *Perception, 52*, 27–32.

Searle, J. R. (1998). How to study consciousness scientifically. *Philosophical Transactions: Biological Sciences, 353*, 1935–1942.

Searles, E. (2008). Inuit identity in the Canadian Arctic. *Ethnology, 47*, 239–255.

Segurel, L., Wyman, M. J., & Przeworski, M. (2014). Determinants of mutation rate variation in the human germline. *Annual Review of Genomics and Human Genetics, 15*, 47–70.

Seifert, F., Strunk, J., Danielsen, S., Hartmann, I., Pokendorf, B., Wichmann, S., . . . Bickel, B. (2018). Nouns slow down speech across structurally and culturally diverse languages. *Proceedings of the National Academy of Sciences, 115*, 6720–6725.

Seiffge-Krenke, I., Persike, M., Besevegus, E., Chau, C., Karaman, N. G., Lanregrad-Willens, L., . . . Rohail, I. (2018). Culture beats gender? *Journal of Adolescence, 63*, 194–208.

Serbin, L. A., Poulin-Dubois, D., & Eichstedt, J. A. (2002). Infants' responses to gender-inconsistent events. *Infancy, 3*, 531–542.

Servin, A., Nordenstrom, A., Larsson, A., & Bohlin, G. (2003). Prenatal androgens and gender-typical behavior. *Developmental Psychology, 39*, 440–450.

Shah, A., Lerche, J., Axelby, R., Benbabaali, D., Donegan, B., Raj, J., & Thakur, V. (2018). *Ground Down by Growth*. London: Pluto Press.

Shariff, A. F., Wiwad, D., & Aknin, L. B. (2016). Income mobility breeds tolerance for income inequality. *Perspectives on Psychological Science, 11*, 373–380.

Sherrow, H. M. (2012). Adolescent male chimpanzees at Ngogo, Kibale National park, Uganda have decided dominance relationships. *Folia Primatologica, 83*, 67–75.

Shiino, A., Chen, Y. W., Tanigaki, K., Yamada, A., Vigers, P., Watanabe, T., . . . Akiguchi, I. (2017). Sex-related differences in human white matter volumes studied. *Science Reports, 7*, 39818. doi:10.1038/srep39818.

Short, S. J., Elison, J. T., Goldman, B. D., Stymer, M., Gu, H., Connelly, M. . . . Gilmore, J. H. (2013). Associations between white matter microstructure and infants' working memory. *Neuroimage, 64*, 156–166.

Siegler, R. S. (1996). Uni-dimensional thinking, multi-dimensional thinking and characteristic tendencies of thought. In A. G. Sameroff & M. M. Haith (Eds.), *The Five to Seven Year Shift* (pp. 63–84). Chicago: University of Chicago Press.

Sigmund, K. (2017). *Exact Thinking in Demented Times*. New York: Basic Books.

Simon, E., Meuret, A. E., & Ritz, T. (2017). Sympathetic and parasympathetic cardiac responses to phobia-relevant and disgust-specific emotion provocation in blood-injection-injury phobia with *and* without fainting history. *Psychophysiology, 54*, 1512–1527.

Sitas, F., Yarnell, J., & Forman, D. (1991). Helicobacter pylori infection rates in relation to age and social class in a population of Welsh men. *Gut, 32*, 25–28.

Slominski, A., Wortsman, J., Luger, T., Paus, R., & Solomon, S. (2000). Corticotropin releasing hormone and proopiomelanocortin involvement in the cutaneous response to stress. *Physiological Reviews, 80*, 979–1020.

Smarsh, S. (2018). *Heartland*. New York: Scribners.

Smit, D. J. A., Wright, M. J., Meyers, J. L., Martin, N. G., Ho, Y. Y. W., Malone, S. M., . . . Boomsma, D. I. (2018). Genome-wide association analysis links multiple psychiatric liability genes to oscillatory brain activity. *Human Brain Mapping, 39*, 4183–4195.

Smith, K. M., Larroucar, T., Mabulla, I. A., & Apicella, C. L. (2018). Hunter-gatherers maintain assortativity in cooperation despite high levels of residential change and mixing. *Current Biology. 28*, 3152–3157.

Snape, S., & Krott, A. (2018). The benefit of simultaneously encountered exemplars and of exemplar variability to verb learning. *Journal of Child Language, 45*, 1412–1422.

Sokolowski, H. M., Hawes, Z., & Lyons, I. M. (2019). What explains sex differences in math anxiety? *Cognition, 182*, 193–212.

Song, M., Vogelstein, B., Giovannucci, E. L., Willett, W. C., & Tomasetti, C. (2018). Cancer prevention. *Science, 361*, 1317–1318.

Sophian, C. (2000). From objects to quantities. *Developmental Psychology, 36*, 724–730.

Sousa, A. M. M., Zhu, Y., Raghanti, M. A., Kitchen, R. R., Onorati, M., Tebbenkamp, A. T. N., Stutz, B., . . . , & Sestan, N. (2017). Molecular and cellular reorganization of neural circuits in the human lineage. *Science, 358,* 1027–1032.

Spector, P. E., & Brannick, M. T. (2011). Methodological urban legends. *Organization Research Methods,* 14, 287–305.

Spelke, E. S. (2005). Sex differences in intrinsic aptitude for mathematics and science? *American Psychologist,* 60, 950–958.

Speth, M. L., & Parent, M. B. (2006). Age and sex differences in children's spatial search strategies. *Psychonomic Bulletin and Review,* 13, 807–812.

Spielberg, J. M., Forbes, E. E., Ladouceur, C. D., Worthman, C. M., Olino, T. M., Ryan, N. D., & Dahl, R. E. (2015). Pubertal testosterone influences threat-related amygdala-orbitofrontal coupling. *Social Cognitive and Affective Neuroscience,* 10, 408–415.

Stafford, T. (2018). Female chess players outperform expectations when playing men. *Psychological Science, 29,* 429-436.

Steenkamp, M. M., Schlenger, W. E., Corry, N., Henn-Haase, C., Qian, M., Li, M., . . . Marmar, C. (2017). Predictors of PTSD 40 years after combat. *Depression and Anxiety,* 34, 711–722. doi:10.1002/da.22628.

Stephens, N. M., Markus, H. R., & Phillips, L. T. (2014). Social class culture cycles. *Annual Review of Psychology,* 65, 611–634.

Styron, W. (1990). *Darkness Visible.* New York: Random House.

Su, R., Rounds, J., & Armstrong, P. J. (2009). Men and things, women and people. *Psychological Bulletin, 135, 859–884.*

Super, C. M., Guldan, G. S., Ahmed, N., & Zeitlin, M. (2012). The emergence of separation protest is robust under conditions of severe developmental stress in rural Bangladesh. *Infant Behavior and Development,* 35, 393–396.

Swahn, M. H., Gressard, L., Palmier, J. B., Yao, H., & Haberlen, M. (2013). The prevalence of very frequent physical fighting among boys and girls in 27 countries and cities. *Journal of Environmental and Public Health,* 215126. doi:10. 1155/2013/215126.

Swanson, H. L., Olide, A. F., & Kong, J. E. (2018). Latent class analysis of children with math deficiencies and/or math learning disability. *Journal of Educational Psychology,* 110, 531–551.

Sylvester, C. M., Smyser, C. D., Smyser, T., Kenley, J., Ackerman, J. J., Shimony, J. S., . . . Rogers, C. E. (2017). Cortical functional connectivity evident after birth and behavioral inhibition at age 2. *American Journal of Psychiatry,* 175(2), 180–187. doi:10.1176/appi.ajp.2017.17010018.

Tackett, J. L., Herzhoff, K., Smack, A. J., Reardon, K. W., & Adam, E. K. (2017). Does socioeconomic Status mediate racial differences in the cortisol response in middle childhood? *Health Psychology,* 36, 662–672.

Tagliaferri, S., Esposito, F. G., Fagioli, R., di Cresce, M., Sacchi, L., Signorini, M. G., . . . Magenes, G. (2017). Ethnic analogies and differences in fetal heart rate variability signal. *The Journal of Obstetrics and Gynaecology Research,* 43, 281–290.

Tai, H. C., Shen, Y. P., Lin, J. H., & Chung, D. T. (2018). Acoustic evaluation of old Italian violins from Amati to Stradivari. *Proceedings of the National Academy of Sciences,* 115, 5926–5931.

Tan, Y., Vandeput, J., Qiu, J., van den Bergh, O., & von Leupoldt, A. (2019). The error-related negativity for error processing in interoception. *Neuroimage,* 184, 386–395.

Tarampi, M. R., Heydari, N., & Hegarty, M. (2016). A tale of two types of perspective taking. *Psychological Science,* 27, 1507–1516.

Tardif, T., Fletcher, P., Liang, W., Zhang, Z., Kaciroti, N., & Marchman, V. A. (2008). Baby's first 10 words. *Developmental Psychology,* 44, 929–938.

Tateno, Y., Komiyama, T., Katoh, T., Munkhbat, B., Oka, A., Haida, Y., . . . Inoko, H. (2014). Divergence of East Asians and Europeans estimated using male- and female-specific genetic markers. *Genome Biology and Evolution,* 6, 466–473.

Telkes, I., Viswanathan, A., Jimenez-Shahed, J., Abosch, A., Ozturk, M., Gupte, A., . . . & Ince, N. F. (2018). Local field potentials of subthalamic nucleus contain electro-physiological footprints of motor subtypes of Parkinson's disease. *Proceedings of the National Academy of Sciences,* 115, E8567-E8576.

Temby, O. F., & Smith, K. R. (2014). The association between adult mortality risk and family history of longevity. *Journal of Biosocial Sciences,* 46, 703–716.

Thomas, R. L., Misra, R., Akkunt, E., Ho, C., & Spence, C. (2018). Sensitivity to auditory-tactile colocation in early infancy. *Developmental Science,* 21(4), e12597. doi:10. 1111/desc.12597.

Thompson, M. S., & Keith, V. M. (2001). The blacker the berry. *Gender and Society,* 15, 336–357.

Timmins, L., Rimes, K. A., & Rahman, Q. (2018). Minority stressors, rumination, and psychological distress in monozygotic twins discordant for sexual minority status. *Psychological Medicine,* 48, 1705–1712.

Tomasello, M. (2018). How children come to understand false beliefs. *Proceedings of the National Academy of Sciences,* 115, 8491–8498.

Tomasi, D., & Volkow, N. D. (2012). Laterality patterns of brain functional connectivity. *Cerebral Cortex*, 22, 1455–1467.

Torrey, E. F., & Yolken, R. H. (2018). How statistics killed the cat. *Psychological Medicine*, 48, 175.

Toscano, H., Schubert, T. W., & Glessner, S. R. (2018). Eye gaze and head posture jointly influence judgments of dominance, physical strength, and anger. *Journal of Nonverbal Behavior*, 42(3), 285–309. doi.org/10.1007/s10919-018-0276-5.

Toscano, H., Schubert, T. W., Dotsch, R., Falvello, V., & Todorov, A. (2016). Physical strength as a cue to dominance. *Personality and Social Psychological Bulletin*, 42, 1603–1616.

Trauffer, N., & Widom, C. S. (2017). Child abuse and neglect, and psychiatric disorders in nonviolent and violent female offenders. *Violence and Gender*, 4, 137–143.

Tromp, D. P., Grupe, D. W., Oathes, D. J., McFarlin, D. R., Hernandez, P. J., Kral, T. R., . . . Nitschke, J. B. (2012). Reduced structural connectivity of a major frontolimbic pathway in generalized anxiety disorder. *Archives of General Psychiatry*, 69, 925-934.

Tryon, R. C. (1939). Studies in individual differences in maze ability. *Journal of Comparative Psychology*, 28, 365–415.

Tsang, T., Ogren, M., Peng, Y., Nguyen, B., & Johnson, K. L. (2018). Infant perception of sex differences in biological motion displays. *Journal of Experimental Child Psychology*, 173, 338–350.

Tuman, D. M. (1999). Gender style as form and content. *Studies in Art Education*, 41, 46–60.

Turkheimer, E., Haley, A., Waldron, M., D'Onofrio, B., & Gottesman, I. I. (2003). Socioeconomic status modifies heritability of IQ in young children. *Psychological Science*, 14, 623–628.

Tzuriel, D., & Egozi, G. (2010). Gender differences in spatial ability of young children. *Child Development*, 81, 1417–1430.

Uller, C., Carey, S., Huntley-Fenner, G., & Klatt, L. (1999). What representations might underlie Infant numerical knowledge? *Cognitive Development*, 14, 1–36.

Ullman, H., & Klingberg, T. (2017). Timing of white matter development determines cognitive abilities at school entry but not in late adolescence. *Cerebral Cortex*, 27, 4516–4521.

Unger, M. J. (2018). *Picasso and the Painting that Shocked the World*. New York: Simon & Schuster.

Updike, J. (2012). *Self-Consciousness*. New York: Random House.

Urbatsch, R. (2018). Things are looking up. *Social Science Research,* 71, 19–36.

Ursano, R. J., Kessler, R. C., & Naifeh, J. A. (2018). Risk factors associated with attempted suicide among US Army soldiers without a history of mental health diagnoses. *JAMA Psychiatry,* 75(10):1022–1032. doi 10.1001/jamapsychiatry.2018.2069.

Van der Stigchel, S., & Hollingworth, A. (2018). Visuospatial working memory as a fundamental component of the eye movement system. *Current Directions in Psychological Science,* 27, 136–143.

Van Drenth, A. (2018). Rethinking the origins of autism. *Journal of the History of the Behavioral Sciences,* 54, 25–42.

Van Hemmen, J., Veltman, D. J., Hoekzema, E., Cohen-Kettenis, P. T., Dessens, A. B., & Bakker, J. (2016). Neural activation during mental rotations in complex androgen insensitivity syndrome. *Cerebral Cortex,* 26, 1036–1045.

Van Loesbroek, E., & Smitsman, A. W. (1990). Visual perception of numerosity in infancy. *Developmental Psychology,* 26, 916–922.

Vandenbergh, J. G. (2003). Prenatal hormone exposure and sexual variation, *American Scientist,* 91, 218–221.

Veldman, S. L. C., Jones, R. A., Santos, R., Sousa-Sa, E., Pereira, J. R., Zhang, Z., & Okely, A. D. (2017). Associations between gross motor skills and physical activity in Australian toddlers. *Journal of Science and Medicine in Sport,* 21, 817–821. http://dx.doi.org/10.1016/j.jsams.2017.12.007.

Verriotis, M., Jones, L., Whitehead, K., Laudiano-Dray, M., Panayvotidis, I., Patel, H., . . . Fitzgerald, M. (2018). The distribution of pain activity across the human neonatal brain is sex dependent. *Neuroimage,* 178, 69–77.

Viana, A. G., Palmer, C. A., Zvolensky, M. J., Alfano, C. A., Dixon, L. J., & Raines, E. M. (2017). Children's behavioral inhibition and anxiety disorder symptom severity. *Behaviour Research and Therapy,* 93, 38–46.

Vock, M., Koller, O., & Nagy, G. (2013). Vocational interests of intellectually gifted and highly achieving young adults. *British Journal of Educational Psychology,* 83, 305–328.

Von Eye, A., Mun, E. Y., & Bogat, G. A. (2008). Temporal patterns of variable relationships in person-oriented research. L., *Developmental Psychology,* 44, 437–445.

Von Kanel, R., Malan, N. T., Hamer, M., & Malan, L. (2015). Comparison of telomere length in black and white teachers from South Africa. *Psychosomatic Medicine,* 77, 26–32.

Voskarides, K. (2018). Combination of 247 genome-wide association studies reveals high cancer risk as a result of evolutionary adaptation. *Molecular Biology and Evolution*, 35, 473–485.

Vouloumanos, A. (2018). Voulez-vous jouer avec moi? Twelve-month-olds understand that foreign languages can communicate. *Cognition*, 173, 87–92.

Waaijer, C. J. F., Sonneveld, H., Buitendijk, S. E., van Bochove, C. A., & van der Weijden, I. C. M. (2016). The role of gender in the employment, career, perception, and research performance of recent PhD graduates from Dutch universities. *PLoS One*, 11(10): e0164784. doi.org10.1371/journal.pone.0164784.

Walia, R., Singla, M., Vaiphei, K., Kumar, S., & Bhansali, A. (2018). Disorders of sex development. *Endocrinology Connection*, 7(2), 364-371. doi:10.1530/EC-18-0022.

Wall, T. L., Luczak, S. E., & Hiller-Sturmhofel, S. (2016). Biology, genetics, and environment. *Alcohol Research*, 38, 59–68.

Waller, G., Thalen, P., Janiert, U., Hamberg, K., & Forssen, A. (2012). A cross-sectional and semantic investigation of self-rated health in the northern Sweden MONICA-study. *BMC Medical Research Methodology*, 12, 154. doi:10.1186/1471-22-88-12-154.

Walsh, D. T. (2002). The development of self in Japanese preschools. *Counterpoints*, 180, 213–245.

Wang, Q., Phillips, N. E., Small, M. L., & Sampson, R. J. (2018). Urban mobility and neighborhood isolation in America's 50 largest cities. *Proceedings of the National Academy of Sciences*, 115, 7735–7740.

Wang, Q., Yang, C., Gelernter, J., & Zhao, H. (2015). Pervasive pleiotropy between psychiatric disorders and immune disorders revealed by integrative analysis of multiple GWAS. *Human Genetics*, 134, 1195–1209.

Wang, X., Pipes, L., Trut, L., Herbeck, Y., Vladimirova, A. V., Gulevich, R. G., . . . Clark, A. G. (2018). Genomic responses to selection for tame/aggressive behaviors in the silver fox (Vulpes vulpes). *Proceedings of the National Academy of Sciences*, 115, 10398–10403.

Ward, E. J., Isik, L., & Chun, M. M. (2018). General transformations of object representations in human visual cortex. *Journal of Neuroscience*, 38, 8526–8537.

Watson, S. B., Alvea, R. A., Hawkins, B. E., Thomas, M. L., Cunningham, K. A., & Jakubas, A. A. (2006). Estradiol effects on the dopamine transporter-protein levels, subcellular location, and function. *Journal of Molecular Signaling*, 5, 1–5.

Webb, S. J., Long, J. D., & Nelson, C. A. (2005). A longitudinal investigation of visual event-related potentials in the first year of life. *Developmental Science*, 8, 605–616.

Wegrzyn, M., Brockham, J., & Kissler, J. (2015). Categorical perception of fear and anger expressions in whole, masked, and complete faces. *PLoS One,* e134790.

Weinberg, S. M., Parsons, T. E., Raffensperger, Z. D., & Marazita, M. L. (2015). Prenatal sex hormones, digit ratio, and face shape in adult males. *Orthodontics and Craniofacial Research,* 18, 21–26.

Weinberger, A. H., Gbedemah, M., Martinez, A. M., Nash, D., Galea, S., & Goodwin, R. D. (2018). Trends in depression prevalence in the USA from 2005 to (2015).*Psychological Medicine,* 48, 1318–1315.

Weisberg, S. M., & Newcombe, N. S. (2016). How do (some) people make a cognitive map? Routes, places, and working memory. *Journal of Experimental Psychology: Learning, Memory and Cognition,*42, 768–785.

Weisberg, S. M., Marchette, S. A., & Chatterjee, A. (2018). Behavioral and neural representations of spatial directions across words, schemas, and images. *Journal of Neuroscience,* 38, 4996–5007.

Werner, E., & Smith, R. S. (1982). *Vulnerable but Invincible.* New York: McGraw Hill.

Wheelan, C. (2017). *Naked Statistics.* New York: W. W. Norton.

White, S. H., & Pillemer, D. B. (1979). Childhood amnesia and the development of socially accessible memory system. In J. F. Kihlstrom & F. J. Evans, (Eds), *Functional Disorders of Memory* (pp. 29–73), Hillsdale, NJ: Lawrence Erlbaum.

Whitehead, A. N. (1916). Presidential address to the British Association for the Advancement of Science (pp. 157–158). (Cited in V. Lowe, 1990, *Alfred North Whitehead,* vol. II, 1910–1947.)

Whiting, B. B. & Whiting, J. W. M. (1975). *Children of Six Cultures.* Cambridge, MA: Harvard University Press.

Whitney, D., & Leib, A. Y. (2018). Ensemble perception. *Annual Review of Psychology,* 69, 105–129.

Wichstram, L. (1999). The emergence of gender differences in depressed mood during adolescence. *Developmental Psychology,* 35, 237–245.

Wiener, N. (1956). *I am a Mathematician.* Garden City, N.Y: Doubleday.

Wierenga, L. M., Bos, M. G. N., Schreuders, E., Vd Kam, F., Peper, J. S., Tamnes, C. K., & Crone, E. A. (2018a). Unraveling age, puberty, and testosterone effects on subcortical brain development across adolescence. *Psychoneuroendocrinology,* 91, 105–114.

Wierenga, L. M., Sexton, J. A., Laake, P., Giedd, J. N., Tamnes, C. K., & Pediatric Imaging, Neurocognition, and Genetics Study. (2018b). A key characteristic of sex differences in the developing brain. *Cerebral Cortex,* 28, 2741–2751.

Wierzbicka, A. (1999). *Emotions Across Languages and Cultures* New York: Cambridge University Press.

Wilhelm, F. H., Rattel, J. A., Wegerer, M., Liedlgruber, M., Schweighofer, S., Kreibig, S. D., . . . Blechert, J. (2017). Attend of defend? *Biological Psychology, 130*, 30–40.

Willard, V. W., Conklin, H. M., Huang, L., Zhang, H., & Kahalley, L. S. (2016). Concordance of parent-, teacher-and self-report ratings on the Conners 3 in adolescent survivors of cancer. *Psychological Assessment, 28*, 1110–1118.

Willetts, P. (1999). Development of means-end behavior in young infants. *Developmental Psychology, 35*, 651–667.

Williams, A. M., Shave, R. E., Coulson, J. M., White, H., Rosser-Stanford, al B., & Eves, N. D. (2018). The influence of vagal control on sex-related differences in the left ventricular mechanics and hemodynamics. *American Journal of Physiology: Heart Circulation Physiology, 315*(3), H687–H698. doi:10.1152/ajpheart.00733.

Wong, A. P. Y., French, L., Leonard, G., Perron, M., Pike, G. B., Richer, L., . . . Paus, T. (2018). Inter-regional variations in gene expression and age-related cortical thinning in the adolescent brain. *Cerebral Cortex, 28*, 1272–1281.

Wood, A. M., Kaptoge, S., Butterworth, A. S., Willeit, P., Walnakula, S., & Bolton, J. (2018). Risk thresholds for alcohol consumption. *The Lancet, 391*, P1513–1523.

Worle, M., & Paulus, M. (2018). Normative expectations about fairness. *Journal of Experimental Child Psychology, 165*, 66–84.

Wu, M., Zhou, R., & Huang, Y. (2014). Effects of menstrual cycle and neuroticism on females' emotion regulation. *International Journal of Psychophysiology, 84*. 351–357.

Wu, Y., Muentener, P., & Schulz, L. E. (2017). One-to four-year-olds connect diverse positive emotional vocalizations to their probable causes. *Proceedings of the National Academy of Sciences, 114*, 11891–11901.

Wuthnow, R. (2018). *The Left Behind*. Princeton, NJ: Princeton University Press.

Wynn, K. (1992). Addition and subtraction by human infants. *Nature, 358*, 749–752.

Xie, W., & Richards, J. E. (2016). Effects of interstimulus intervals on behavioral, heart rate, and event-related potential indices of infant engagement and sustained attention. *Psychophysiology, 53*, 1128–1142.

Xie, W., Mallin, B. M., & Richards, J. E. (2017). Development of infant sustained attention and its relation to EEG oscillations. *Developmental Science, 21*(3). doi:10.1111/desc.12562.

Yang, F., Choi, Y. J., Misch, A., Yang, X., & Dunham, Y. (2018). In defense of the commons. *Psychological Science, 29*, 1598–1611.

Yang, J., Kanazawa, S., Yamaguchi, M. K., & Kuriki, I. (2016). Cortical response to categorical color perception in infants investigated by near-infrared spectroscopy. *Proceedings of the National Academy of Sciences, 113,* 2370–2375.

Yokoi, I., Tachibana, A., Minamimoto, T., Goda, N., & Komatsu, H. (2018). Dependence of behavioral performance on material category in an object-grasping task with monkeys. *Journal of Neurophysiology, 120,* 553–563.

Young, S. K., Fox, N. A., & Zahn-Waxler, C. (1999). The relation between temperament and empathy in 2-year-olds. *Developmental Psychology, 35,* 1189–1197.

Zaruli, V., Jones, J. A. B., Oksuzyan, A., Lindahl-Jacobsen, R., Christensen, K., & Vaupel, J. W. (2018). Women live longer than men during severe famines and epidemics. *Proceedings of the National Academy of Sciences, 115,* E832-E840.

Zavrsnik, J., Pisot, R., Simunic, B., Kokol, P., & Blazun-Vosner, H. (2017). Biomechanical characteristics of skeletal muscles and associations between running speed and contraction time in 8- to 13-year-old children. *Journal of international Medical Research, 45,* 231–245.

Zell, E., Krizan, Z., & Teeter, S. R. (2015). Evaluating gender similarities and differences using metasynthesis. *American Psychologist, 70,* 10–20.

Zhan, L., Jenkins, L. M., Wolfson, D. E., GadElkarim, J. J., Nocito, K., Thompson, P. N., . . . Leow, A. D. (2017). The significance of negative correlations in brain connectivity. *The Journal of Comparative Neurology, 525*(15), 3251–3265. doi:10.1102/cne/24274.

Zhao, G. (2006). Reinventing China. *Modern China, 32,* 3–30.

Zhao, M. (2018). Human spatial representation. *Journal of Neurophysiology,* 2453–2468.

Zhu, J., Manichaikul, A., Hu, Y., Chen, Y. L., Liang, S., Steffen, L. M., . . . Lin, X. (2016). Meta-analysis of genome-wide association studies identifies three novel loci for saturated fatty acids in East Asians. *European Journal of Nutrition, 12,* 1–8.

Ziv, T., & Sommerville, J. A. (2017). Developmental differences in infants' fairness expectations from 6 to 15 months of age. *Child Development, 88,* 1930–1951.

Zosuls, K. M., Ruble, D. N., Tamis-LeMonda, C. S., Shrout, P. E., Bornstein, M. H., & Greulich, F. K. (2009). The acquisition of gender labels in infancy. *Developmental Psychology, 45,* 688–701.

Zundorf, I. C., Karnath, H. O., & Lewald, J. (2011). Male advantage in sound localization at cocktail parties. *Cortex, 47,* 741–749.

Index